THE HOMEOWNER'S ENERGY GUIDE

By John A. Murphy

Thomas Y. Crowell Company
Established 1834   New York

Cover Photo: Courtesy of National Bureau of Standards

Energy waste in this test house is registered as white and red areas when the house is recorded by a special TV camera which picks up infrared rays, or heat.

The white areas represent the areas of major heat loss. In this house, areas of major heat loss are the windows, the gable vent, the chimney, and the bandboard. What other areas of heat loss do you observe? What steps might this homeowner take to reduce the heat losses from these areas and thus reduce heating costs?

PREFACE

THE HOMEOWNER'S ENERGY GUIDE, How to Beat the Heating Game is designed to help you win the energy battle. The basic approach to the book is to show you how to reduce your energy use based on economical trade-offs. How much does it cost? How much will you save? And when will you get your money back? These are the types of questions that the author examines in order to assist you in making decisions that will reduce your energy use at a direct payback.

By converting heat loss into heating dollar costs, the author helps you analyze all the components of your home—the ceilings, walls, doors, windows, floors, and basements, and shows you how much each is costing under a variety of conditions. Using this approach of examining each component of your home, you will discover there are many energy saving measures that don't cost a lot of money. In addition, the author helps you examine gains, hot water, fireplaces, solar heat, heat pumps, and other costs besides heating.

Basic definitions are explained in terms you can understand—BTU, weather data, thermal resistance (R values of insulation), fuels, their ratings, and what these terms really mean to you. You will learn how to calculate a fuel cost factor for your home which will enable you to calculate potential savings, costs, and payback of energy reducing items.

A Work Section, divided into two parts, is provided to guide you through your home analysis. Part One is an 83-point checklist which shows you step-by-step many ways to reduce your energy use. Part Two uses a basic arithmetic approach to show you how to calculate the (1) heat loss of all components of your home, (2) heat loss due to air infiltration, and (3) paybacks of making thermal corrections.

Before you buy any insulation, replacement windows, or energy saving device, you should read this book to find out the answers to such questions as how much you will save, how much the heat loss is costing you, and when you will get your money back.

Energy conservation should and can make sense from an economical and practical standpoint. Invest in those items that will save you money and investigate before you invest. Once you have read this book you will not have to depend on sales pitches for much information. You will be able to ask questions that will enable you to **beat the heating game.**

So, Good Luck!

TABLE OF CONTENTS

Preface iii

Beginnings THE THERMAL WOODS 1

Chapter One THE ENTIRE STRUCTURE 7
Conductance Rate • Fuel Cost Factor • Payback

Chapter Two DEFINITIONS 13
Cold • Heat • Radiation • Convection •
Conduction

Chapter Three THERMAL RESISTANCE 16
British Thermal Unit (BTU) • Flow of Energy •
Time Factor • Temperature Factor • Area Factor •
Arithmetic Relationship of R Factors and U Values •
Total Heat Transmission Rate (U_t)

Chapter Four WEATHER DATA 23
Discovering Temperature Differences for Your Area •
NOAA • Degree Hour • Degree Day • Degree
Month • Degree-Day Year • Ground Temperatures •
Frost Lines • Temperatures in Ducts

Chapter Five FUELS AND THEIR RATINGS 28
Electric Resistance • Combustion Fuels •
Comparing Fuels • C.O.P.

Chapter Six FUEL COST FACTOR 32
Calculating Fuel Cost Factor • Heat Transmission
Rates Revisited

Chapter Seven THE BUILDING OF A BUILDING 36
Workmanship • Costly Shortcuts

Chapter Eight EXTERIOR WALLS 39
Insulation Materials • Heat Transfer in Walls •
Economics Applied • Reducing Studs in the Wall •
Cost of Insulation

Chapter Nine CEILINGS 47
Ceiling Construction • Triangular Roof Correction •
Loose Fiberglass • Cellulose in the Attic •
Cost of Ceiling Heat Loss •

Chapter Ten WINDOWS 53
Heat Loss of Window Panes • Types of Windows •
Total Window Performance • Solar Gain on
Window • Effects of Storm Windows

Chapter Eleven DOORS 62
Dollar Cost of Heating a Door • Effects of Storm
Doors • Sliding Glass Doors

Chapter Twelve FLOORS AND BASEMENTS 67
Rings and Bandboards • Slabs • Basements •
Crawl Spaces • Basement Floors • Foundations

Chapter Thirteen THE HEAT TRANSFER SYSTEM   76
Ducts • Heat Loss of Duct System • Insulating
Ducts

Chapter Fourteen AIR INFILTRATION   80
Costs of Air Infiltration • Stopping Air Infiltration •
Air Turns

Chapter Fifteen GAINS, GAINS, AND MORE GAINS
Other Heat Sources • Appliances • Solar Gains

Chapter Sixteen HUMIDITY AND ODOR   92
Relative Humidity • Perm Ratings • Odor

Chapter Seventeen SOLAR HEATED HOMES   97
Payback for Solar Heating Unit • Solar Heat Today •
Costs of Solar Units

Chapter Eighteen THE HEATING OF WATER   103
Hot Water Use in Home • Water Temperatures •
Heat Loss from Hot Water System • Solar Collector
Systems for Hot Water

Chapter Nineteen FIREPLACES   109
Dampers • Types of Fireplaces • Efficiency of
Fireplaces

Chapter Twenty HEAT PUMPS   114
Heat Output at Various Temperatures • Winter and
Summer Cycles • Efficiency

Chapter Twenty-One BESIDES HEATING COSTS   120
Operation Costs • Automatic Temperature Set-
backs • Air Conditioning • Energy Shortage

Chapter Twenty-Two PRACTICAL STEPS TO
                                        REDUCING HEATING
                                        COSTS   124
Types of Homes • Taking Measurements •
Drawings • How Much Money Should You Spend •
Insulation • Caulk • Insulating Heating Ducts
and Water Lines • Storm Windows and Storm Doors •
Weather Sealing Doors and Windows • Electrical
Outlets • Plumbing • Fireplaces • Furnaces and
Heating Systems • Venting Baths, Laundry Areas •
Do It Yourself Manuals

WORK SECTION

Part One CHECK LISTS   136

Part Two CALCULATIONS   152

Appendices   193

Bibliography   215

BEGINNINGS
THE THERMAL WOODS

What certainly seems like just yesterday, I started my journey through the Thermal Woods, not a typical woods, but a living forest of darkness and strange sounds. Strange voices called out "R-10," "R-15," "U-6," "U-7," "solar heat," and "transmission rates." Bravely and undauntedly, I called back: "A couple of R's and U's to you." Seductive sounding voices wooed me with "Save 30%! Save 50%!" In agony I called out, "Where are you? Where are you?"

This Thermal Woods looked dark and foreboding to a small country builder looking for the Wizard. Maybe, if I could find the Wizard, he would tell me how to build a solar-heated house that would save both me and my customers from assigning our equities over to the utility companies. Days and more days were spent looking for the

1

great Wizard who, I knew, had the secrets of the Thermal Woods and who most certainly would give me all the answers. "Where are you ol' Wizard? Where are you?"

But search as I would, I couldn't find the great Wizard. Furthermore, there were no imps giving me directions to the Yellow Brick Road. So I set myself to the task of studying. Maybe the clue was in a book. But the more I studied, the more the Thermal Woods took on the aspect of a jungle instead of a mere forest. Frankly, it was becoming difficult to see the forest because of the many trees.

Although the project seemed simple at first, it grew in complexity. This reminded me of a Murphy Law: *Whatever you set out to do, something else must be done first.* So true! In other words, before I could begin to design a solar collector, I must first study solar heat, heat transfer, and related engineering data. This kind of study meant refreshing my math and mastering new terms. Quickly, I hid behind a rock and began to study these subjects. Ah, the cosine of the theta angle, plus the viscosity of the fluid . . . depending upon the what-ma-heg-it of the du-flumb. "Oh Wizard! Oh Wizard! Where are you?" my aching mind cried in agony. "Oh Wizard, show me the way out of the Thermal Woods."

Days, more days, nights, and more nights went by as I studied more and more. Finally, the dawn came. Yes, mathematically, I could easily angle the collector in the right direction, use *fluid 3145*, transfer the fluid at *delta T* to the thermal collector, and then, with a mere flick of a switch . . . Presto! . . . solar heat. "Step right in, folks, and get out of that nasty cold. Enter and enjoy free heat from the sun. Don't worry about the cost because we have just defeated that crafty utility man with scientific endeavor. Come in and enjoy the newest technical wonder—solar heat!" Ha, I could see my name in lights.

2

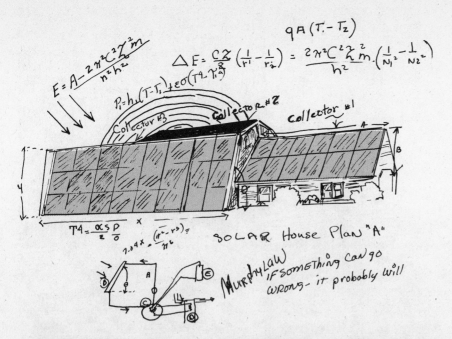

SOLAR House Plan "A"

Murphy Law: IF something can go wrong — it probably will

With sophomoric enthusiasm, I ran pell-mell to my drawing board to clearly set down on paper my ultimate design for the world to see. Scribble, scribble, erase, erase—diligently I worked through the night. Finally, I was done! Quietly I wrote across the bottom of the sketch: "Remember Murphy's Law, *If something can go wrong, it probably will.*" There, above my inscription was my design. The solar collector was twice as large as the house! With a long, depressed sigh, I went back to the Thermal Woods.

Standing on the edge of the Thermal Woods I called out, "Wizard, where are you? Come out, wherever you are, nice Wizard." As I sat on a tree stump, an inner voice spoke, "The house—it is just using too much energy." "Yes! Yes!" I responded. "How stupid of me; reduce the energy consumption of the house and everything will fall into place. Simple! The solution is simple!" Yet another Murphy Law clearly contradicted this: *Nothing is ever as simple as it first seems.*

Tackling the problem of thermal losses in a home was not simple. Even though I had collected great amounts of "free" information, much of it was contradictory. But this was a mere detail for one who had ventured so far into the depths of the Thermal Woods. I decided to evaluate the heat loss of a structure, construction methods, heat transfer systems, and, of course, insulation methods and products, to find a solution. There just had to be a way out of the Thermal Woods. Frankly, I was very encouraged by the claims coming from the corners of the insulation world.

One fellow boasted of a 50% savings if I used his product. Another "scientifically" showed me I could save a whopping 30% with his product. This guy even said that if I used his new furnace gizmo, deluxe or standard, I would save 50%! It looked as if my fears were over. My trip looked as if it would end. Bravely, I faced the utility man and said, "Look you beast," (I was feeling very confident now) "I have been told that if I buy three products, I will save 130% on my energy bill and the way I see it, you owe me money. I want to give you my mailing address so you can send me what you owe me." Utility men just don't have a sense of humor. The laughter was bad enough, but he didn't have to say things like "idiot," "dummy," and "stupid."

Back to the Thermal Woods. Because I was caught up in a perplexing tangle of confusing claims, the Thermal Woods seemed even more

3

foreboding. "Wizard, where are you? I cannot give up," I said to myself, "Don't give up. I must find the Yellow Brick Road."

Looking under each stone, sorting through paper after paper, I began the search again. There had to be a way and there was. ECONOMICS! Yes, that would be an excellent tool to help ferret out the truth of the Thermal Woods. Economics, by George! HOW MUCH DOES IT COST? HOW MUCH WILL IT SAVE? HOW SOON WILL I GET MY MONEY BACK? Aptly, Murphy has a law to cover this situation: *Everything you decide to do costs more than you first estimated.*

Armed with economics, I had to convert energy into dollars and heat savings into tangible dollars. To do this, I had to sift through brochures which by now had begun to occupy an entire corner of my office. Back to the books on thermal heat transfer, rereading of papers on doors, windows, heating systems . . . the task seemed endless. Slowly the light came. It was dim at first, then brighter. Soon the small pieces of the puzzle started to fall into place. Finally, a picture began to emerge.

The morning sun was bright, indicating a good day. I was pleased, yet tired, from the last surge of effort that had taken me through the night. Exhausted, I fell asleep to replenish my energy so I could go back to the Thermal Woods, not in search of anything, but to prove once and for all that I had mastered its secrets.

Armed with a math formula, working knowledge of heat transfer, and building materials, I entered the Thermal Woods again. This time the woods did not look foreboding and strange. Even its darkest shadows did not spark any fear. A voice met me a few steps into the woods . . . "Sir, sir, I have a solar unit that costs only $800.

4

It will surely save you 2 million BTU per season!" "Yes," I answered, "it will certainly do that. However, converted into dollars, this investment means a savings of only $18.00 in electric, straight resistance heat, a savings of only $9.00 with electric heat pump, and a mere savings of $4.45 with natural gas. Under the best circumstances, it would take me forty-four years to even begin to think about getting my $800 investment back. Besides, because of the molecular deterioration of components you are using, I would have to replace your unit in fifteen years." What, at first, appeared to be a giant faded into the woods with his tail between his legs and I have never seen him since. Great confidence swelled inside me.

Another voice called out, "You, there, you. Did you know that ten inches of my insulation in your attic will save you many dollars?" "How much?" I asked. He wasn't too sure but 30% seemed like a good figure. "Well, sir," I spoke out, "with the four inches of insulation I have in my attic now, and taking into consideration the triangular correction factor because of the pitch of my roof, economics dictate that the ideal amount and the most I need is eight inches total; and sir, it won't be done with your insulation product, but with another." The voice was quiet and I heard movement in the brush. The movement was away from me! He left me. I had won! Knowledge won! Wow, did I feel exhilarated. With juvenile exuberance I sped through the Thermal Woods, first this way, then another. Forward two steps, back one, then three giant steps forward (I didn't even forget to say "Mother, may I?"), through the Thermal Woods and out! Free, I had actually made it through the Thermal Woods. I was out!

A large, bearded man approached. His hair was silver and even had touches of gold. The Wizard! The Wizard was coming to me. "Over here," I called. "Over here, oh great Wizard. Are you the great Wizard?" I asked. "Yes," he answered. The Wizard asked "Did you just come through the Thermal Woods?" Proudly (and a little boastfully) I replied in the affirmative. "Good," he said, "then you can help me."

*   *   *   *   *

Well, friend, I made it through the Thermal Woods and I am quite willing and prepared to take you through. Certainly this trip should prove to be profitable to you with the savings you will realize if you follow the plan. Yet, let me caution you, this trip will take some effort on your part. But you look like the person who is both willing and quite able to complete the journey.

Before we begin, let us examine the claims about an energy shortage in the far or near future. Frankly, I cannot reach a conclusion with the information I have on hand at the moment. One thing I am sure about . . . energy, like most other things, will cost more in the future. So, by defining areas of heat loss and by examining and applying appropriate methods for correcting heat loss within economic limits, you can get the most for your energy dollar. To help you maximize the value of your energy dollar is the purpose of this book. We will certainly try to make the trip as pleasant as possible, but *you* are the person who has to make up your mind to follow through.

First, we will cover definitions, weather data, and some basic arithmetic. Then we will look at areas in the home such as ceilings, walls, floors, basements, windows, and doors. Next we will examine fireplaces, hot-water systems, solar heat, and appliances in the home. Finally, we will help you examine, step-by-step, the areas in *your* home which may be eating up your energy dollars. By evaluating these areas, calculating their heat conductance rate before and after thermal corrections, and assigning dollar values to these corrections, you will be able to maximize your energy dollars. Each step of the way should be a revelation to you and help you get to know *your* home better. So, welcome and good luck.

CHAPTER ONE
THE ENTIRE STRUCTURE

The complexity of the heating problem is manifested in the variables of yesterday's and today's building components. Wide variations in construction techniques, differing degrees of home maintenance, and the never-ending flow of new materials on the market prevent a person from making broad and easy statements about heat losses and gains in a home. Thus, it is the job of each and every home owner to inspect his or her own home and to arrive at conclusions based on facts peculiar to the situation of that home owner.

7

Our method of energy saving is really the best way for the home owner. First, we will examine heat transfer rates (U) of various materials. Second, we will calculate a fuel cost factor. Then, by multiplying the U value of a material by a fuel cost factor we will be able to judge heat loss based on economics and to interpret our results in dollars, not percentages.

In many dramatizations, we will show you that often, although a material or combination of materials will save you 50% of heat loss for a given section of the house, it will save you very little in dollars. Also, by comparing heat cost with the cost of new insulation (thermal correction), we will show you how you can decide whether the capital investment is worth the heating savings you may realize.

We will point out to you the function of internal and external heat gains in the home. Most "energy-saving experts" rarely consider the heat gains of a home. In a separate chapter, we discuss heat gains and show you not only how to discover them but also how to take advantage of them in your home.

Most thermal leaks in a home are related to the amount and type of insulation (thermal impedance or thermal barriers) in the walls, ceilings, floors, and other places in the home. The function of insulation is to impede or delay heat transfer. There is no effective method to *stop* heat transfer. However, insulation, as you know it and as often advertised, is not the only cure for high energy consumption. Stopping air infiltration and exfiltration (air leakage into and out of the structure) is very important.

Instead of looking at one separate part of the home, we want to examine every component and then relate the parts to the whole. In this manner, we can decide whether we should add insulation to ceilings or spend our insulation money in the basement area. Many home owners are confused as to how to reduce energy consumption in the home. Also, many home owners do not know how their home heating dollars and operational dollars are really being used.

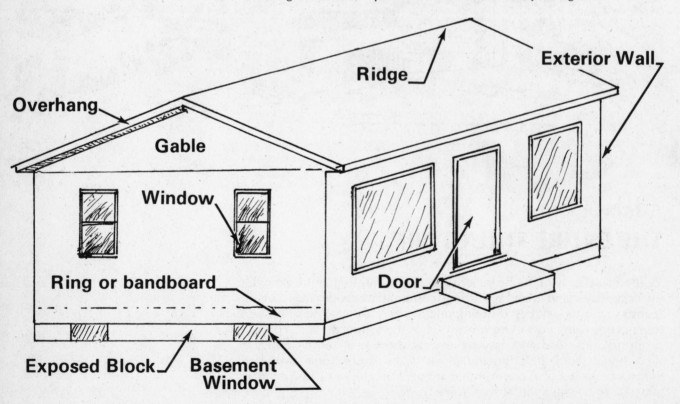

To add to the confusion, most heating experts are telling us to add insulation and stop air leaks without telling us which areas in the home are the most important to correct. They feel the American consumer either cannot or will not take the time to follow through. From my personal experiences with home owners I have not found this to be true.

The heating industry has been given part of the burden of providing a "comfort" system. The usual method of selecting a furnace for your home is first to calculate the heat loss of your home and then to add a heating unit with the appropriate size to make up the heat loss of the home. The heating unit or furnace is designed to operate by a thermostat to keep your home comfortable during the heating season. This same thermostat also controls the cooling unit which keeps your home at some designed comfort level. Energy experts all over this country tell us to turn the thermostat down or up to save energy. At least in part, they are correct with this instruction; however, as you will discover, this may not be the only way to save heating dollars and stay comfortable.

Solar heat units are coming on the market and may be widely used someday in the distant future. The need to be able to evaluate the *cost* efficiency of any given solar unit is very important. If the purveyor of the solar unit is claiming he will save you two-thirds of your heating bill . . . both you and he must be able to know and agree on two-thirds of what? Is his solar unit going to save you two-thirds of $1200 per heating season or two-thirds of $100?

Our method will determine the heat loss of your home and will also dramatize the effect of heat loss on the heating cost of your home for one heating season. We will point out in later chapters that the heating unit of your home is actually a supplementary heating source, or at least it can be reduced to the role of one of several heat sources for your home.

We must *want* to save our supply of energy in this country *now*. We must reduce the tremendous energy squandering that is going on today and conserve existing energy resources. However, we cannot afford many of the suggestions being offered today. Seeking the most efficient ways to use and conserve energy is an educational process and that is the intent of this book. We want to teach the rudiments of heat loss and economics of heating and thermal corrections. We certainly could teach many minute details but this would prove to be both tedious and boring to many readers. To those of you who demand thoroughbred definitions and explanations, refer to our bibliography or search your library shelves to continue your education on heat transfer.

SOME DEFINITIONS

We now want to introduce two terms to you. These terms are *conductance rate (U)* and *fuel cost factor*. The conductance rate, U_t of a home is its total heat conductance rate subject to exterior temperatures. You can get an approximate value of the U_t of your home from your heating unit. To do this, divide the BTU rating of your furnace by your interior design temperature. The interior design temperature is another name for the average interior temperature or the comfort level of your home. In most cases, the design temperature is 70°F.

For example, suppose that your furnace is rated at 80 000 BTU and the design temperature of your home is 70°F. The conductance rate value of your home can be calculated by dividing 80 000 by 70. Thus, your heat conductance rate value would be about 1143. The heat

9

conductance rate is important because it is the basis of heat transfer in the home or wall section. To find our heating dollars for a given heating season, we need only to multiply our calculated heat conductance rate value by our fuel cost factor.

Let's jump many steps ahead and demonstrate the usefulness of conductance rate and fuel cost factors. Let's say we know a particular building has a conductance rate of 722.89. Suppose we also know the fuel cost factors for many fuels in different areas of this country. With some degree of accuracy, we could estimate the annual heating bill of this proposed home in various cities. Table 1-1 contains estimates of annual heating bills for this proposed home if located in various cities.

Table 1-1. Potential Heating Cost of a House with a Heat Transmission Rate (U_t) of 722.89

LOCATION	FUEL			
	Elec. 1**	Elec. 2†	Fuel Oil (0.70)*	Nat. Gas (0.70)*
Atlanta, GA	$655	$366	$226	$180
Columbus, OH	$1200	$600	$500	$320
Syracuse, NY	$1408	$704	$488	$370

*The number beside the type of fuel represents the efficiency of the heating unit.

**Electric heat—straight resistance

†Electric heat pump

The dollar figures represent the upper limits of heating this home. These figures are subject to internal heat gain and external heat gain. Adjusting the dollar value for heat gains, the resulting dollar value is your actual heating bill for operating your furnace! In Chapter 15, we will discuss this in greater detail.

In our example, we can see that natural gas, when compared with other fuels in these cases, appears to be a bargain. In fact, many home owners are buying natural-gas heated homes in fear of high operational or heating costs of the all-electric home. This may not actually be true in real life. The heating cost is a function not only of the type and cost of the fuel, but also of the design of the thermal barriers of the home. The lower the conductance rate of the home, the less fuel the home will consume regardless of the type of fuel. To demonstrate this point, let's look at three homes with different conductance rates (U_t values) and which use different fuels for heating.

Table 1-2 Estimated Fuel Costs For Homes with Different U_t Values and Different Fuels

	Conductance Rate (U_t)	Fuel	Estimated Annual Heat Cost
Home 1	865	Fuel Oil	$854.00
Home 2	1225	Natural Gas	$558.00
Home 3	485	Electric Heat Pump	$396.00

Although the all-electric home's fuel is more costly per million BTU of heat, the all-electric system including the house and heating unit proves superior economically in the above case.

10

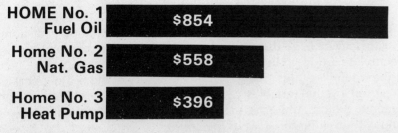

HOME No. 1 Fuel Oil	$854
Home No. 2 Nat. Gas	$558
Home No. 3 Heat Pump	$396

You will also be able to answer other questions as a result of your study. Based upon dollar savings of your heat conductance rate and fuel bill, how much insulation should be placed in the attic area and what type of insulation should be used? Are suppliers selling and not telling? Are suppliers purposely misleading you or do they just not know?

Remember, the heat loss (conductance rate) or U_t of a given home is a function of its components. As an exercise, let's look at a home with a U_t of 1928.33 before and after thermal correction of its components.

Table 1-3. Comparison of the Heat Transmission Rate (U_t) of a House Before and After Thermal Corrections

| Component | Heat Transmission Rate (U) | |
	Before Corrections	After Corrections
Exterior walls	221.16	88.07
Ceilings	693.33	35.88
Doors	88.33	35.88
Bandboards	54.70	5.09
Windows	228.35	129.84
Basement	166.79	111.08
Air Leakage (infiltration)	475.67	34.66
Total Heat Transmission Rate (U_t)	1928.33	445.52

This case house is a good example of houses existing today. Let's examine its dollar performance in Dayton, Ohio, and see what its operational cost of heating loss might be.

Table 1-4 Dollar Performance of a House Before and After Thermal Corrections

	Elec. 1	Elec. 2	Fuel Oil (0.70)	Nat. Gas (0.70)
Before correction	$3,094	$1,546	$1,304	$873
After correction	$713	$356	$300	$210
Annual Savings	$2,381	$1,190	$1,004	$663

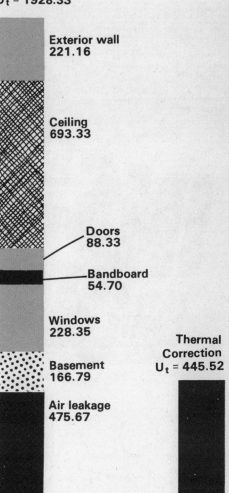

House Uncorrected
$U_t = 1928.33$

Exterior wall 221.16

Ceiling 693.33

Doors 88.33

Bandboard 54.70

Windows 228.35

Basement 166.79

Air leakage 475.67

Thermal Correction $U_t = 445.52$

11

The cost of operating the uninsulated house is extremely high and, even by intuition, we could make the correct choice in this case that insulation does pay. Let's say our thermal correction would cost us $900 in the natural gas-heated home. With an annual savings potential of $663, we would get our invested thermal correction dollars back in about 1.35 heating seasons. This savings is called payback.

So, before we buy insulation, a solar heat unit, a heat pump, or any energy gimmick, we should first learn for *ourselves* how to calculate heat loss and then how to apply heating costs. In this manner, we will avoid being misled by the salesman. We will also be able to decide for ourselves through our own study, calculations and knowledge of money we have available for thermal correction, what will be our best approach to thermal corrections.

You will discover that we are over-insulating many parts of homes and are leaving large thermal leaks uncorrected. We could not give you a complete listing of thermal leaks for your home because, as we stated in the opening of this chapter, the complexity of the heating problem is caused by the variables of yesterday's and today's building components. Besides, there are many different weather conditions to contend with in different areas of the country.

In this chapter, we have briefly examined heat transfer, weather data, fuel efficiencies, fuel costs, and certainly some considerations about your own home. Armed with this bit of knowledge, you can begin your correction of thermal leaks and realize reduction of fuel bills. By all means, start saving energy now, both for yourself and for future generations.

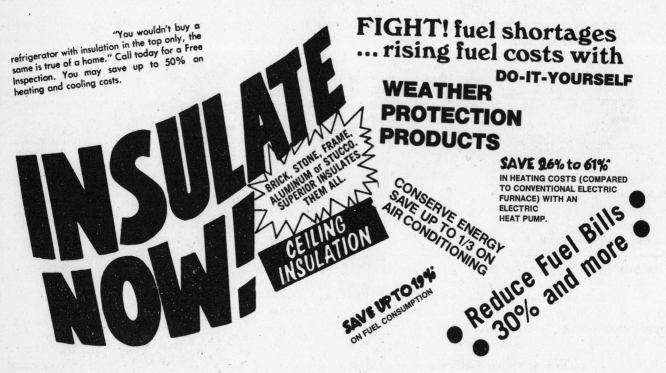

SOLAR HEATING
Solar Pioneers Convert Their Own Homes

12

Conduction

$$q = h(T_1 - T_2)$$

Radiation

$$P_1 = h_1(T_1 - T_2) + \varepsilon\sigma(T_1^4 - T_2^4) + m!(w - w_1)$$

Convection

$$\rho\left(u\frac{\partial u}{\partial x} + v\frac{\partial u}{\partial y}\right) = g(\rho_\infty - \rho) + \mu\frac{\partial^2 u}{\partial y^2}$$

CHAPTER TWO
DEFINITIONS

After years of tedious struggle—the combined effort of engineers and scientists, and, of course, financed by hard-earned tax dollars—man stepped onto the surface of the moon. This great moment was further dramatized by the words spoken on this occasion . . . "One small step for man; one giant leap for mankind." This message was flashed to all corners of the earth. Man was in awe of man.

13

The behind-the-scene effort of propelling man to the moon would, undoubtedly, show sequences of people laboring over minute details. The work of most research people carries very little glory, yet it carries a tremendous amount of personal satisfaction. Luckily for us, many people in the past pored over the details of heat transfer. In fact, Sir Isaac Newton laid down the mathematical foundation of heat transfer centuries ago. His work has since been refined and defined. Since our goal is to reduce our heat bill with the least amount of expense, we must first get a basic understanding of what our work will involve.

The heat transfer within our home is a function of both outside and inside temperature changes. It is also a function of thermal gradients such as insulation or lack of insulation and, of course, time. The transfer of heat is always from the warm side to the cold side. During the winter or heating months, the flow of heat is from indoors to the great outdoors. During the summer months, the reverse is true. Also, the flow of heat is from the hot attic and hot walls to the cooler indoor areas. The greater the heat **transfer rate,** the more money we have to pay the utility company.

Intuition tells us that the more insulation we have in the ceilings, side walls, etc., the lower our heating bill will be. In part, this is true. First, we must realize that there are both internal and external heat gains to consider. We must also consider air infiltration. Air infiltration has little to do with insulation as we know it.

The heat loss of your home is a function of the heat transfer rates (U) or conductivity of wood, glass, and insulating materials, etc. It is also affected by the amount of air infiltration. Conversely, sunshine, body heat, and heat from cooking and other sources constitute a heat or energy gain within the home. So, to make your journey through the Thermal Woods easier, let's identify some of the terms we will be using repeatedly.

COLD

Cold is the absence of heat. Cold is a relative concept. For example, although a steel ingot with a temperature of 800°F may be too cold for a given process, it certainly is too hot for us to touch with our fingers.

HEAT

Heat is mechanical energy of random motion on a microscopic scale. The direction of heat flow is always from the warm side to the cold side. The cold side is also called a heat sink. The rate of heat flow is directly proportional to the temperature difference between the warm side and the heat sink. This rate is also a function of the thermal resistance or impedance of the combination of materials between the temperature gradients.

Heat transfer takes place from molecule to molecule and is identified in three distinct terms: radiation, convection, and conduction.

RADIATION

Radiation is the emission of energy from a body or object. This energy travels at the speed of light. The sun radiates its light and heat energy out into space. Luckily for us, the sun radiates sufficient energy to keep this planet in a livable condition.

CONVECTION

Convection is the transfer of heat by a fluid. A fluid is anything that flows. Examples of fluids are air, water, and any liquid or vapor state of matter. Convection is classified as either free convection or as forced convection.

Free convection is the movement of a fluid by natural imbalances caused by a thermal process. The more excited molecules within the

14

fluid move more rapidly than the less excited molecules. These faster molecules move further apart, and this portion of the fluid becomes warmer, expands, and rises. Hence, the misconception was born that ALL heat rises. It is true, however, that the majority of heat will rise in still air spaces, liquids, etc. All heat transfer is subject to temperature differences. The direction of motion is toward the cold side. Forced convection is the movement of a fluid by a fan or pump.

Air is composed of molecules which are relatively far apart. The less dense the air is, the fewer molecules it has per cubic unit and the slower is the rate of heat transfer. As we compress air by force, we bring its molecules closer together and its heat transfer rate increases. The wind, when it blows on the outside wall of your home, compresses the air film next to the structure. When this happens, the density of the molecules in the air film increases and so does the heat transfer rate. If the wall is colder than the air or wind, the transfer of heat will be from the wind into and through the wall. The reverse is true if the wind is colder than the wall. So, actually, convective heat transfer of air is really dependent upon the conductive thermal resistance of its film.

If the wind is blowing, the thermal resistance value of the air film will be low and will allow a more rapid transfer of heat than the air film on the interior side of the house. However, if there is an air leak in the wall or the window, the cold air will enter the structure. This we call INFILTRATION. Infiltration, as you will discover, is the easiest thermal leak we can correct in the home. Naturally, the heat transfer will be from the warm inner air within the house to the newly introduced cold air.

CONDUCTION

Conduction is the transfer of heat energy through or within a solid. The rate of heat transfer is a function of the density of the solid and its molecular makeup. Because of low thermal resistance (R), the rate of heat transfer through one inch of concrete is much faster than it is through one inch of wood, insulation, or glass. Through efforts of many scientists and engineers, the heat transfer rates have been firmly established for many materials used in the construction of a home. Also, mathematical formulas which allow the heat transfer rate to be measured have been derived. We will cover these formulas later.

For purposes of our economical trade-offs, an overview is more than enough to give you a basic knowledge of heat transfer. Some excellent texts are listed in the bibliography for the more serious-minded student of heat transfer.

Just keep in mind that the rate of heat transfer depends not only on thermal barriers but also on temperature differences. Heat transfer is also a function of time. The direction of heat transfer is from the warm side to the cold side.

In summary, radiation is the transfer of heat from an object. Convection is the transfer of heat by a fluid. Conduction is heat transfer through a solid.

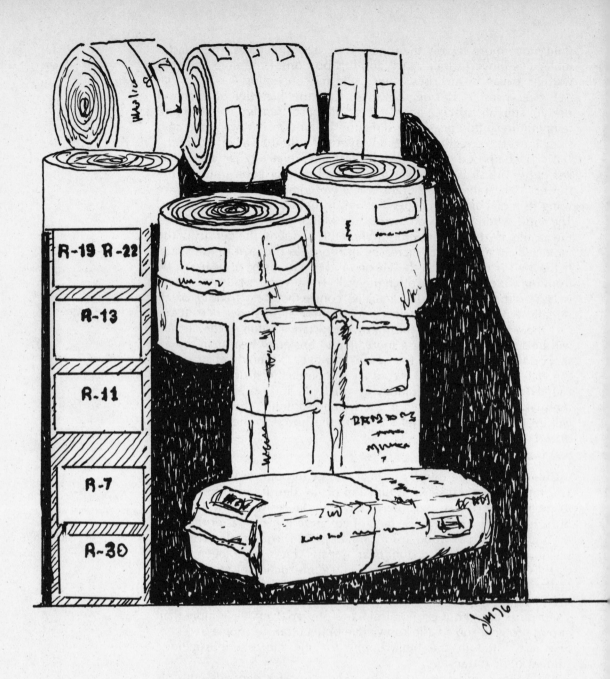

CHAPTER THREE

THERMAL RESISTANCE

Advertisers on TV try to induce us to use insulation with a high R factor in the attic. One builder claims he uses R-13 insulation in the side walls of his home and R-30 insulation in the attic. Another builder tells us that R-8 on the basement wall is a must.

Before my trip through the Thermal Woods, I, like most consumers, thought that the greater the R factor, the lower the heat loss in my home. My assumption was basically correct. However, I also discovered that correcting the many sources of heat loss is just as important as using insulation with an appropriate R factor in reducing energy costs.

The thermal resistance value of a material is called an R factor. The R factor of various materials can be discovered by subjecting the material to a simple test. This testing is done in a laboratory on a special

16

machine called a "K" machine. The test results are expressed as U values rather than as R factors. A U value is the heat transmission rate of a material expressed as the rate of heat flow (British Thermal Units, BTU) per square foot of area, per stated thickness, per hour of time subject to a temperature difference. This is often stated as $BTU/hr/ft^2/F°$ for some specific thickness. Rather than writing $BTU/hr/ft^2/F°$ every time the U value is expressed, engineers and scientists prefer to refer to the heat transmission rate as just U.

Knowing that U is a function of area stated in terms of one square foot, we can easily find the U for larger or smaller areas simply by multiplying the U per one square foot by the number of square feet of area we are considering in the calculation.

We will be discussing the U_t of a house, a wall, a door, a roof, and various combinations of materials. The subscript "t" designates *total*. Therefore if we are discussing U_t of a window, we are giving the heat transfer rate of that window including frame. If we note U_t of a house, we know it is the heat transfer rate of all the components of the house.

We will need to have a working knowledge of some heat transfer definitions before we go more deeply into the relationship of R values and U values. Ready?

BRITISH THERMAL UNIT (BTU)

One British Thermal Unit (BTU) is the amount of heat energy needed to raise the temperature of one pound of water by one Fahrenheit degree (F°). Furnaces and air conditioners are rated in terms of British Thermal Units. Fuel oil, natural gas, electricity, and all other heat sources are rated in BTUs. In fact, all transfer of heat is rated in BTUs.

FLOW OF HEAT ENERGY

Flow of heat energy takes place only where there is a temperature difference. Regardless of how much insulation we have in the side wall, there will be no heat loss or heat gain if the inside temperature is the same as the outside temperature. The greater the difference in temperature between the inside and the outside of your home, the greater is the flow of heat (expressed in BTUs). The direction of heat flow or transfer is from the warmer side to the cooler side.

THE TIME FACTOR AND THE TEMPERATURE FACTOR

Remember that U is the flow of heat expressed in $BTU/hr/ft^2/F°$. Note that the time factor is expressed in hours (hr). The temperature factor, which is expressed in Fahrenheit degrees (F°), is the temperature difference between the two sides. The flow of heat energy is expressed per hour of time because of certain limitations of the testing equipment.

We are most interested in the costs of heating for one month and for one heating season. This cost of heating can be estimated very simply if we know the temperature differences for one given heating month or for one heating season. In Chapter 4, we will show you how to make these estimates. Just keep in mind that heat flow is subject to some amount of time.

THE AREA FACTOR

Knowing area is paramount in discussing heat flow. Heat flow is always expressed in terms of volume. However, conductance rate (U) for solid materials is given in terms of area, not volume. The assumption made here is that each material has a standard thickness. Should your material have a thickness other than its standard thickness, this must

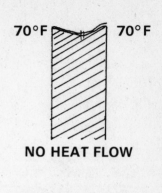

NO HEAT FLOW

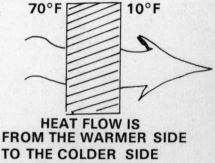

HEAT FLOW IS FROM THE WARMER SIDE TO THE COLDER SIDE

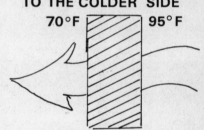

17

also be taken into consideration. Examination of solid materials in your home for thickness is important so you can factor in U correctly.

Heat flow in liquids is expressed in volume (cubic feet) rather than in area (square feet) as are solid materials. When time is taken into consideration, heat flow in liquids is expressed as cubic feet per minute (C.F.M.).

Heat flow in air films is expressed in area units (square feet) and the assumption is made that the thickness is known—the same as for solid materials. However, the thickness of the air film is subject to the pressure exerted on a surface due to the movement or velocity of the air expressed in feet per minute.

Heat flow rate depends on time, area, and temperature difference. Now let's consider what the U value (heat transfer rate) has to do with the R factor (thermal impedance). It's basic arithmetic!

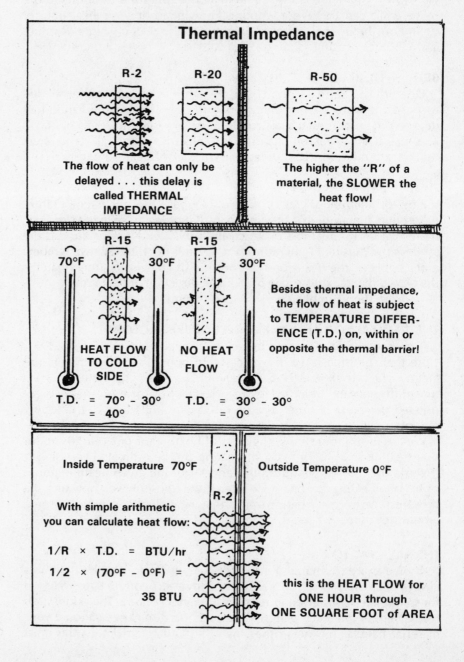

Thermal Impedance

R-2   R-20   R-50

The flow of heat can only be delayed . . . this delay is called THERMAL IMPEDANCE

The higher the "R" of a material, the SLOWER the heat flow!

R-15   R-15

70°F   30°F   30°F

HEAT FLOW TO COLD SIDE

NO HEAT FLOW

Besides thermal impedance, the flow of heat is subject to TEMPERATURE DIFFERENCE (T.D.) on, within or opposite the thermal barrier!

T.D. = 70° - 30°
    = 40°

T.D. = 30° - 30°
    = 0°

Inside Temperature 70°F   Outside Temperature 0°F

R-2

With simple arithmetic you can calculate heat flow:

1/R × T.D. = BTU/hr

1/2 × (70°F - 0°F) =

35 BTU

this is the HEAT FLOW for ONE HOUR through ONE SQUARE FOOT of AREA

18

ARITHMETIC RELATIONSHIP OF R FACTORS AND U VALUES

You have probably already realized that U values and R factors are closely related. They are, in fact, related in such a way that for any material, the product of its U value and its R factor is equal to one. This kind of relationship is called an inverse proportion. In the case of U values and R factors, this relationship is expressed very simply as

$$U \times R = 1$$

This relationship can also be expressed in two other forms:

$$U = \frac{1}{R} \quad \text{or} \quad R = \frac{1}{U}$$

Suppose that a builder tells us that he used R-20 insulation on a wall. Knowing that R is the thermal impedance of a given material which is one square foot in area and at some stated thickness, we can use simple arithmetic to find the heat transfer rate per hour for this insulation. Substituting R-20 into the expression for U, we get

$$U = \frac{1}{R} = \frac{1}{20} = 0.05$$

This tells us that the U value for R-20 insulation is 0.05. If the temperature difference for one hour was 60° and the area covered by the R-20 insulation was 1000 square feet, its heat transfer rate could be calculated.

70°F   **Inside Temperature**
-10°F   **Outside Temperature**
60 F°   **Temp. Diff.**

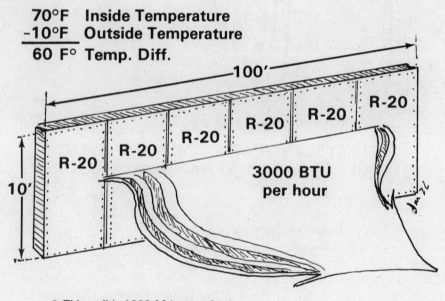

● **This wall is 1000 ft² (square feet)**
● **It has a thermal impedance of R-20/ft²**
● **The temperature difference is 60 F°**

Heat transfer per hour = 1/R × Temperature difference (TD) × area

                  = 1/20 × 60 × 1000

                  = 3000 BTU per hour

This simple arithmetic is the very foundation of the way out of the Thermal Woods.

19

Heat transmission rate (U) is subject to time, area and temperature difference. Be sure you clearly state all of these factors and their units when you calculate U. This will help you arrive at a correct figure for total heat transmission rates (U_t) for various home components such as walls, ceilings, etc., as well as for the whole house.

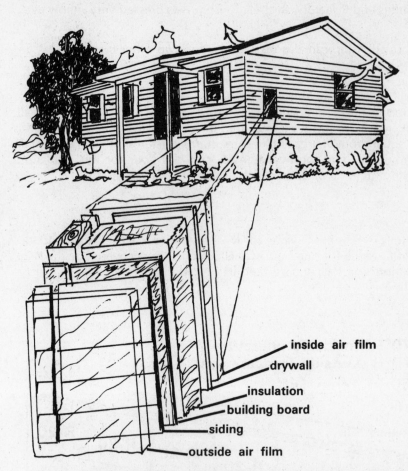

inside air film
drywall
insulation
building board
siding
outside air film

THE HEAT TRANSFER RATE OR "U" IS SUBJECT TO THE COMBINED THERMAL RESISTANCE OR "R"

TOTAL HEAT TRANSMISSION RATE (U_t)

Suppose a builder tells us that he wants to use R-8 insulation in the side wall but a friend suggests insulation with a rating of R-16. The friend's rationale is that R-16 insulation has twice as much thermal resistance or impedance as the R-8 insulation. Therefore he thinks it should save you 50% of your heating cost. Is he right?

The insulation inside the wall is just one of the components of the wall. We must consider the R factor of the inside air film, ½" thick drywall, the insulation, the outside building board, the siding (stucco, in this example), and the outside air film. In Appendix N, we list the R factors of these materials for one square foot of area. Let's list these in Table 3-1.

Eureka! The total conductance rate (U_t) of our R-8 wall per square foot is 0.0960 and the U_t of our R-16 wall is 0.0543. Percentage-wise, the U_t for the R-16 wall was not 50% of the U_t for the R-8 wall, but only 43.4%. Furthermore, when we apply economics, the answer becomes even clearer.

20

Table 3-1. Comparison of Heat Transfer Rates of Walls with R-8 and R-16 Insulation

	R-Value (R-8 Wall)	R-Value (R-16 Wall)
Inside Air Film	0.65	0.65 (same)
Drywall (½")	0.20	0.20 (same)
Suggested Insulation	8.00	16.00
Insulation Board	1.20	1.20 (same)
Siding (Stucco)	0.20	0.20 (same)
Outside Air Film	0.17	0.17 (same)
Total Impedance per ft^2 (R_t)	10.42	18.42
Total Heat Transfer per ft^2 (U_t)*	0.0960	0.0543

*Recall that $U = 1/R$

To dramatize this point, let's assume we know the fuel cost factor is $0.50. By multiplying the U_t by the fuel cost factor we can find the heating cost for some area in the country for one heating season.

For the R-8 wall:

$$\begin{aligned} \text{Cost per heating season} &= U_t \times \text{fuel cost factor} \\ &= 0.0960 \times \$0.50 \\ &= \$0.048/ft^2 \text{ per heating season} \end{aligned}$$

For the R-16 wall:

$$\begin{aligned} \text{Cost per heating season} &= U_t \times \text{fuel cost factor} \\ &= 0.0543 \times \$0.50 \\ &= \$0.027/ft^2 \text{ per heating season} \end{aligned}$$

The savings which would result from changing from R-8 to R-16 insulation is $0.021 per square foot per heating season.

However, the builder informs us that changing from R-8 to R-16 insulation would cost us $4.00 per square foot! By dividing our savings of $0.021 into our cost of $4.00 we discover it would take 190 heating seasons to get our investment back!

Of course, the above is just a dramatization to prove a point. One must also consider interest on money and probable increase of fuel costs in the future. The point is, examine each detail and understand

WHERE IS THE HEAT GOING?

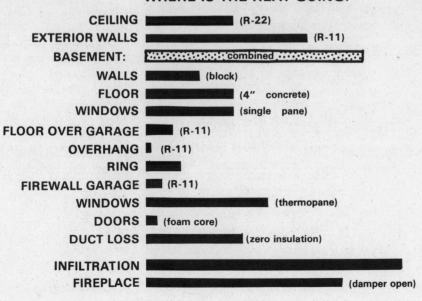

21

for yourself all considerations before you invest in thermal corrections. Look for thermal corrections that will give you the greatest and quickest return on your money.

By using this detailed method of examining thermal weaknesses, I aided Ryan Homes, Inc. of Pittsburgh, PA, in getting 30% to 40% decrease of heating costs with minimum increase in the sales price of the house.

A friend of mine is enjoying a $350.00 investment in his home that will save him $100.00 per heating season! The bonus is that it added at least $1000 to the resale value of his home. His investment? A wood burning stove in his basement. In another case, a neighbor invested $300 and got his money back from lower heating bills in one heating season!

U is important. You, too, are important. Your heating dollars can never be reduced to zero. But in most cases, the reduction will be dramatic and often profitable!

The successful heating game consists of using dollars normally spent on heating to improve your home instead!

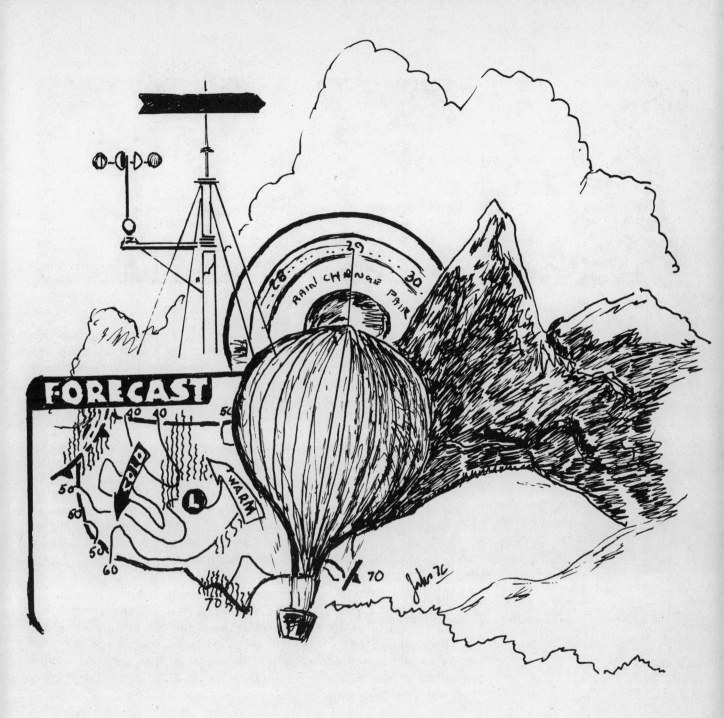

CHAPTER FOUR

WEATHER DATA

Every second, the temperature outside is changing as transfer of heat is taking place. Wind may introduce warm temperatures from the South or a cold chill from the Arctic. The sun's rays may be heating the earth, which is, in turn, reflecting or radiating energy into the air. Because temperatures outdoors are constantly changing, we must have some idea of what the average temperature is so that we have a representative temperature to use in our calculations.

23

DISCOVERING TEMPERATURE DIFFERENCES FOR YOUR AREA

Certainly I will not, and I am sure you will not, stand outdoors to record outside temperatures every minute for one hour, much less for an entire heating season. Fortunately, these measurements are made for us by the National Oceanic and Atmospheric Administration (NOAA), more commonly called the weather bureau.

NOAA

The National Oceanic and Atmospheric Administration, through its hundreds of weather stations, takes temperature readings minute by minute and records average hourly temperature readings. These weather stations also record cloud cover, rain, snow, wind, sun radiation, and other weather data. For only 15 cents (1976 quote), you can obtain a report on the annual weather data for your area by writing to:

National Climatic Center
Federal Building
Ashville, North Carolina 28011

In Appendix K, some of the data you will need in your study of heating costs for your area are listed by cities and states.

You may find the NOAA report interesting because in it you will find temperatures for months recorded in heating degree days and months, just as the temperatures for a year are recorded. So we must understand the *degree hour*, the *degree day*, the *degree month*, and the *degree year*.

DEGREE HOUR

A degree hour is a difference between the base temperature of 65°F and the outside temperature. This base temperature of 65°F is an assumed temperature established many years ago when interior temperatures were set at 75°F in the home. The 10F° difference assumes some solar gain, heat gain, etc., in the home. If the outside air temperature is below 65°F, the degree hour is recorded as a *heating degree hour*. If the outside temperature is above 75°F, the degree hour is recorded as a *cooling* degree hour. For example, if the temperature outside is 20°F, the degree hour is recorded as a 45 degree heating hour (65° – 20°= 45 DH). A heating degree hour is a temperature difference recorded below 65°F. A cooling degree hour is a temperature difference recorded above the base temperature of 75°F. Since we are primarily concerned with heat loss, our reference to degree hour, degree day, etc., assumes heating.

TIME: 7:00 A.M.
TEMPERATURE: 10°F
D.D. HOUR:

65 – 10 = 55

24

DEGREE DAY

By adding all the degree hours for one 24 hour period and dividing by 24 we get the average degree hour for that day. This average is called a *degree day*. Suppose we are told that an area recently had a 55 degree day, or 55 DD. This means the average outside temperature was ($65°F - 55°F$), or $10°F$ As with all averages, there is room for error, but over the span of one heating season this average can be surprisingly representative.

In the home there are heating gains which include solar gain, heat rejection from freezers, refrigerators, etc. The base temperature for the degree day is calculated from $65°F$, assuming a $75°F$ interior temperature in the home. Especially since the energy crunch of 1972, many home owners keep the interior temperature from $60°F$ to $70°F$. We recommend $70°F$ for comfort. The choice of interior temperature is up to you, the home owner. Nevertheless, in the well-sealed and insulated home there is often enough heat gain to compensate for any heat loss with outside temperatures as low as $50°F$.

This means there is no fuel consumption for heating unless the temperature outside goes below $50°F$! Because of this, the degree day calculation will always give you the upper limits of heating cost. In the Work Section, we show you by arithmetic how to compensate for heating gains in calculating actual heating cost.

DEGREE MONTH

At the end of one month, NOAA adds up the degree days and totals them. This total gives us the degree days for that given month. As in the case of a cold January, the degree days for that month will naturally be all heating degree days. January will most likely have the largest degree-day month figure for the entire year.

DEGREE-DAY YEAR

By totaling all the degree-day months for heating, we have a degree-day year for a given year. As you can imagine, the value for each year will be different. For this reason, the NOAA report contains the normal DD year for a given area. This is the figure we have given in Appendix K. The normal DD year for heating in one given area is the average DD year over a period of ten years.

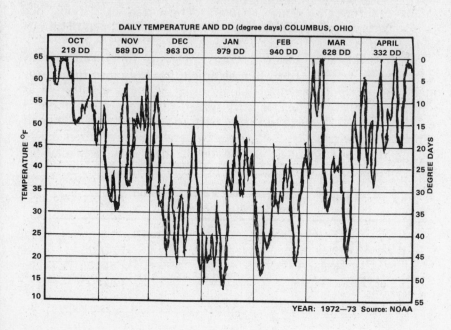

DAILY TEMPERATURE AND DD (degree days) COLUMBUS, OHIO

OCT 219 DD	NOV 589 DD	DEC 963 DD	JAN 979 DD	FEB 940 DD	MAR 628 DD	APRIL 332 DD

YEAR: 1972—73 Source: NOAA

DATE: 12-5-76	STATION: 625-A
TIME:	TEMPERATURE:
0100	50
0200	50
0300	50
0400	45
0500	40
0600	40
0700	35
0800	35
0900	32
1000	33
1100	34
1200	40
1300	42
1400	43
1500	44
1600	44
1700	40
1800	45
1900	45
2000	40
2100	30
2200	35
2300	20
3400	21

AVERAGE TEMPERATURE: $39°F$
DEGREE DAY: $65 - 39 = 26$

DEGREE DAY MONTH: Nov. 1970

DAY	D.D.	DAY	D.D.
1	10	17	19
2	15	18	21
3	10	19	22
4	5	20	50
5	2	21	60
6	5	22	60
7	10	23	60
8	20	24	61
9	40	25	40
10	40	26	41
11	40	27	18
12	10	28	19
13	10	29	20
14	11	30	21
15	12	31	21
16	14		

TOTAL D.D. 787

DEGREE DAY YEAR (HEATING)

SEPT.	165
OCT.	325
NOV.	787
DEC.	1405
JAN.	1510
FEB.	1375
MAR.	695
APR.	265
MAY	105

TOTAL: 6632   NORMAL* 6135
* Ten-year average

25

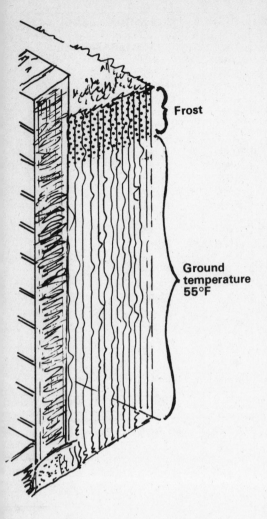

Frost

Ground temperature 55°F

GROUND TEMPERATURES

Below the frost line, the ground stays at a relatively even temperature of about 55°F. Since we will be concerned with heat loss from parts of the home extending into the ground, let's explain a method of converting ground temperatures into DD years.

Assuming a 65°F base temperature in the home and a 55°F base temperature in the ground, our temperature difference or degree hour would be 10 DH. Naturally, our degree day would average out to 10 DD, also. Since in most areas the average heating season is 250 days (check this for your area), we would have a 2500 degree year for the ground temperature.

$$(65° - 55°) \times 250 \text{ days} = 2500 \text{ DD year}$$

In reverse, the cooler ground temperature will absorb heat during the warmer summer months.

FROST LINES

In some areas the frost lines can go as deep as four feet or more. However, in most cases the frost line goes down to about 12 inches or less during the heating season. During the early heating months of September, October, and often November, there is very little frost in the ground because of solar heat radiation. In the latter part of the heating season, the sun is beginning to defrost the ground and the surface ground temperature tends to climb above 32°F. To calculate the actual degree-day year of the frost line, follow the method we outlined for ground temperatures. Estimate degree-day months to establish a degree year.

In our calculations referring to a frost line degree-day year, we will use the figure of 3500 degree-day year. The frost line average temperature will often be colder than the average ground temperature and warmer than the average air temperature during the heating season. The accuracy of this assumption is suspect because very little information has been printed regarding temperatures of the frost line in many parts of the country.

TEMPERATURES IN HEATING DUCTS

Much heat loss occurs via heating ducts. Heat loss by way of heating ducts is often overlooked in the garage, sidewalls, and crawl space of a home. Much of the heat loss which takes place through heating ducts in the basement could actually be used to heat the basement. We have devoted an entire chapter to heat transfer systems, but for now we want only to establish DD years for heating ducts of various heating systems.

The air temperature inside the ducts of gas or fuel-oil furnaces is in the range of 110°F. The warm air in electric resistance furnaces is often only 95°F. In heating systems using heat pumps, the air is only about 85°F. The metal duct system often gives low thermal resistance values. The heat loss from ducts should be closely examined by the home owner.

Using the same rationale of the degree-day year, let's establish degree-day years for our three basic heat transfer systems:

Table 4-1. Degree Day Years for Basic Heat Transfer Systems

Type of System	Degree-Day Year
Fuel oil *or* Natural gas	10 000
Elec. 1 (Resistance)	6240
Elec. 2 (Heat Pump)	3750

Of course, the leat loss of your heating duct is subject to the hours the furnace is in operation and to many other factors. Nevertheless, the range of temperature difference or DD year shown here is high when you consider that in Fairbanks, Alaska, the normal degree day heating year is 14 000.

TO SUMMARIZE

The degree day method gives us the net temperature difference between a 65°F temperature interior and the exterior air temperature. This method simplifies and shortens by many hours the calculations used to discover total heat loss for one given month or for one given heating season.

CHAPTER FIVE

FUELS AND THEIR RATINGS

Propane gas, natural gas, fuel oil, and wood are combustion fuels that we burn in the home. For these fuels we need a chimney (stack) or exhaust to remove gases resulting from combustion. Some of the heat value of the fuel is lost up the stack. This wasted energy ranges from 20% on a new, well-designed heating unit to as high as 50% on a poorly maintained heating unit. In essence, money goes up the stack. It pays to keep your furnace in top operating order.

The percent efficiency of conversion of electricity to heat in the home is 100%. However, at the generation plant where coal is used, energy waste is high, as it is in all fuel combustion units. Energy is also wasted in the transfer of electricity from the generation plant to your home. In the case of forced air electric furnaces and gas furnaces, electricity is required to operate the fan in the system. We do not factor this in most calculations but it is a cost.

Resistance baseboard heating units do not require the operation of a fan. Instead, their heat is transferred by free convective currents. Heat pumps generate more heat per unit quantity of electricity used than resistance furnaces and thus are more efficient.

In home heating, natural gas and fuel oil are bargains when compared to electricity. Because of the low economical trade-offs of adding insulation, many home owners using fuel oil and natural gas may defer thermal correction.

ELECTRIC RESISTANCE

Electricity is sold to the customer in units of kilowatts or kilowatt hours (Kwh). One kilowatt hour will generate 3413 BTU. Heat pumps can generate about 6826 BTU/Kwh on the seasonal average in its operation. In our dramatizations (see Table 1-4), we indicate resistance electric (baseboard and electric furnace) heating as *Elec. 1* Heat pumps are designated as *Elec. 2*. The notation *Elec. 1* indicates a 100% conversion of a Kwh to 3413 BTU. The notation *Elec. 2* indicates a potential of 200% conversion of a Kwh to 6826 BTU. This principle is explained in Chapter 20 on heat pumps. We rated the heat pump higher in our trade-offs than it may perform in actual practice. We did this because of the present popularity of the heat pump at this writing.

COMBUSTION FUELS

Natural gas is sold to the customer by the cubic foot, but is billed to them in increments of 1000 cubic feet (mcf). For convenience we will refer to 1000 cubic feet (mcf) of natural gas as one unit of natural gas.

One unit of natural gas delivered to the home owner is rated as being able to yield one million BTU of heat energy. However, since the home owner is losing at least 30% of his heat energy up the stack, the useful energy delivered to the heating of the home can only be rated as 700 000 BTU. In our cost dramatizations, we show natural gas as *Natural Gas (0.70)*. This notation reflects our assumption that only 70% is useful heat delivered to the home.

Fuel oil is sold to the customer by the gallon. No. 2 fuel oil has a theoretical rating of 140 000 BTU per gallon delivered to the home. Correcting this figure for a 30% waste factor up the stack, we find that the useful energy available from fuel oil for home heating is only 101 000 BTU per gallon. Note that *Fuel Oil* in our dramatizations is also labled *0.70*. Owners of fuel oil furnaces should take great care in keeping their units in top operating condition to get the maximum heat from their furnace units.

Wood is mentioned here because of the popularity of fireplaces. The fireplace is a subject that deserves some attention. (We treat the operation of fireplaces in depth in Chapter 19.) Most wood-burning fireplaces lose 80% of the heat from combustion up the stack. There are many species of wood. Each kind has a characteristic BTU rating but we will stick to an average BTU rating only. According to this average, one pound of wood will yield about 5400 BTU during combustion.

29

Since 80% of this energy is lost up the stack (chimney), the useful heat is only 1080 BTU per pound into the room and the home.

Some homes use coal and others use propane. Check with your dealer about the BTU rating of the fuel you are using. Convert the BTU rating to useful heat after stack (chimney) losses. Be sure to consider only useful heat to the home.

COMPARING FUELS

Heat loss, even in the well-insulated home, will climb into the millions of BTUs for one heating season. Let's use a unit of one million BTU and compare the number of units of different fuels it takes to get this much useful heat to your home.

Table 5-1. Fuel Units Required for One Million BTU Useful Heat

Fuel	Amount Required
Natural gas	1.25 units (1250 ft³)
Fuel oil	9.92 gallons
Elec. 1 (Resistance)	293 Kwh
Elec. 2 (Heat Pump)	147 Kwh
Wood	934 pounds

You can see that natural gas *is* a bargain, especially after examining the costs of other sources of heat from the home. Let's compare the cost of useful heat per million BTU for some commonly used fuels. The fuel costs listed in Table 5-2 are the fuel costs which we will use throughout this book.

Table 5-2. Cost of Useful Heat per Million BTU

Fuel	Cost/Unit	Gross Cost (after stack loss)
Nat. gas	$2.25	$ 3.15
Fuel oil	$0.45	$ 4.46
Elec. 1	$0.04	$11.72
Elec. 2	$0.04	$ 5.86

30

Our figures are not a guarantee that a natural gas heated home is the best bargain. In fact, if the thermal defects are high in the natural gas heated home, it may cost more to heat than an all electric home. But we want to reduce energy loss with a relatively small investment and to approach this energy problem with some degree of intelligence and confidence.

Fine opportunities for rehabilitating old homes, apartments, and commercial establishments are available by the thousands in the real world. New construction methods on homes should assure that energy bills will be less in new homes than in many older homes and thus should make new homes more competitive on the market. Our idea is to keep the energy costs down in existing homes but not to go broke in the process.

C.O.P.

C.O.P. designates estimated **C**oefficient **O**f **P**erformance. Very simply, this describes the estimated operating performance of your heating unit as compared to potential performance of fuel consumed.

We noted that the waste factor on a new gas furnace is 30%. The C.O.P. of this heating unit would be 0.70. A coefficient of performance (C.O.P.) of 0.70 tells us that only 70% of the fuel is converted to useful heat. On older heating units laboring under poor design and poor maintenance, the C.O.P. could be lower than 0.70.

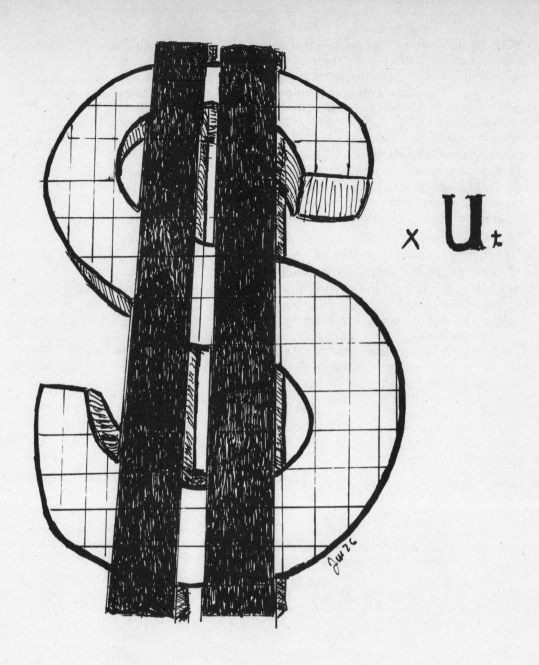

$\times U_t$

CHAPTER SIX
FUEL COST FACTOR

Let's review some of the items we have already covered. A degree-day year is the temperature difference outside for a given year. Each fuel has a different capacity for delivering heat to your home (C.O.P. of the heating unit) and each fuel has a different cost. The heat loss from your home is a result of thermal barriers (insulation, etc.) and can be translated by arithmetic into dollars and cents. In fact, if we knew the above mentioned information in some given place we could calculate the cost of heating a particular home for a given year. We could also calculate the estimated fuel to be consumed for a coming heating season by using averages of the normal degree-day year.

FUEL COST FACTOR

We are interested in how much it is costing us to heat our home, how much it will cost to reduce the heat bill, and how long it will take us to get our improvement money back. To do this, we must use some basic arithmetic. The formula for interpreting the cost of heating for one year is:

$$\text{Heating cost for one season} = \frac{\text{DD year} \times 24}{\text{BTU rating of fuel} \times \text{C.O.P. of furnace}} \times \$ \text{ cost of fuel} \times Ut$$

This formula will give us the estimated heating cost of our home if Ut is the heat transmission rate of the home. Since we will want to calculate the cost of heating through a wall section, window, door, or other components of the house it would be unhandy to continually carry out the entire function of the above formula. Therefore, if we leave the number Ut as an unknown and calculate the rest of the formula, we will then have our fuel cost factor for the area and at the cost of fuel including the estimated efficiency of the heating unit.

We have covered all of these items and we can get the required information for your area with little effort. Since we will be considering different insulations and methods, we will be talking about heat loss in heating dollars and not heat loss in BTUs. Expressing heat loss in dollars will have more meaning to you.

For example: Let's assume your DD year normal is 5150. The fuel used in your home is electricity (baseboard) which gives a C.O. P. of one. Let's also assume the cost of electricity is \$0.04 per kilowatt hour (Kwh). This gives us the information needed to find our fuel cost factor. Remember, the formula is:

$$\text{Heating cost for one season} = \frac{\text{DD year} \times 24}{\text{BTU rating of fuel} \times \text{C.O.P. of furnace}} \times \$ \text{ Cost of fuel} \times Ut$$

With our knowns established above we have:

$$\text{Heating cost for one season} = \frac{5150 \times 24}{3413 \times 1} \times \$ \, 0.04 \times Ut$$

$= \$1.44 \, U_t$ for one heating season in this above mentioned area.

Now all we have to discover is the value of the heat transmission rate (U_t) of your home or some wall section or any other component of your home and then we can discuss heating dollars and not heat loss. That is the name of the game! Heating dollars . . . our cost of heat in money-out-of-pocket terms and not BTUs or percentages.

Knowing the fuel cost factor will allow us to concentrate on the arithmetic value of the heat transmission rate only. As you can see, the larger the rate of heat transmission, the greater will be our cost of heating for one heating season.

You may want to use the fuel cost factor to discover the dollar amount of heating for one or more months in your area. All you need to do is to substitute DD month for DD year in the formula to know what the fuel cost factor would be for that given month.

If you want to discover what your home will cost if you use another fuel, just rework the formula, but substitute the known BTU rating and the C.O.P. of the heating unit and also change the fuel cost factor. For example, we have carried out calculated costs for different fuels using 5150 DD year.

**Table 6-1. Estimated Fuel Costs for
Different Fuels for a 5150 DD Year**

Fuel Type	Cost
Elec. 1 at $0.04/Kwh	$1.44 U_t
Elec. 2 at $0.04/Kwh	$0.72 U_t
Fuel oil at $0.45/ gallon	$0.55 U_t
Natural gas at $2.25/1000 ft^3	$0.39 U_t

Notice that as the DD year decreases, the fuel cost factor also decreases. The same is true if the cost of fuel is reduced. We show you in more detail how to use this formula in the Work Section.

You can now see the importance of discovering heat transmission rate, the U_t of a material. The better we define the heat transmission rate of a material or combination of materials, the more accurately we can define the heating cost for these materials.

Remember that the fuel cost factor will give us the upper limits of fuel costs only and not the actual amount. Chapter 15, which discusses heat gains, will clarify this statement.

If any fault can be found with many energy saving advertisements it is that the ad men are assuming that few, if any, people will take the time to understand a few basic principles. In fact, one wonders if even the writers and creators of the advertisements understand what they are selling. Because of this weakness, you as a consumer could unwittingly be buying some very shaky logic. Worse yet, you could be throwing away hard-earned money because of this misleading information.

TRANSMISSION RATES REVISITED

In the home, the heat transmission rate is subject to the insulation, lumber, and all materials constituting a wall, ceiling, or floor. Since our fuel cost formula will take into consideration the dollar costs and temperature differences in your area, we can now concentrate only on the transmission rate (U_t) or heat conductance of a particular wall or any other component of your home.

By examining each minute detail of one wall section, we can establish the conductance rate of the wall section. Armed with the fuel cost factor, we can interpret the insulation in terms of heating dollars and then can compare various materials with respect to dollar savings and the cost of materials. Then with these figures, we can decide if the cost of the improvement is worth the savings we might experience.

If you can slip a piece of paper through a locked window or between boards, you have discovered an air leak.

34

An important factor in considering the heat transmission rate or the insulation value of a given material is workmanship, both idealistically and practically. Because of wire chases, lumber, and many problems involved in building a wall section, it would be improper to consider the entire wall as having 100% R-11 insulation in it. The compressing of fiberglass insulation, air pockets, etc., would realistically reduce the insulation value of the material by 20% or more. In fact, the heat loss of a wall could be increased 35% just because of the method of installation of the insulation. For some materials, the R value is a laboratory number which may be quite different from the actual R value experienced in the field. This difference results from methods used in applying the insulating material.

In examining heat loss of windows, we must consider not only the construction of the frame and the glass but also the anticipated air flow through cracks. By looking at each separate component, as you will do in the Work Section, you will be able to decide with reasonable accuracy whether or not that component needs thermal correction.

In the next section we will cover the major components of your home in some detail. We will use the maximum range of potential heat loss, not the true cost of heating. The true cost of heating a home is subject to the insulating efficiency of materials, heat gains, and air infiltration. To understand what is really happening in your home, you must examine every detail in the light of maximum heat loss cost and not minimum.

Some of the factors which you will want to consider are your living style, the method by which your home was built, the efficiency and the type of heating unit you own, the orientation of your home to the sun, and the varying wind velocities in your area. The small effort of understanding this first section will pay handsome dividends to you as a home owner.

When you use the base formula

$$\frac{DD \text{ (for your area)} \times 24}{BTU \text{ rating of fuel used} \times C.O.P.} \times \$ \text{ Cost of heat} \times U_t = \text{Fuel Cost Factor in Dollars} \times U_t$$

for your calculations, you will be using it over and over again for various parts of the house. Try to keep your calculations in an organized manner and label U_t accordingly (e.g., U_t (House) or U_t (North Wall) or U_t (All Windows). Remember, U_t is the transmission rate of heat out of or into your home, or wall section, floor, etc. Good Luck!

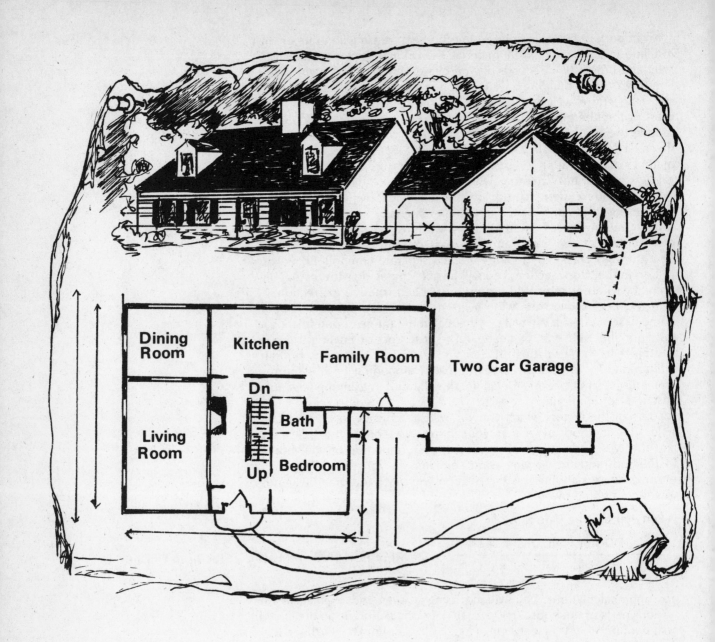

CHAPTER SEVEN
THE BUILDING OF A BUILDING

Let me share with you a sign I have in my office. I do not know the author's name, but if he is reading this, I'd like to thank him. The sign reads: "The object of all dedicated builders should be to thoroughly analyze all situations, anticipate all problems prior to their occurrence, have answers for these problems, and move swiftly to solve these problems when called upon . . . . However, when you are up to your ass in alligators, it is difficult to remind yourself that your initial objective was to drain the swamp."

36

As a builder for many years in a small country area, I was not plagued with regulations and building inspectors. However, I was plagued by ignorance (some on my part), incompetent people, suppliers, and home owners who grew to like or dislike me. As a builder you get to see the best and worst of society in all of its trappings and misgivings. Egos clash, but somehow a balance must be achieved, as you are at one moment working with an apprentice helper who makes you wonder if he knows one end of the hammer from the other, and at the next moment discussing technical problems with a civil engineer.

There are always two factors that builders fight about with subcontractors. These factors are deadlines and techniques and are usually heard in the form of "tomorrow" and "That's not the way we are used to doing it." Tomorrow may well be the busiest day in the construction industry—because that's when the subcontractor and suppliers always promise to do something. Resistance to changing ways and using new materials is a serious problem with many subcontractors.

Let's move back to a construction site and see what is going on. The carpenters are here now and the noise is unbelievable. Hammers banging, power saws are whining, and men are shouting. It looks like a happy, productive affair. It's exciting to see a house being built. Pencil lines from drawings become walls and everything looks so permanent. The excitement runs through the air. The outside walls are going up; building boards are being nailed to the frame. There's a slight gap here and there, but no matter. After all, we are going to stuff the wall full of insulation. A hammer strikes the soft fiberboard and makes a hole, but it's a small hole and no one seems concerned.

Here come the plumbers. Plumbers are happy chaps on the whole. They are well paid for their skills and it is reflected in their attitudes. Zap! A large saw cuts through the roof to make room for the vent pipes. Zing! A small hole drill flies through the studs to make room for the smaller vent pipes, the waste lines, and the water lines. Up through the top plates and down through the bottom plates, then farewell plumbers.

Here come the electricians. Electricians have the fastest and longest drills in town. They can drill through three studs on the wall without even moving. You should see them go around corners and down through lower plates . . . zzip, zzam, buzzz . . . bang!

Now the furnace man arrives. The furnace installer seldom fools with drills. He likes saws, hammers, and axes. Away he goes, up and down and all around.

Look, here comes our thermal friend . . . the insulation man. Stuff here, stuff there, stuff, stuff, stuff. He is gone in no time at all.

The drywall man is here now. The production of this house is really going fast! The drywall installer cuts a board the wrong way and over-cuts the electrical outlets. No worry, the finish man will cover that . . . we hope!

Have you really seen what is happening here? All too often the thermal barrier is being destroyed as we build houses. There is no chance of building a good insulating barrier as long as we are required to drill holes on the outside thermal wall and have to place heat-sucking plumbing stacks there also. As long as there are holes to allow air to flow from the inside to the outside (or vice versa), the wall will never approach its insulating potentials!

This situation does not have to exist. Experience has shown me time and time again that the building trades can and will respond to intelligent direction. By learning the fundamentals of thermal barriers and by passing this knowledge on to others, you can play an important role in this education process. Ferreting out small leaks before, during, and after construction is where some of the largest dividends lie for you, the home owner. For low heating bills the importance of paying attention to details and good workmanship looms larger and larger as fuel costs become dearer to all of us.

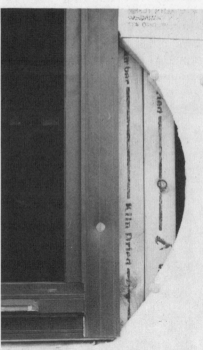

CHAPTER EIGHT
EXTERIOR WALLS

"We always seem to have time to come back to fix something but we never seem to have enough time to do it right in the first place."

The quality and value of a home, could be improved 100% by just taking a trifle more care. Unfortunately, quality building is something nearly every builder claims but very few provide. The public's definition of quality too often reflects the nice pretty lights or some unique finish but does not entail quality construction including

completion of all details during the framing and insulation process. Laws, codes, and thousands of regulations often hinder efficiency and the very quality we all are seeking.

The thermal barrier of exterior walls in homes throughout this country and most likely throughout the world are being compromised because of the many functions they must perform. The exterior walls of a home support the roof or floor above. In addition to providing support, the exterior walls must function as wind shields (often poor ones), chaseways for electrical wires and outlets, and receptacles for windows, doors, and plumbing. The exterior walls must also function as thermal barriers.

The real secret of providing a proper thermal barrier on the exterior wall lies in doing the job right. The wall should be carefully sealed before the insulation goes in. Also, the insulation should be carefully tucked, not stuffed, into place. The electrical wire chaseways and outlet boxes as well as the plumbing chases should be sealed. If the job is done correctly with regular building board, the exterior building board does not have to be foam board, even though foam board may have a higher R rating. The drywall should be carefully glued and nailed into place. The electrical outlet holes should be done a little bit more carefully and the outside wall snugly fitted into place. Windows and doors should be installed correctly and sealed around the frames. If all these things were done, the energy consumption in modern homes could be reduced by 35% or more!

On a cold winter day when the wind is blowing and penetrating the wall system or sucking warm air outside, the economics of heating can be devastating. Air penetration takes place under and around the siding, at starter strips, at corners, and around window and door frames. The channels for air penetration through the wall are the electrical and plumbing chases. This can be corrected by the home owner in existing homes by applying caulk rope, by taping electrical outlets shut with tape, or with a waterproof electrical cover. Careful inspection and just a little bit of effort will pay handsome dividends. On new construction, the use of building paper to cover cracks and crevices and the use of construction glue as a sealer will save the home owner many heating and cooling dollars and will ultimately increase the years of usable fuel supplies.

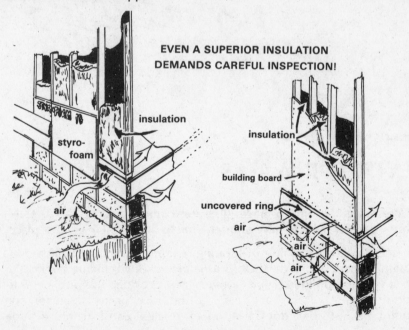

EVEN A SUPERIOR INSULATION DEMANDS CAREFUL INSPECTION!

40

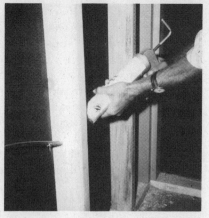

INSULATION MATERIALS

On the microscopic scale of heat transfer, trapped air is a deterrent to the transfer of heat from one molecule to another. Actually, slowing the transfer of heat is the true function of insulation. The factor that determines the thermal resistance (R) value of an insulating material is trapped air. All insulating materials depend upon trapped, still air to slow the transfer of heat. In the market place, both the builder and the home owner have basically the same materials to choose from—fiberglass batts or wool (loose), cellulose, ureaformaldehyde foam (solid or liquid), styrenefoam boards (Styrofoam® is a trademark of the Dow Chemical Co.), and urethane foam (solid or liquid). The insulating properties of these materials depend upon trapped air or trapped inert gas as in the case of urethane. Their insulating properties also depend upon *workmanship*, the care with which they are installed. Each material has a cost and certain limitations. Because liquid foams can be applied only within certain temperature ranges, they have limited usage by the builder during cold winter months and hot summer months.

Urea-formaldehyde foam is a good product. However, during the application and drying processes its odor can be overwhelming. Also, if it is put on too thick, the outer membrane solidifies and traps moisture in the inner core where the foam may not dry for a long time.

Styrene foam or Styrofoam® boards are highly flammable and can be an extreme fire hazard if not covered with the proper fire retardant material. Styrofoam® or a bead board type of styrene board applied to the outside stud walls is dependent upon the fire protection of the drywall and the exterior materials of the home for its fire protection. If these materials are used correctly, the fear of creating a fire hazard with them is no greater than it is with any other combustible material. However, under all circumstances this type of foam or any other type of foam should be protected with a fire retardant material.

Cellulose, blown in the sidewalls of existing homes, will act as an excellent thermal barrier and is superior thermally to fiberglass type of insulation. However, care must be taken to prevent bridging of wires in the wall because bridging causes an area not to have insulation. Settling of all blown insulation in the wall cavities must be considered. Cellulose (made of macerated paper) must be treated for fire resistance and must also be vermin proof and insect proof.

Fiberglass wool (in loose form) has the same bridging problem as cellulose. However, it is fireproof, vermin proof, and insect proof to a certain dgree. Fiberglass wool in batt form has a lower thermal resistance value than other materials but, with everything else taken

41

into consideration, it must rank as the best overall thermal insulator available for exterior walls.

Many "sandwich" boards are available for new construction. The sandwich board consists of two sheets of plywood or other construction material with a solid foam core. With the solid center core, air penetration is limited and because of fabricating methods a smaller quantity of lumber is required in the wall system. Cost per lineal foot of wall construction is often less and thermally this sandwich board may prove to be one of the best for lowering heating energy costs in the future. Universal acceptance of this method of construction is extremely limited, however, because of code acceptance.

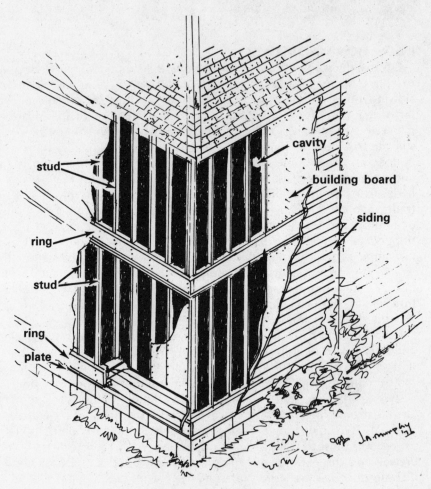

TWO STORY FRAME

HEAT TRANSFER IN WALLS

Let us examine the problem of heat transfer in the wall under static air conditions (no air infiltration). The thermal weakness of an exterior wall is in the stud and wood framing members. One must keep in mind that this is relative to the insulation in the stud cavity only. The stud cavity is the area between the vertical framing members.

In the building industry, much has been said about using less wood in the exterior walls and reducing the amount of window space in order to conserve energy and reduce potential heating bills for the home owner. Two by fours are placed 16" on center in order to provide the proper strength to carry the load of the roof or the floor

42

above the plate. Two by four studs, 24″ on center can be used but suitable plywood must be used as a bracing material to give the proper strength to the wall. This plywood has a special glue to take the punishment from moisture. This exterior glue could cause problems in the inner wall because of the condensation of moisture caused by the low transmission of water vapor through it. This transmission or migration of moisture through the wall would be subject to the vapor barrier of the warm side of the wall. We will discuss this problem in greater detail in Chapter 16 on humidity and moisture. Another proposed method for reducing heat transfer involves the use of two by six studs on the outer wall 24″ on center and the filling of the cavity with more insulation (5½ inches worth). Still another method involves the use of a foam board (styrene or Styrofoam®) in place of insulating board to decrease the amount of heat transfer through the exterior walls.

Exterior materials such as brick, aluminum, and wood have about the same thermal resistance. Stucco has one of the lowest thermal resistance values per thickness (applied). However, unlike all the rest of the exterior materials, stucco when properly applied creates the best windshield. Air infiltration is the lowest with stucco. The anti-infiltration qualities of stucco can be achieved with aluminum siding if the envelope of the structure is sealed **before** the siding is installed. If the structure is not sealed, aluminum siding will allow air penetration into the wall system and into your home because of moisture vent holes. Judging from past observations of field applications of aluminum siding, it would be safe to say that most families with aluminum-sided homes have a heating problem.

Brick has about the same thermal resistance value as aluminum or wood siding. Since the mortar joints and the bricks themselves act as an excellent windshield, infiltration through the side wall is less than that of aluminum, wood shingles, etc., with the possible exception of stucco. However, brick must be vented to allow potential moisture condensation to escape. These vents will, under certain conditions, allow inside air to escape or cold air to enter the wall system.

You can select a material to use on your home for beauty or for whatever reason or reasons turn you on. Just be sure the envelope under the exterior material is sealed. Sealing, workmanship, and thoroughness will pay handsome dividends to the home owner over the operating life of the home.

So far, we have looked at the negative end of heat loss through exterior walls. We will cover solar heat in greater detail in a separate chapter but let's keep in mind that because of heat from sunshine on the east, west and especially the south walls we have a potential heat gain during the heating season. Under the proper conditions, solar heat will often reduce heat loss to zero for many hours during the solar day. Unfortunately, due to lack of research it is difficult to factor the economics of solar heat gain into our calculations.

ECONOMICS APPLIED

On page 34, certain fuel cost factors subject to the heat transmission rate of material were presented (Elec. 1, ($1.44) U_t; Elec. 2, ($0.72)U_t; Fuel oil ($0.55)U_t; and Natural gas, ($0.39)$U_t$). These figures were calculated for areas with a 5150 degree-day year at fuel costs slightly higher (in most cases) than 1976 prices. By using these fuel cost factors and the heat transmission rates of various wall components, you should be able to get an idea as to relative savings. In the Work Section at the end of this book, you will do this study for your own home. The method is extremely effective for determining where your heating dollars are going.

REDUCING STUDS IN THE WALL

Consider a 1000 square foot wall area. Excluding windows and doors, the amount of wood used in the wall system and its heat transmission rate (U_t) are listed in Table 8-1.

Table 8-1. Effect of Stud Area on Conductance

Method	Area of Wood	Conductance Rate (U_t)
16" on center	106.8 ft² (10.68%)	14.84
24" on center	98.1 ft² (9.81%)	13.63
48" on center	68.0 ft² (6.8%)	9.45

The wood area of the 1000 square foot opaque wall area using two-by-fours, spaced 24" on center changes only slightly because we still must use the same amount of lumber for top and bottom plates in the wall. By multiplying the transmission rate by the fuel-dollar factor, we are ready to examine the Thermal Woods.

Table 8-2. Effects of Using Fewer Studs on Exterior Wall

System	Transmission Rate (U_t)	Elec. 1	Elec. 2	Fuel Oil (0.70)	Nat. Gas (0.70)
16" on center	14.30	$20.59	$10.29	$7.86	$5.57
24" on center	13.66	$19.67	$9.83	$7.51	$5.32
48" on center	9.49	$13.67	$6.83	$5.21	$3.70

Certainly every little bit helps. However, one must balance the amount of heat gain to be realized against the expense of correction. One must also consider the heat loss due to air leaks caused by cracks and crevices. Nevertheless, let's look at another consideration.

COST OF INSULATION

Many gas homes and fuel oil homes have no insulation in the sidewalls at all. Let us compare the dollar cost of heating a wall with 1000

44

square feet of wall area which has 0.00 (zero) inches of insulation with a wall which has 3.5 inches of filberglass insulation. Since we may be considering a new home, let's look at the possibility of replacing the insulboard with 1 inch of foam (R = 5.5). Let's also compare the insulating effect of 3.5 inches of styrene type foam in the wall with that of 3.5 inches of cellulose insulation. The wall area will have studs 16" on center.

Table 8-3. Cost Comparisons of Different Types of Insulation on a 1000 Square Foot Wall

Method	Transmission Rate (U_t)	Elec. 1	Elec. 2	Fuel Oil (0.70)	Nat. Gas (0.70)
0.00 insulation	221.16	$318.47	$159.24	$121.63	$86.25
3.5" fiberglass	88.07	$126.82	$63.41	$48.44	$34.34
3.5" cellulose	64.37	$92.70	$46.39	$35,40	$25.70
Fiberglass w/foam	58.78	$84.65	$42.32	$32.33	$22.92
3.5" foam	57.98	$83.49	$41.74	$31.88	$22.61
2 × 6 Stud w/5.5" fiberglass	64.37	$92.37	$46.39	$35.40	$25.10

From this table, you can see that adding insulation in the cavity areas of an exterior wall really saves on heating cost. Also, this table demonstrates that dollar savings are a function of the type of heating unit and cost of fuel. These dollar figures are based on a 5150 DD year area and will change from area to area. In Wisconsin, the heating dollar cost will increase and in Tennessee it would certainly be less. However, we have yet to factor in heat gains. Heat gains will be covered in Chapter 15.

We have assumed good workmanship for all of the systems in Table 8-3. To account for workmanship is very difficult. If sealing is not done properly, all of these figures could be increased 30% to 40%! In addition, each system here is considered under unreal static heat transfer conditions. In colder areas where the degree day or the length of winter is longer, the costs of heating will naturally increase. In the warm southern states of this country, the cost will decrease proportionately to the degree days and solar gains. Even though the seller of insulation may factor in 40% savings, what you must find out is 40% of what as well as the actual dollar value of this 40% savings.

To find out the length of payback, you must get separate cost bids for the system you have in your home or anticipated new home. Then, by using one system as standard to other systems, you can compare extra cost and potential savings.

TO SUMMARIZE

The net heating cost of exterior walls is subject to heat loss through cavities between construction members (wood), the construction members themselves, air infiltration into the wall system, and internal and external heat gains.

In the Work Section we show in greater detail how to discover the total heat transmission rate (U_t) of exterior wall sections of your own home. Our next step is to look at ceilings.

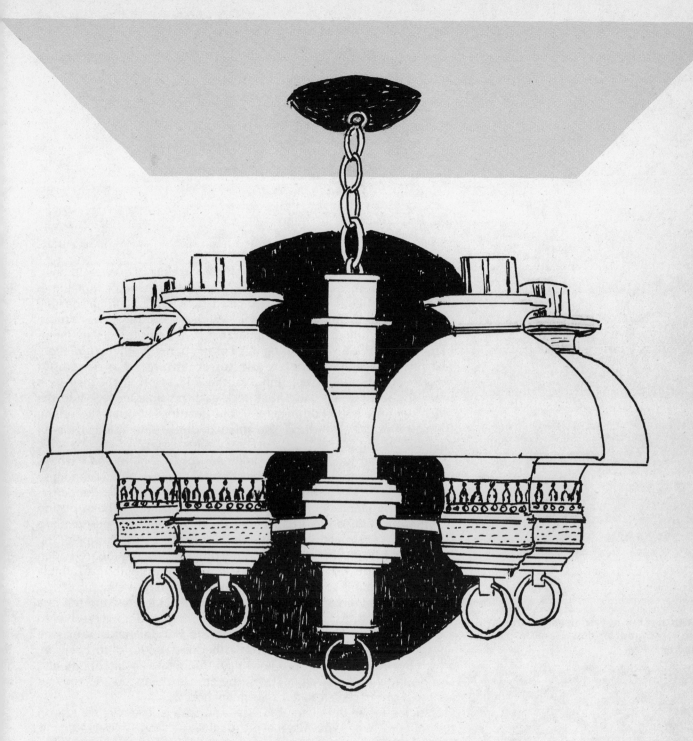

CHAPTER NINE
CEILINGS

Ceilings are getting a lot of attention today. They are easy to get at in the average home. Ceiling materials are easy for suppliers to sell, and their sales are further enhanced by the misconception that all heat rises. As you will find out, it is possible for a basement window to lose more heat than the entire ceiling!

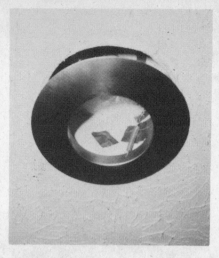
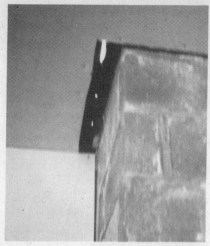

The ceiling of your home is probably a composite of drywall, lumber, and hopefully, insulation. The ceiling's insulation value or function as a thermal barrier is often compromised by wires, plumbing, heating ducts, chimneys, and access panels. Air leaks around light fixtures, chimneys, heating ducts, or anything that penetrates the ceiling membrane will increase your heating bill. For the homes with no insulation, seal off these air leaks before the correction project is started. Or before you add more insulation, seal these leaks off. If the insulation is already present, go back and check each possible air leak into the attic. Certainly insulation is helpful, but heat loss through the ceiling from air moving into or from the attic will do considerable harm even after you insulate.

Often we introduce moisture-laden air from the baths and kitchens into the attic area. If this air is not properly vented, it will condense and freeze as it comes in contact with the cold roof. After condensation or subsequent melting, the water will drip down to the insulation and thereby reduce the thermal values of the ceiling. The best method of ventilation is to vent high-moisture air directly to the outside of the home, not into the attic! The math needed to calculate the free open air spaces of the vents is presented in Appendix G. With this formula you can find out if your attic is over-vented or under-vented.

During the summer we all recognize that an attic gets very hot due to solar heating. As a result, the rooms below become very uncomfortable. In cases like this, especially in the warmer states, it may be cheaper to operate a vent fan with a thermostat control to keep the attic temperature at a desired level than to operate an air conditioner. During the winter in colder states, the attic air heats up and reduces heat loss of the ceiling to zero for many hours.

Shingles are an excellent absorber of solar rays. The ceramic bits on the shingles (what you may have thought was sand is really ceramic bits) absorb solar rays and then transmit the heat to the air and to the attic. In this way, heat loss of rooms below is reduced during the heating season. Note how the roof exposed to the south clears itself of snow first. This melting is caused by solar heating. Rapid, spotty snow melting on a cloudy day is an indication of a heat leak in your ceiling below.

In summary, the heat transfer of the ceiling is subject to heat transfer from below, through the wood ceiling members, insulation in the cavities, air seeping up from cracks and crevices, and the rate of air ventilation within the attic area. If the ventilation is too great, the heat loss from the ceiling naturally will be increased

With the use of Styrofoam® at truss ends, we can control air flow as well as humidity and heat loss.

48

Too often, attics are overventilated. This overventilation actually increases the net heat loss of ceilings. Closer examination of ventilation and vapor barriers are in order.

Heat gains from the sunshine on the roof to the interior of the attic actually decrease some of our cost of heating over the heating season. By insulating gable ends we will keep the interior temperature of the attic higher than outside air temperatures and reduce the heat loss from rooms below. Surprisingly, in a well-designed home, very little if any ventilation is in order if adequate vapor rejection is implemented.

Solar heat gains during the summer months through the roof to the attic air are not wanted. Removal of solar heated air from the attic is in order in summer. Sometime in the future, especially in the southern states or areas where air conditioning is mandatory most of the year, rejected heat could be put to practical use for preheating our hot water instead of heating the outdoors.

In Appendix G, we outline the necessary and recommended ventilation of attics. Also, in our Work Section, we outline the different areas to check for heat loss from the ceiling into the attic area.

TRIANGULAR ROOF CORRECTION

As we begin to add more and more insulation in the attic area (some schools of thought recommend ten inches or more), we come into direct conflict with a physical limitation. The roof has a pitch. The roof configuration is the shape of a triangle. The top part of the triangle is called the peak or ridge and the corners of the triangle are where the roof trusses are set on the outside walls. At the point

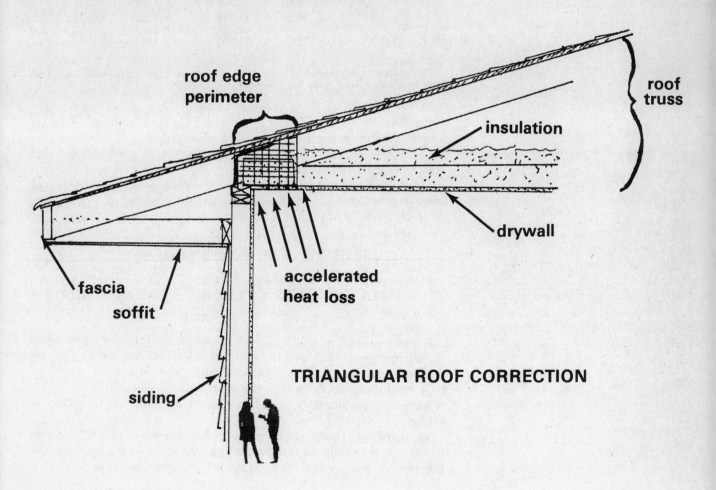

TRIANGULAR ROOF CORRECTION

49

where the roof trusses are set on the outer walls (see diagram), we have only about four inches of head room from the top of the wall to the bottom of the roof. Naturally, we cannot get ten inches of insulation in this space. As a result, we have a thermal leak along the front and rear of the roof edge. The thermal loss or heat leak at this point will be considerably more than it will be in the center of the ceiling. In fact, because of this problem, most ceiling insulations do not do the insulating job as claimed on roofs with 4/12 pitches. We must take this triangular area into consideration in all of our calculations.

In the now-famous Arkansas house, it is recommended that the truss be built up so that more insulation could be placed at the perimeter. Fortunately, there is a better and less expensive way to reduce the loss of heating dollars through the ceiling.

Let's first examine what the triangular correction factor does to the thermal resistance (R) as we pile insulation into the attic space. (See Appendix D for math.)

LOOSE FIBERGLASS

Let us consider loose fiberglass wool at the density that gives us an R rating of 2.20* per inch per square foot of ceiling area.

Table 9-1. Loose Fiberglass Wool Insulation in Ceiling

Depth	R Rating	U/ft^2	Triangular Correction	Final U/ft^2
6″	13.2	0.075	× 1.07	0.081
8″	17.5	0.056	× 1.14	0.064
10″	22.0	0.045	× 1.16	0.053
12″	26.5	0.038	× 1.20	0.045
14″	30.8	0.032	× 1.31	0.041

*The R rating of loose insulation is subject to many variables. I have seen loose fiberglass insulation "rated" from $R = 2.20/in/ft^2$ to $3.33/in/ft^2$.

Regardless of which material is used, the higher the depth of insulation fill, the more the trangular-correction factor.

CELLULOSE IN THE ATTIC

Let us now use a more dense material, in this case we shall consider cellulose, which is really treated paper. BE SURE YOU USE A PERMANENT, FIRE-RATED CELLULOSE!

Table 9-2. Cellulose Insulation in Ceiling

Depth	R Rating	U/ft^2	Triangular Correction	Final U/ft^2
6″	22.8	0.043	× 1.06	0.0456
8″	30.4	0.32	× 1.14	0.0375

When you look at the final heat transmission rate per square foot (U/ft^2) for the six-inch and the eight-inch fill, you can see that we are reaching the point of economical return for insulating a ceiling. It is interesting to note that the final U/ft^2 is about the same for 6 inches of cellulose ($R = 3.8$ per inch) as it is for 12 inches of fiberglass!

Naturally, we could use a more dense fiberglass to get a higher R. In fact, we really should be putting insulation in the attic area by the pound, not by the inch. Manufacturers should label their bags

50

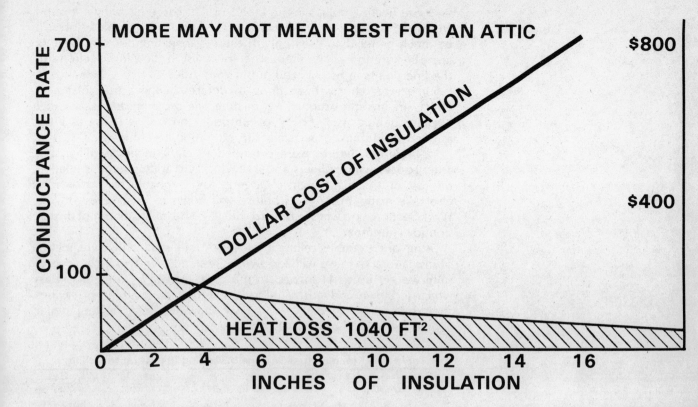

MORE MAY NOT MEAN BEST FOR AN ATTIC

CONDUCTANCE RATE — 700, 100

DOLLAR COST OF INSULATION — $800, $400

HEAT LOSS 1040 FT²

INCHES OF INSULATION — 0 2 4 6 8 10 12 14 16

accordingly and installers should certify that the density of the insulation which has been put into the attic meets the manufacturer's specifications.

COST OF CEILING HEAT LOSS

Let's examine the economics of heat loss through a ceiling that has an area of 1040 ft². We will consider both the heat transmission taking place through the trusses and the triangular-roof correction. Assume a 5150 DD representation of the Indiana and Illinois areas.

Table 9-3. Cost Comparison of Varying Insulation Depths of 1040 Square Foot Ceiling

Fiberglass Depth	Transmission Rate (U)	Elec. 1	Elec. 2	Fuel Oil (0.70)	Nat. Gas (0.70)
0"	693.44	$998.55	$499.29	$381.39	$270.44
4"	86.65	$124.74	$62.39	$47.66	$33.79
6"	68.63	$98.83	$49.41	$37.75	$26.76
8"	54.70	$78.76	$39.38	$30.08	$21.33
Cellulose Depth		**Cellulose Insulation**			
6"	48.55	$69.91	$34.95	26.70	$18.93
8"	35.87	$51.66	$25.83	$19.73	$13.99

The first big savings comes from the first four inches! Over all, in most areas of 6000 DD or less, a depth of six inches is within the limitations of attic insulation. In colder areas, a depth of eight inches pays off if cellulose or a dense fiberglass is used.

On TV and in magazines, there is a push for the home owner to install insulation in the attic in the form of batts. Forget it. This method will not cover the trusses or ceiling joists. Instead, blowing insulation in by yourself or having it done professionally will actually

51

save you heating dollars in the long run. The loose fill will get around and over trusses, wires, and pipes in the attic. This complete job will be much better than batts only. If there are heating ducts in the attic area, be sure to insulate them. The check list in the Work Section lists the fine points to be checked out in your attic.

Some research has been done to determine the actual solar gain effects in an attic during the heating season. Indications are that because of solar gains, heat loss through the ceiling is not as great as one would think, especially if air infiltration is kept low.

In Table 9-3, figures were extended to eight inches of fill in the attic. Today, many builders and individuals are adding more insulation on top of the eight inches. Does it pay? Probably so. But it may also take many, many years before you begin to break even. In the Work Section, you will see how to calculate the ideal amount of insulation for your area.

Using our example ceiling of 1040 ft^2, let's start with eight inches of insulation. Then we will add two inches and then two inches more, until we get up to 14 inches. In this case, we will be using fiberglass which is blown and not cellulose. Nevertheless, the ratio of savings should be dramatized. We will now show the total heating dollar savings per year in a 5150 DD year area.

Table 9-4.   Incremental Savings of Adding Insulation to Ceiling

Depth	Elec. 1	Elec. 2	Fuel Oil 0.70	Nat. Gas 0.70
8"	base	base	base	base
10"	($17.54)*	($8.77)	($6.69)	($4.75)
12"	($11.34)	($5.67)	($4.33)	($3.07)
14"	($6.98)	($3.49)	($2.66)	($1.89)

*These savings, in brackets, are from one step to the next step with added insulation.

If you went from 8 inches to 14 inches with Elec. 1, you would save $35.86 for one heating season. At today's prices, it would cost a home owner about $280.80 to add six more inches of insulation in this example attic. So the trade-off would take 7.83 years to get the money back. However, in the case of a home with a heat pump, the trade-off could go to 12 or 14 years or even longer if fuel oil or natural gas is used. In the Work Section, you will see how to get the trade-off on your home.

52

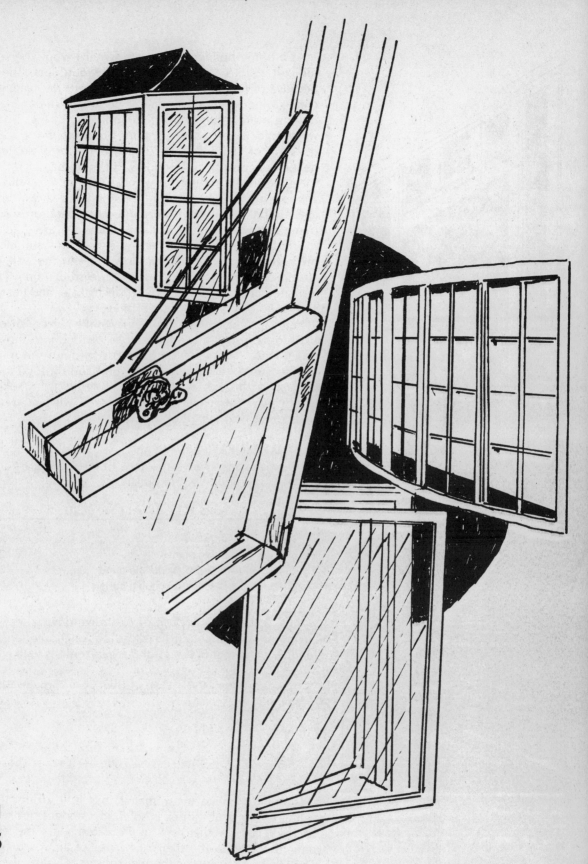

CHAPTER TEN
WINDOWS

Windows provide for ventilation, visibility, and escape. Recently, they have come under fire by the construction industry as a primary source of heat loss. There are suggestions for reducing windows in size and number. Are all these claims based upon objective facts or is it just the easy way for heating experts to dodge the real issue?

53

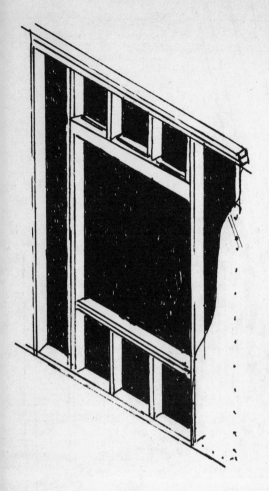

As a home builder and home owner I would personally find it very difficult not to be able to view the outdoors. The lack of sunlight because of fewer windows would be very depressing. Also, if we decrease window area, we may be adding to the energy problem by requiring more artificial light. In addition, during the summer months, we would have less ventilation. Then we must consider the safety question of escape. So, as objectively as possible, let us examine the heat loss and gains of a window in the home.

Notice in the figure the wood frame of the wall required to set a window in place. In the Work Section we treat windows by lineal footage of the wall, which takes into consideration the heat loss of the frame and the window. For this study, we are going to examine just the individual window. There is a note of caution about using this method because, when a window is set in the wall, there is often an air gap between the window and the stud frame. This area must be insulated and sealed. Otherwise, air leakage and heat loss will increase and make our calculations worthless.

Heat loss and heat gain may take place through a window. Heat loss through a window can be divided into three classes: (1) heat loss through the glass, (2) heat loss through the frame, and (3) heat loss because of air infiltration around and through the window sashes. Heat gain through a window will result from solar heat. Even on cloudy days ultraviolet and visible rays will penetrate a window and reduce the heat loss of a window.

HEAT LOSS OF WINDOW PANES

Let's compare single-pane glass to insulated glass and then see what the heat saving effect is in dollars.

Table 10.1.   Heat Loss of Window Panes

Type of Glass	Transmission Rate (U)
Single pane glass	$1.13/ft^2$
¼" Air space on double pane	$0.65/ft^2$
½" Air space on double pane	$0.58/ft^2$

We will cover the function of storm windows after we touch some other bases first. Since our heat loss is a function of area, let's examine a window pane that is $3' \times 3'$, or 9 ft^2, in regions with a 5150 DD year.

Table 10-2.   Cost of Heat Loss Through Glass

Type of Glass	Transmission Rate (U)	Elec. 1	Elec. 2	Fuel Oil (0.70)	Nat. Gas (0.70)
Single pane	10.16	$14.64	$7.32	$5.59	$3.96
¼" Air space	6.20	$8.93	$4.42	$3.41	$2.42
½" Air space	5.84	$8.41	$4.20	$3.21	$2.27

Glass, not unlike many metals, has little if any thermal resistance value. Its thermal barrier is solely dependent upon the air films next to the glass. In the case of insulated glass the thermal barrier is dependent upon the thermal barrier of air space between the glass. The insulation value or thermal resistance value of ¾ inch air space is equivalent to a four inch air space as often found in storm windows. As the depth of air space decreases from the ¾ inch space the thermal resistance value of the air space decreases. As the air space becomes larger than four inches, the air space becomes subject to convective currents causing a greater loss of heat. For this reason, storm windows

54

In homes and many other types of buildings, much heat loss takes place through wide expanses of windows.

properly installed often create a thermal barrier due to air space thickness slightly greater in value than many so-called thermal pane or insulated windows.

Judging from Table 10-2 and comparing the savings of a ½ inch insulated window to the single pane window there appears to be a significant savings. In fact, if I were selling windows I would claim a 50% savings over the single pane window. This is often the case on today's market. However, if I were clever enough not to inform you that a storm window would be just as effective as my insulated glass, you would most likely buy what I was selling you.

Before we approach the heat loss of the frame of the window let us make an observation. Large picture windows and massive glass walls in homes are not uncommon. If we had a fixed window pane that took up an entire wall and it had insulated glass with a ½ inch air space, its heat loss would be $1.03 per square foot of glass area in a 5150 DD year area, especially if it faced north. If the wall were eight feet high and twelve feet long, the heat loss would cost us $98.88 per heating season with electric heating. If we removed the mass area of glass and replaced it with a frame wall with just 3.5 inches of insulation, we would only spend $10.81 in heating dollars for the same area.

Both the frame of the window and the amount of glass area contribute to the heat loss of the entire window. Most modern homes have aluminum windows, not wood windows. The question is which of the two is better? The answer is that they are about the same if everything is considered. In fact, some wood windows may prove to become thermally defective during extreme cold spells because of the expansion and contraction of the wood itself. In this case, a storm window is in order.

Depending on the grain of the wood, you may be able to see the separation of wood window sashes as they move outward during cold spells. During cold spells, the crack between the sashes of a double-hung window will become larger and allow cold air to move through. This air penetration will ruin any thermal effectiveness the wood framing may have. Most wood frames have to be at least two inches in width and at least one inch thick to hold a window pane in place. The heat transmission rate (U) per square foot of wood is 0.557.

The gap between these window sashes is demonstrated with this piece of heavy paper.

The heat transmission rate per square foot of aluminum is 1.21, about twice that of wood. These values include both inside and outside air films. Aluminum is stronger than wood and easier to mold and put into place. Thus, less area is required to achieve the same result with aluminum as with wood. Often, the ratio of the amount of aluminum to that of wood is one to two. Taking this into consideration, the frame of the aluminum framed window and the frame of the wood framed window are about thermally equal.

The true measuring device for windows is the quality of window construction and the quality of the method by which it is installed. The true problem with any window is air infiltration.

The air penetration through cracks and crevices is dependent upon the type of window and the manner in which the window is installed by the carpenters. A fixed pane of glass with no movable parts will have little if any air penetration through it. These are referred to as casement type windows. A window that has one pane fixed and one which slides horizontally is referred to as a slider or a movable casement. The most common window is the type where the lower and upper sashes can be opened or closed vertically. These are called double hung windows. In a single hung window only the lower sash is movable and the upper sash is fixed. A bow window or picture window can be classified as a fixed-pane if it does not vent. Jalousie windows have a number of small glass panes that can be opened outward with a crank. Some casement type windows can be opened outward with a crank.

With the many hundreds of manufacturers in the market with hundreds of different styles of windows it is difficult to single out any as the best because of the many varieties available. Each style has a different level of air penetration. Movable windows will have the most air penetration because of the greater amount of lineal footage where air can penetrate. Fixed windows will naturally have the lower amount of air infiltration.

A simple test for you to perform to see if your windows require sealing is to tape a plastic cover on the interior side of your window. Be sure the cover goes over the entire trim of your window. If the plastic billows at 10 to 15 mile per hour wind velocities you have a leaky window.

Often little, if any, insulation or sealant is placed around the frame of the window as it is set into place. The removal of the trim from the inside or outside of your home will tell you the story on your windows. Seal and insulate around the window frame.

The window manufacturers subject their windows to a standard wind test. This standard was established many years ago. According to this standard, the lower the penetration of wind through cracks and crevices, the better the window. Unfortunately, this criterion is too often ignored by builders and home buyers altogether. Builders and home buyers just kept asking, "How cheap is it? How pretty does it look? Does it have insulated glass?"

Without naming manufacturers, let's examine some small windows with an area of 9 ft² for the economical effects of air penetration over one heating season. See Table 10-3.

Look at the low cost of number three and four windows. Since the low cost of air infiltration is primarily a result of window design rather than materials used, neither insulated glass nor for that matter the thermal resistance value of the frame are such critical factors.

After examining the three potential areas of heat loss of a window, one can see how much shady salesmanship is taking place by many window manufacturers. Certainly, they have a product to sell. Natur-

56

Table 10-3. Cost of Air Infiltration of Various Windows

Window Brand	Transmission Rate (U)	Elec. 1 0.04 Kwh	Elec. 2 0.04 Kwh	Fuel Oil (0.70) 0.45 gal	Nat. Gas (0.70) 2.25 mcf
1	7.15	$10.29	$5.14	$3.93	$2.78
2	12.65	$18.21	$9.10	$6.95	$4.93
3	0.33	$00.47	$0.23	$0.18	$0.13
4	0.47	$00.67	$0.33	$0.25	$0.18
5	8.80	$12.67	$6.33	$4.84	$3.43
6	8.25	$11.88	$5.94	$4.53	$3.21
7	3.30	$4.75	$2.37	$1.81	$1.28
8	4.40	$6.33	$3.16	$2.42	$1.71

ally the advertising agency is going to make their presentation as attractive as possible so you will buy their product. Certainly, it will be to their advantage to inform you of great savings of 30% to 50%, but 30% to 50% of what?

TOTAL WINDOW PERFORMANCE

Let's take three windows and compare their overall potential performance over one heating season. The windows are all the same size, 9 ft^2, and have the following specifications:

Window one: aluminum frame, insulated glass with air space 1/4"

Window two: vinyl-coated aluminum frame, insulated glass with air space 1/4"

Window three: wooden frame, insulated glass with air space 1/4"

Table 10-4. Total Cost of Window

Window	Transmission Rage (U)	Elec. 1	Elec. 2	Fuel Oil (0.70)	Nat. Gas (0.70)
1	16.45	$23.68	$11.84	$9.04	$6.41
2	7.73	$11.13	$5.56	$4.25	$3.01
3	10.80	$15.55	$7.77	$5.94	$4.21

These costs represent worst-case situations. Hopefully, you do not have one of the poor performers in your home. If you do, a storm window or some plastic covering over the window will save you many, many dollars, just by reducing the energy costs of the infiltration factor. Right here is a prime example of the mazes in the Thermal Woods. The entire spectrum of heat loss must be analyzed! More facts must be presented. So far, I have found little evidence of thorough research in heat loss study. I hope it is forthcoming shortly.

If window manufacturers, builders, and the public understood the **total** heat loss of windows, the problem would be given more attention. Window manufacturers should make wind tests, starting at 10 mph wind velocity and extending their tests through 40 mph wind velocity. With this published information we could check weather charts and come within a 5% estimate of how well the window will perform as a result of wind infiltration over one heating season. It would separate the junk from the good windows!

Before you become too horrified at the cost of heating a window, we must cover one more topic . . . the topic of solar heat. In Columbus, Ohio, one can expect an average solar contribution of 1156 BTU/ft^2 on the southern exposure and 578 BTU/ft^2 on the eastern and western exposures during the winter per day! This is calculated at the December 21 solstice. In March and September, the solar contribution is even

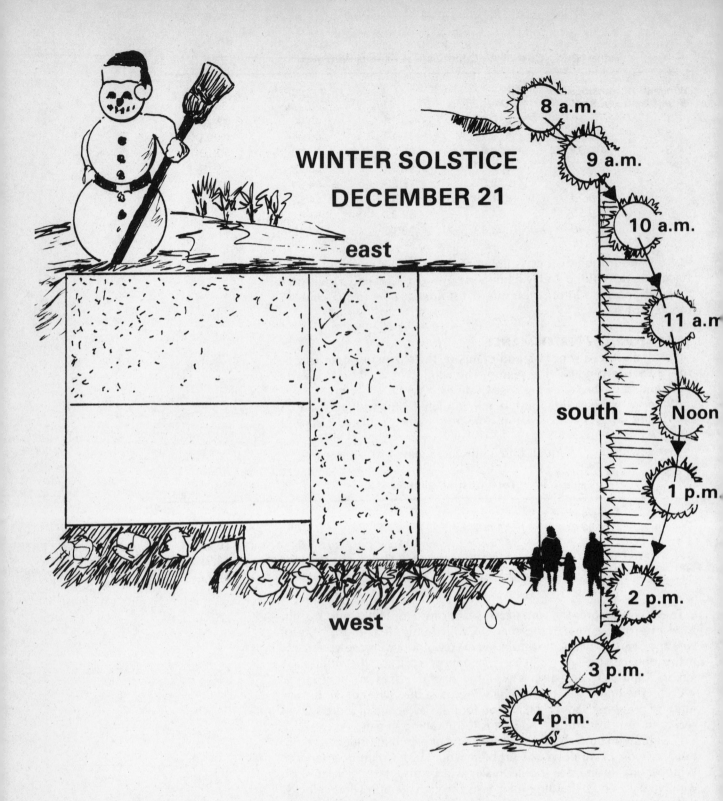

WINTER SOLSTICE
DECEMBER 21

east

south

west

8 a.m.
9 a.m.
10 a.m.
11 a.m
Noon
1 p.m.
2 p.m.
3 p.m.
4 p.m.

From sunrise to sunset the sun is changing bearing (direction) and altitude (height) "in" the sky in relation to a fixed object on the earth.

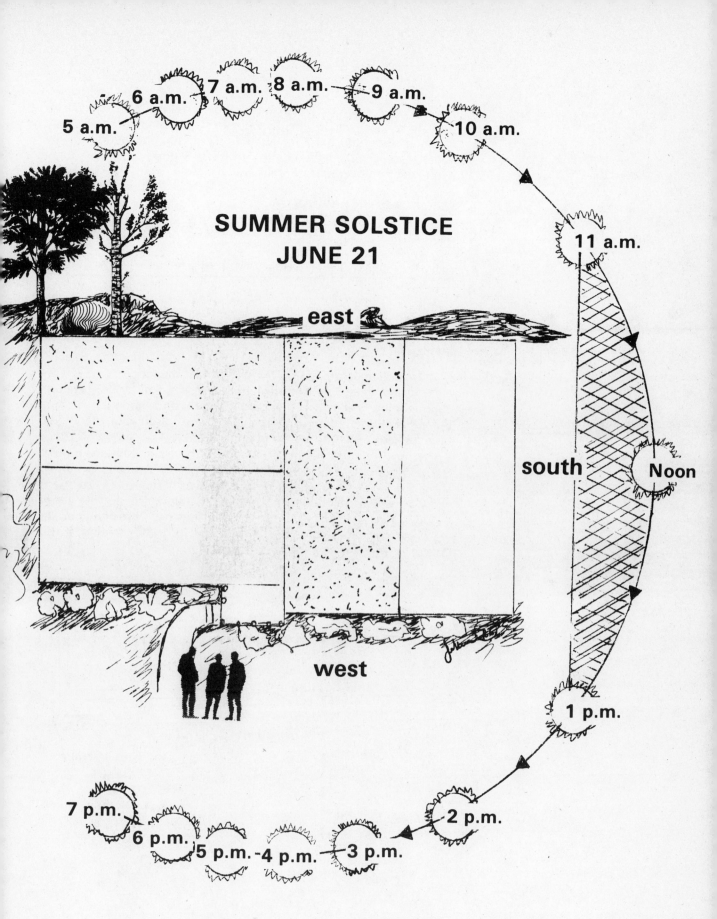

SUMMER SOLSTICE
JUNE 21

5 a.m. 6 a.m. 7 a.m. 8 a.m. 9 a.m. 10 a.m. 11 a.m.

east

south Noon

west

1 p.m.

7 p.m. 6 p.m. 5 p.m. 4 p.m. 3 p.m. 2 p.m.

Sunlight entering windows on the wall opposite the wall shown here is a source of heat gains.

higher, 1450 BTU/ft² on the southern exposure and 626.1 BTU/ft² on the eastern and western exposures per day. These values are affected by cloud cover, temperature differences, wind velocities, etc. Nevertheless, you can see that solar contribution is still the redeeming factor for even a poorly-made window. Solar heat gain is an important point in emphasizing the need for good workmanship and design for the better manufacturer because a low heat loss window would represent a net heat gain over a heating season.

SOLAR GAIN ON A WINDOW

Let's interpret what **one half** of the potential of solar heat would be on our 9 ft² window area for 250 days in terms of heating dollars.

Table 10-5. Potential Solar Heat Gain per Window

Exposure	Transmission Rate (U)	Elec. 1	Elec. 2	Fuel Oil (0.70)	Nat. Gas (0.70)
Southern	11.93	$17.19	$8.59	$6.56	$4.65
East/West	5.96	$ 8.59	$4.29	$3.28	$2.32
North	—	—	—	—	—

These dollar figures are on the plus side of the ledger. Can you see what is happening? As we calculate heat loss, we must also take into consideration heat gains. This approach works on windows, doors, and the entire house. These solar gains allow you to tell your friends you have a *solar assisted house.*

The most important thing is to reduce the air infiltration through the window sash and frame. On a really poorly designed or poorly air sealed window, a storm window is worth the cost. Use storm windows which can be easily removed. Caution: Do not use storm windows that are difficult to remove and thus may threaten your life in an emergency, such as fire. Also, if the storm has screens, it will reduce summer heating loads.

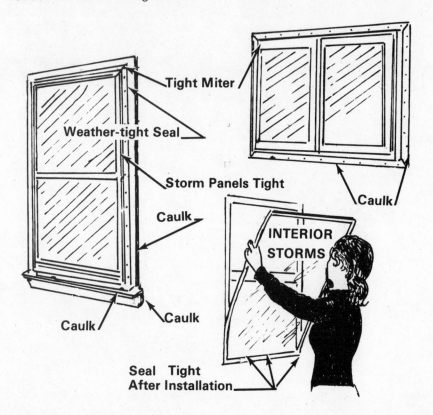

60

EFFECTS OF STORM WINDOWS

Let's examine the economics of placing a storm sash over a single glazed window and a double glazed window with a ½ inch air space in between the glazing.

Table 10-6. Advantage of Storm Sash over Single and Double Glass

Type	Transmission Rate (U)	Elec. 1	Elec. 2	Fuel Oil (0.70)	Nat. Gas (0.70)
Single glazed	5.11	($7.36)	($3.68)	($2.81)	($1.99)
Double glazed	2.56	($3.69)	($1.84)	($1.40)	($0.99)

The dollar figures in the brackets indicate the dollar amount of heating cost reduction over one heating season in a region with a 5150 DD year. As we factor in the dollar savings of heating cost reduction for the window sash and reduction of air penetration, it becomes easy to justify the economics of adding a storm sash. In fact, as we reduce direct thermal losses from the window sash, glazing and air penetration, the solar gains on the east, west and southern exposures become more positive in reducing our heating cost of the home.

In Chapter 16 on humidity and odors, we will approach the problems of frosting and condensation on windows. Now let's examine the thermal values of doors.

61

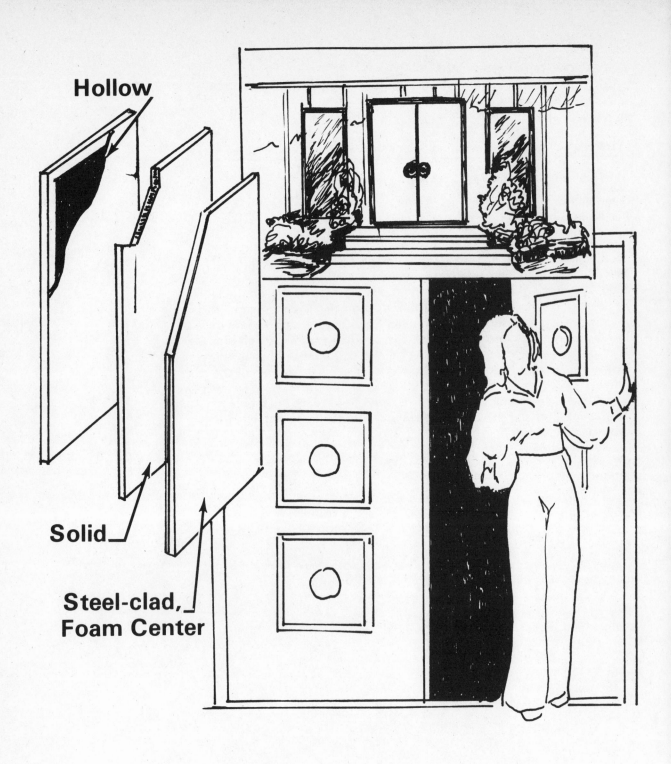

Hollow

Solid

Steel-clad, Foam Center

CHAPTER ELEVEN

DOORS

We are interested in finding out what the cost of heating the door is when the door is shut. If keeping the door shut tightly is a problem in your home, consider investing in a good automatic door closer. In addition to reducing the heating bill, a good automatic door closer might help reduce the noise pollution that results from constantly yelling at someone to shut the door.

62

Most modern builders have gone to steel-clad exterior doors for the front and back entries. These doors function well as thermal barriers because of their foam insulating core and because of good weather stripping and adjustable thresholds. Other types of doors that are used are the solid wood doors and the hollow-core doors. Hollow-core doors should be considered in our discussion because many builders install them as an exit door to the attached garage.

Its molecular structure makes pine a far better insulator than oak or maple. Pine has more air spaces than the other wood. However, the difference is not really great enough to warrant the elimination of the oak or maple door altogether. Most interior doors used today consist of a solid wood frame with a veneer of birch or mahogany. This is what we mean by hollow-core doors.

Again, air infiltration plays an important part in the comparison of thermal performances of doors. As with the window, the reduction of air infiltration by weather stripping is of utmost importance.

DOLLAR COST OF HEATING A DOOR

Let's compare the three main types of exterior doors on the market for heating cost in Indiana. These types are (1) hollow-core, (2) solid pine, and (3) steel-clad with urethane core.

Table 11-1. Cost of Heat Loss Through an Exterior Door in One Heating Season

Door Type	Transmission Rate (U)	Elec. 1	Elec. 2	Fuel Oil (0.70)	Nat. Gas (0.70)
1	12.45	$17.92	$8.96	$6.89	$4.85
2	7.78	$11.20	$5.60	$4.27	$3.03
3	4.23	$ 6.10	$3.05	$2.33	$1.65

The high performance of the steel-clad door is quite evident. Of course, this performance is subject to door opening size and air infiltration.

Notice in the illustration the wood framing during the rough construction stage of a home. The door assembly fits into this opening. On each side of the door there will be a slight gap that must be insulated. All spaces which provide for potential air leaks must be thoroughly caulked. In homes with heavy air leaks around the trim of the door, it would be worth the while to remove the trim and fill in this gap.

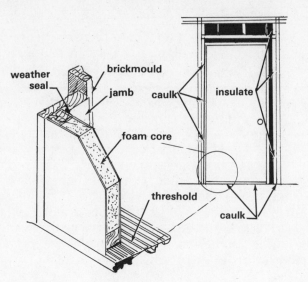

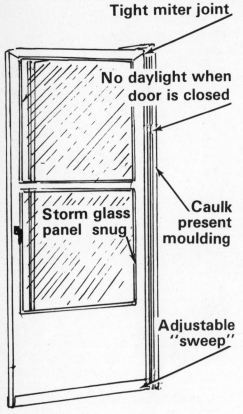

Tight miter joint

No daylight when door is closed

Storm glass panel snug

Caulk present moulding

Adjustable "sweep"

STORM SCREEN DOORS

This storm door is cooled during the summer by shade from the overhang. During the winter, the sun shines into the home and provides a heat gain.

We mentioned the importance of keeping the door shut. Let's look at the economics of leaving the door open for one day with the outside air temperature of 40°F, and with a wind velocity of 8 mph.

Table 11-2. Cost of Heating an Open Door Per Day in Akron, Ohio

Elec. 1	Elec. 2	Fuel Oil (0.70)	Nat. Gas (0.70)
$29.42	$14.71	$12.05	$8.31

If the air temperature is near 20°F, the cost could easily double. Also, if the wind velocity increases, so does the heating cost. This example was given because the above figures exceed the total heating cost of a tightly closed door for a heating season.

The dynamics of life dictate that we enter and leave the house through a door. During cold weather, it is important to make the trip through a door as quickly as possible. Also, because of the possibility of leaving the door ajar, it is very difficult for a builder to give any type of heating guarantee on any given home.

EFFECTS OF STORM DOORS

If your door is well weather-stripped, it would be difficult to justify a storm door. However, you can certainly justify a screen door. Since the cost of a screen and storm door are comparable, it would be wise to consider a storm door-screen door combination. On steel-clad doors which have plastic decorations and a storm door, the plastic often melts when the opening has a southern exposure. Why? This combination is, in effect, a solar collector! The sun's rays are absorbed by steel. The center core insulation prevents a rapid transfer of heat to the interior, so most of the heat is re-radiated. In addition, the storm glass has a low transmission rate of heat in the infrared range. The resulting temperature of 150°F, or higher, is enough to melt the plastic used for door decorations. It could be possible to have the temperature rise over 200°F! The trick is to crack the inside door slightly during a sunny winter day. Let the heat be circulated into the home.

Table 11-3. Savings in Dollars for a Storm Door

Type	Transmission Rate (U)	Elec. 1	Elec. 2	Fuel Oil (0.70)	Nat. Gas (0.70)
1	1.53	($2.20)	($1.10)	($0.84)	($0.59)
2	1.16	($1.67)	($0.83)	($0.64)	($0.45)
3	0.63	($0.90)	($0.45)	($0.35)	($0.25)

The values in Table 11-3 indicate the dollar savings of a combination of storm door, low air infiltration, and tightly sealed door for one heating season in Pittsburgh, PA. From experience, the air test rating determined at the factory, when compared with the actual performance in the field, can be as different as night and day. This is a judgment call by you the home owner and you the builder. If you are experiencing ice build-up on the threshold and you cannot stop it, or if you are having difficulty keeping your weather stripping in good repair, add the storm door. Air penetration into or out of the door frame may certainly justify a storm door on homes.

Sidelights, transom lights, etc., should be considered and treated just like windows. Glass in the door will also change the heat cost for the door. Home owners having openings with single-pane glass should consider a thermal barrier such as heavy-gauge drapes or a storm sash of some type.

64

WILL THEIR BEAUTY COME BACK TO HAUNT US?

Sliding glass doors are really rather new to the art of building. They burst on the scene in the sixties. Builders by the score used them to a great extent. In fact, I can remember homes with six such units in them. As a builder, I always felt the sliding glass door was a window and a door combined. In fact, this is what you really have. One pane is fixed and the other is a slider. The heat loss just about equals what one would have with a window and a door combined. Just like a window, a sliding glass door has a heat loss through the glass and frame, along with air infiltration. The ratio of heat loss per lineal foot of wall area is naturally higher than in a good exterior door. If you want to eliminate a few sliding glass doors, this is your justification. First, let's look at three different types of sliding doors. These types are (1) an aluminum sliding door (as per the 1970s market), (2) a wooden door with average air infiltration, and (3) a wood or aluminum sliding glass door with low air infiltration.

Table 11-4. Cost of a Sliding Glass Door in Denver, Colorado, for one Heating Season

Type of Sliding Door	Transmission Rate (U)	Elec. 1	Elec. 2	Fuel Oil (0.70)	Nat. Gas (0.70)
1	87.15	$125.49	$62.77	$47.93	$18.69
2	55.90	$ 80.49	$40.24	$30.74	$21.80
3	33.20	$ 47.80	$23.90	$18.26	$12.94
Wall (R-11) and 3/0 Door	5.31	$7.65	$3.82	$2.92	$2.07

PATIO DOORS

WILL THEIR BEAUTY COME BACK TO HAUNT US?

65

The wall R-11 has siding and insulation and a 3/0 door. If you have the misfortune of owning a sliding door of Type 1, the economics indicate that the sliding glass door should be changed into a wall or replaced with an exit door and partition wall. However, before you jump to any conclusions, let's consider the effects of solar heat.

The heat loss in BTUs for one heating season in Dayton, Ohio, would amount to 6.678 million BTU for a sliding glass door of Type 2. For a sliding glass door of Type 3, which has a lower air infiltration factor, the heat loss would be 3.957 million BTU. On the southern exposure, the solar gain on one sunny day would be 1156 BTU per square foot of glass. If discounted by 50% over one heating season, it would amount to a heat gain of 6.068 million BTU. This would mean that a door of Type 2 would have a net heat loss of only 609 538 BTU per heating season. However, a sliding glass door of Type 3 would have a net heat gain of 2.11 million BTU. On the eastern and western sides of the house, a Type 2 door would represent another loss, but we would be losing only one-half the net heating dollars.

Whether or not to remove a sliding glass door in an existing house is a judgment call for the home owner. The builder should be very selective in deciding where to place a sliding glass door and in deciding how many to use. The builder should also compare the heat losses of a window and door opening to those of a good low air infiltration sliding glass door unit. The little time it takes to inquire about the infiltration tests from the manufacturer could pay handsome dividends to the builder and the home owner.

Sliding glass doors should not come back to haunt us if they are approaching the heat loss of a Type 3 door. Many changes are taking place in the window and door industry in the area of actual testing. Make yourself aware of the changes and be ready to discuss the changes intelligently.

CHAPTER TWELVE
FLOORS AND BASEMENTS

The majority of modern homes have little, if any insulation in the floor system. Let's examine the heat loss of floors, basements, and crawl spaces. Some of the easiest and most rewarding thermal corrections for the home owner present themselves here. In most homes, heat loss through the floor system is equal to or larger than heat loss through the ceilings. As warm air is circulated in the home, its heat will be transferred to the colder component.

If we look at your home as a cube and follow most insulating schemes, we will quite likely discover the bottom of the cube, or your floor, unprotected. Besides the lack of insulation, you will find that air infiltration through basement windows, imperfections in siding material, electrical wires, etc., will tend to keep the floor cold. Floors above garages, crawl spaces, and basements demand minute inspection by the home owner. Sealing all potential air leaks is extremely important before adding any insulation.

67

Most of the heat loss of any uninsulated floor in a home takes place at the perimeter or the edges of floor exposed to outside temperatures and air infiltration. The exception to this is a floor which is above a garage, a crawl space, or a basement. The flow of heat downward to the heat sink of the garage is constant in the center. The infiltration under the siding into the home's floor system is often quite large when aluminum, wood paneling, or similar siding is used. The infiltration at floor edge is lower in all-brick or stucco homes. This is why it is extremely important to caulk all cracks and crevices before adding any insulation. We will also demonstrate the tremendous heat loss of many basement windows.

Looking at the illustration, you can see that the ring or bandboard is the outer joist of the floor system. The figure also shows the amount of lumber in the floor. This lumber must be considered in our heat loss calculations. Before we discuss insulating a floor, let's compare heat loss of a ceiling having an area of 1040 ft^2 and insulated with 8" of fiberglass with the heat loss of a bandboard or ring having a lineal footage of 132 feet both before insulation and after the addition of 6" of insulation (with the barrier—kraft paper—facing inside).

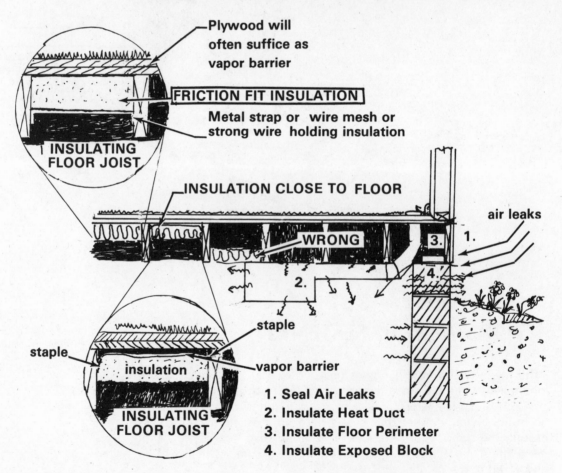

Table 12-1. Cost of Heat Loss of Ceiling in a 5150 DD Year Region

	Transmission Rate (U)	Elec. 1	Elec. 2	Fuel Oil (0.70)	Nat. Gas (0.70)
Ceiling with 8" insulation	54.70	$78.76	$39.38	$30.08	$21.33
Bandboard (uninsulated)	29.70	$42.76	$21.38	$16.33	$11.58
Bandboard with 6" insulation	5.08	$ 7.32	$ 3.66	$ 2.79	$ 1.98

Originally, the heat loss of the small bandboard area was almost equal to one-half of what the entire ceiling was losing. By adding 6" of insulation to the bandboard, the home owner corrected this thermal leak and greatly reduced the heating cost.

If the floor above the basement is insulated, the temperature of the basement will tend to average the ground temperature of about 55°F. However, there are other approaches which will be discussed later. The floor above a crawl space or garage should definitely be insulated.

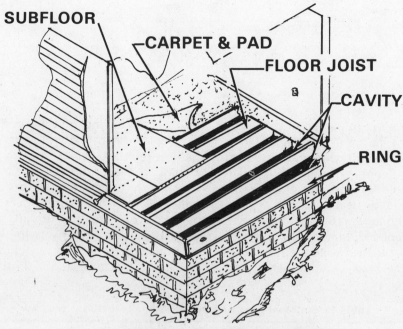

WOOD FLOOR SYSTEM

The cost of heat loss through a floor is subject to floor materials such as carpeting, the floor joists, and the cavity space between the joists. Let's examine a wood floor, 24 feet × 24 feet, above a garage. The following figures are shown without carpet.

Table 12-2.   Heat Loss of an Uncarpeted Floor
Above a Garage in Massachusetts

Insulation	Transmission Rate (U)	Elec. 1	Elec. 2	Fuel Oil (0.70)	Nat. Gas (0.70)
none	161.05	$231.91	$115.95	$88.57	$62.80
3.5"	41.01	$ 59.05	$ 29.52	$22.55	$15.99
7.5"	27.88	$ 40.15	$ 20.07	$15.33	$10.87

When installing insulation in the floor, be sure the vapor barrier is **facing the warm side.** Again, with just this small area, the heat loss, even after insulating with 3.5 inches of insulation almost equals the 1040 square feet of ceiling's loss. If we can get a lot more people looking at the floor heat loss, we could save millions of cubic feet of natural gas and gallons of fuel oil. A bonus you will get by insulating the floor is warm feet. Warm feet make for a warm body.

SLABS

Concrete slabs act as a large heat sink in the home. New construction permits easy correction of this problem. However, thermal corrections

69

This entire slab will be insulated before concrete is poured.

for an existing home are a little more difficult. Carpet would reduce the heat loss and so would insulation added to the outside edge. Adding insulation to the outside edge calls for digging a ditch around the house and installing good foam. Dow Chemical's Styrofoam® is very effective here. It is dense and has low moisture absorption.

Perimeter insulation is called for because the edge of the slab is exposed to the tantrums of winter temperatures. Let's examine the dollar cost of heating a 960 ft^2 slab (24 feet × 40 feet) both in the center and around the perimeter. Remember, the ground temperature in the center of the slab is about 55°F, creating a 2500 degree-day year for us. Let us first examine the slab without insulation, then with carpeting, and finally with carpeting and 2″ of foam at the edge and 1″ in the center.

Table 12-3. Heat Loss of 1040 ft^2 Slab in Dayton, Ohio

Without Carpet	Transmission Rate (U)	Elec. 1	Elec. 2	Fuel Oil (0.70)	Nat. Gas (0.70)
Edge Loss	151.28	$217.85	$108.92	$83.20	$59.00
Center Loss	203.86	$293.57	$146.78	$112.12	$79.50
With Carpet					
Edge Loss	63.73	$ 91.78	$ 45.89	$35.05	$24.85
Center Loss	85.88	$123.67	$ 61.83	$47.23	$33.49
With Carpet and Insulation					
Edge Loss with 2″ additional Insulation	18.50	$ 26.64	$13.32	$10.17	$ 7.21
Center Loss with 1″ Additional Insulation	47.23	$ 68.02	$ 34.01	$25.98	$18.42

Looking back at our original potential losses, we can say we have brought the cost of heating this slab under control.

BASEMENTS AND CRAWL SPACES

Crawl space floors should have a vapor barrier on them. Vinyl plastic sheets make an excellent vapor barrier on the ground. All cracks should be sealed and air vents should be closed during the winter. All ducts exposed in the crawl space should be insulated. Then, your family could comfortably stretch out on the floor and watch TV, or maybe even reread this book.

70

Note how we have numbered the blocks in the next illustration. The first block is above grade and is subject to the entire temperature change during the heating season. The second block is exposed to the frost line. The rest of the blocks are exposed to the ground temperature of 55°F. These last blocks give us a constant heat sink, measured as a 2500 degree-day year. Fortunately, the ground is acting as an insulator in this instance. In fact, the ground's thermal resistance value is rated at R-15. Knowing this, we can work with Mother Nature, and get the greatest results with the minimum amount of insulation.

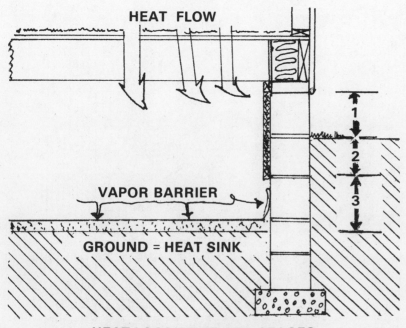

HEAT LOSS OF CRAWL SPACES

In some hillside homes, all the blocks, except a few, are exposed to the outside air temperature. In homes with a sloping grade, the amount of the foundation on the ground varies. Most of the heat loss in the foundation wall takes place through the blocks out of the ground and the blocks exposed to the frost line. Insulate these blocks for maximum return. However, if your aim is heat recovery, which I explain in detail in Chapter 15, insulate the entire wall. For furring strips, use 2×4 studs, 24 inches on center as shown in the diagram.

Let's look at a 12 course block wall, 132 feet long, with just one block exposed. The frost depth is 8 inches.

Table 12-4. Potential Heat Loss of a Basement in a 5150 DD Year Region

Area	Transmission Rate (U)	Elec. 1	Elec. 2	Fuel Oil (0.70)	Nat. Gas (0.70)
		Cost Before Adding Insulation			
Top Block	71.57	$103.06	$51.53	$39.36	$27.91
Frost	5.45	$7.84	$ 3.92	$ 2.99	$ 2.12
Below Frost	22.51	$15.82	$7.91	$6.20	$4.27
		Cost After Adding Insulation			
Top Blocks with R-8	15.83	$ 22.80	$11.40	$ 8.71	$ 6.17
Savings per year		$ 88.10	$44.05	$33.64	$23.86

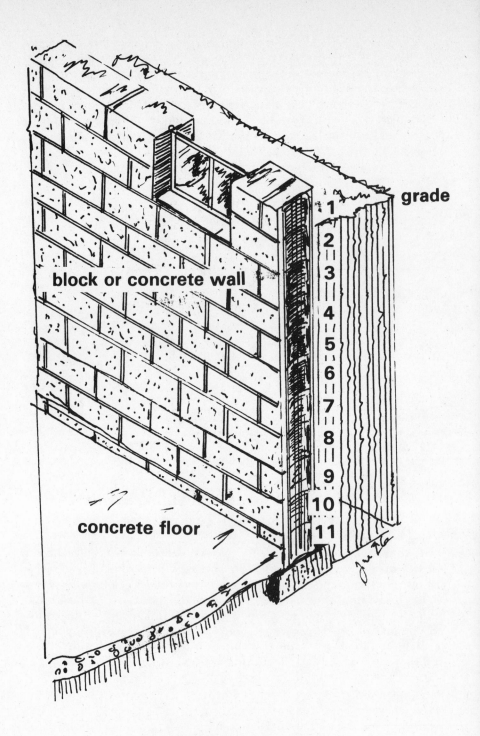

grade

block or concrete wall

concrete floor

1 2 3 4 5 6 7 8 9 10 11

HEAT LOSS OF A MASONRY BASEMENT

Wood foundations are beginning to come on the market. Many homes have this system. I have built some of the units and will only say that, when I build, I prefer poured concrete foundations. Nevertheless, a wood foundation unit is equal in heat loss to a block wall without insulation. The advantage of a wooden foundation is that more insulation can be added quickly with a minimum of fuss.

72

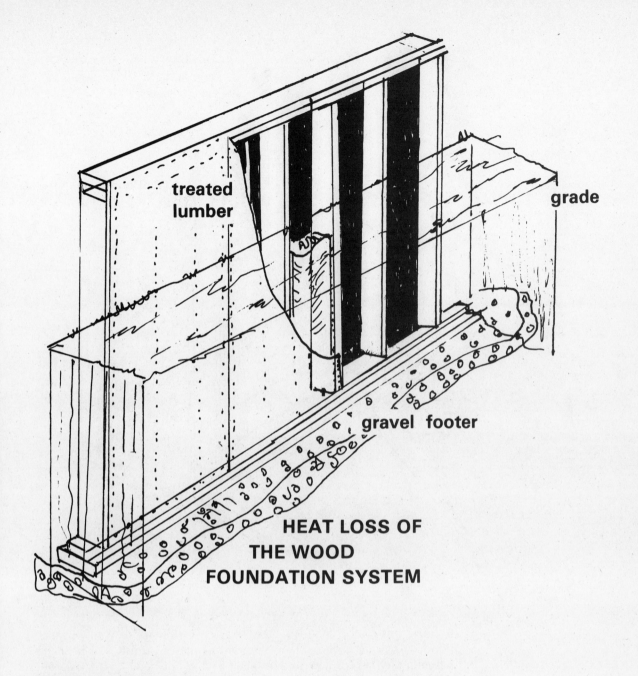

treated lumber

grade

gravel footer

HEAT LOSS OF THE WOOD FOUNDATION SYSTEM

BASEMENT FLOORS

Basement floors constantly lose heat in the home, and the amount of heat they absorb is similar to slabs above grade. However, their edge losses are not as great as slabs except when the water table is high. With the high water table and rapid water movement at the edges, the basement floor's heat loss could exceed the edge loss of a slab above grade. Because of water movement, the insulation qualities of the ground are negligible. The ground temperature is 55°F, thereby creating the following costs when considering a 1040 ft² floor. By the way, the figures presented here are valid across the nation.

Table 12-5. Heating Cost of an Uninsulated Basement Floor

Transmission Rate (U)	Elec. 1	Elec. 2	Fuel Oil (0.70)	Nat. Gas (0.70)
62.27	$89.67	$44.83	$34.25	$24.28

73

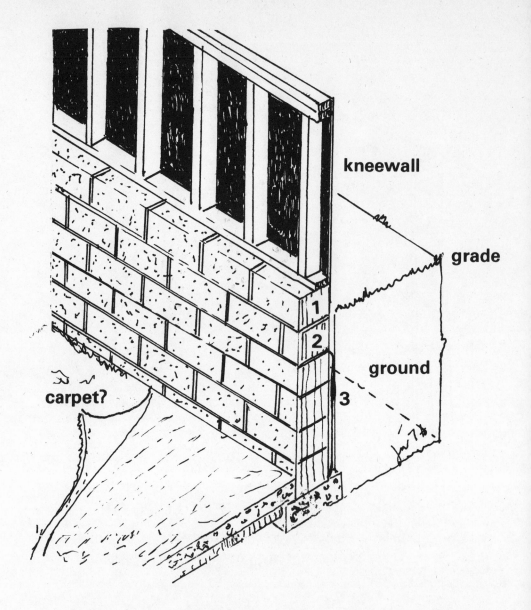

Labels on illustration: kneewall, grade, ground, carpet?, 1, 2, 3

Because this area (1040 ft^2) is very large, it is difficult to justify insulation in a basement floor. However, if you plan to finish and heat the basement, either insulate under the area to be finished or plan to carpet the floor.

The average air temperature in most basements is about 62°F, which is higher than the ground temperature of 55°F. The higher temperature indicates there is a source of heat. This heat source is often the heat loss from the hot-water tank, dryer, water lines, freezer, washer, etc. Full wall insulation on the basement walls, etc., will lower heat loss cost to zero by enabling the home owner to recover heat from the aforementioned items.

Most basement windows leak air profusely. The window frame is often steel or aluminum. Many basements have at least two to four windows. Let's examine just one basement window in a 5150 DD year region. Remember that these costs are for one window only!

Table 12-6. Heat Loss of a Basement Window

Transmission Rate (U)	Elec. 1	Elec. 2	Fuel Oil (0.70)	Nat. Gas (0.70)
30.60	$44.07	$22.03	$16.83	$11.93

74

Home owners who have heating systems using combustion fuels such as propane, natural gas, and fuel oil need planty of air for combustion. The cost of adding an insulated air duct directly to the furnace and hot water tank would pay great dividends over the years. Not only will you save money while the furnace is on, but also you will save warm air from going up the stack when the furnace is off! To be sure the proper amount of air will flow into the furnace, an expert should install this system. The size of the fresh air duct would approximate the size of your chimney stack. A barometric damper is recommended to prevent downdrafts of fumes.

All of you who have basement windows with high air infiltration rates should install storm windows, plastic, or something similar to reduce the air flow and consequently the dollar cost of heating.

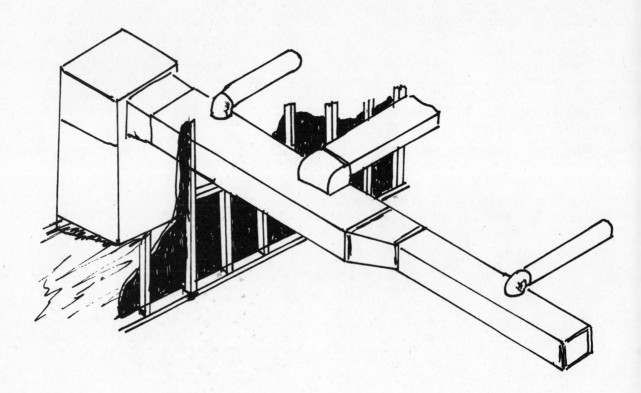

CHAPTER THIRTEEN
THE HEAT TRANSFER SYSTEM

The heat transfer system should be carefully examined because it is often a major source of heat loss. Heating experts are telling us to add "tons" of insulation in the ceiling, to add insulated glass windows, etc. Occasionally, they tell us to insulate our basement.

The true function of the duct system or heat transfer system is to distribute warm air to individual rooms and to return air (often referred to as the cold air side) to the furnace so that there will be a proper supply of heated air to keep house temperatures even. With the use of a fan to propel the air through the ducts, we have controlled convective transfer of heat. By the way, heating companies often arbitrarily add 10% to the heat loss of a structure for the makeup of heat loss from the ducting system. The question is, are they right in their assumption of this 10% heat loss?

With few exceptions, heating ducts are made of metal. The thermal resistance value of metal is so low that we will consider it to be zero. The only thermal resistance value we have in a duct is a result of the inside and outside air films of the duct. Warm air leaking from the heat duct system adds to the problem of calculating heating costs of duct transfer system. We shall be cautious in establishing a transmission rate per square foot (U/ft^2) of 1.21 for our heating costs.

Heat loss is dependent upon a thermal barrier, temperature difference, area, and time. The air temperature inside the duct varies according to the type of heating system. The farther the register is away from the heating source (furnace), the greater the amount of air leakage and consequently the lower the delivered air temperature will be. For our calculations we shall establish air temperatures inside of the heat ducts as follows—*Elec. 1, 95°F; Elec. 2, 85°F; Fuel Oil (0.70), 110°F; and Nat.Gas (0.70), 110°F.*

On page 26 we established the total DD year for duct systems. These tables assumed that the heating unit was operating 100% of the time. For our demonstration, let's establish operating time of your furnace at 75% during the heating season. As you make thermal corrections, operating time will decrease. Nevertheless, let's establish the DD year (temperature difference) of the duct system as given in Table 13-1.

Table 13-1. Degree-Day Years of Various Duct Systems

	Inside Air Temperature	DD Year in Basement or Crawl Space
Electric Forced Air (Elec. 1)	95°F	7187
Heat Pump (Elec 2)	85°F	5312
Fuel Oil	110°F	10 000
Natural Gas	110°F	10 000

We can now estimate the heating cost of the heat transfer system in your home. To demonstrate duct losses, we shall look at 6-inch round and 8 inch × 14-inch rectangular shaped heating ducts.

Table 13-2. Heat Transfer Rate (U/lineal foot) in Air Ducts

Duct	No Insulation	Add R-7 Insulation
6" round	1.89	0.20
8" × 14" rectangular	5.39	0.56

These uninsulated heat ducts in the garage will be a source of considerable heat loss.

We now have enough information to see how much our heat loss from the duct system will cost. Consider Vermont and assume a 6500 DD year. We shall also assume the ducts are in a garage or outside wall and a basement area and that unit fuel costs are $0.45/gallon for fuel oil, $2.25/unit for natural gas, and $0.04/Kwh for electricity. Note what the heat loss will be for one lineal foot of uninsulated duct and keep in mind that the duct loss in the basement would be about the same all over the country.

77

Wrapping the heat ducts in garage areas will save many heating dollars.

Table 13-3.   Heat Loss for 6" Insulated Round Duct

Type	DD Total	Basement	DD Total Garage	or Outside Wall
Fuel Oil	10 000	$1.07	14 000	$1.49/lin.ft
Natural Gas	10 000	$0.77	14 000	$1.08/lin.ft
Resistance Elec. (Elec. 1)	7187	$2.02	11 187	$3.14/lin.ft
Heat Pump (Elec. 2)	5312	$0.74	9312	$1.30/lin.ft

These figures are for **one lineal foot dollar cost** in fuel for one normal heating season in Vermont. If you would add R-7 insulation on the pipes you would reduce their heating cost 90%

Let's look at our rectangular duct under the same circumstance in Vermont. Again, R-7 insulation would reduce the heating dollar cost of heat ducts 90%!

Table 13-4.   Heat Loss for 8" × 14" Uninsulated Rectangular Duct

Heating System	Basement	Garage
Fuel Oil	$3.04/lin. ft	$4.23/lin. ft
Natural Gas	$2.18/lin. ft	$3.07/lin. ft
Resistance Elec. (Elec. 1)	$5.76/lin. ft	$8.95/lin. ft
Heat Pump (Elec. 2)	$2.11/lin. ft	$3.70/lin. ft

Now that we have discovered a large heat leak, here are some options for you. Insulate any and all heating ducts in the garage, crawl space, and attic. Add damper controls before you insulate because the heating ducts will most likely turn out to be oversized after insulation is added.

As to adding insulation to the heating ducts in the basement, the true barometer is what you use your basement for or what your future plans are. The heat loss from the ducts, plus heat loss from water lines, hot water tanks, and other heat producing equipment tends to keep the air of the basement above the ground temperature of 55°F. If you insulate the heat ducts, the air temperature in the basement will naturally drop toward the ground temperature of 55°F and cool the floor above. This means you could insulate the floor and the duct and forget the basement walls. If you do this, insulate the hot water and cold water lines. By the way, if the basement is cooler, it will cost you less to operate the freezer if your freezer is in the basement.

Too often, the small cost of adding insulation is overlooked at the time of construction.

Another option you have is to insulate the basement walls, seal for air infiltration, and let the heat loss of the ducts heat the basement and the floor above. It's six of one and a half dozen of the other. Regardless of what you choose to do, at least do something!

Now, let's examine the assumption made by heating companies that in calculating heat loss it is reasonable to add 10% for heat loss of the ducts to the structures. Is this assumption valid? No. They should not throw in 10%. Most likely, they should use smaller ducts and smaller heating units with the proper calculations of heat loss and heat gains of a home. Closer examination is in order.

Let's examine a home where all of the heat ducts are in the basement (a typical ranch home). This basement has 132 lineal feet of block wall with one block exposed to the outside air and the rest in the ground. It also has four standard, leaky, drafty, basement windows and 1040 square feet of floor area. We will oversimplify the heat transfer system by using 30 feet of 8" × 14" heat duct and 160 feet of 6" round duct. The heat transmission rate (U) of the basement is 287.00 and the U of the heat transfer system is 333.03.

78

As you can see, the heat loss of the duct exceeds the total heat loss of the entire basement. The air temperature in the basement is most likely above the ground temperature of 55°F. If you insulated the basement, its air temperature would climb above its present temperature. If you insulate the heating ducts the temperature will drop; however, it will not drop lower than 55°!

Frankly, if you do not use your basement as a living area and do not plan to do so in the very near future, seal it up for air infiltration—the bandboard, sill plates, basement windows, etc.—and then insulate the ducts and the basement ceiling. You heating vill will drop accordingly.

CAUTION! Do not endanger your home by placing any type of flammable material near or on the plenum (the bonnet) of a combustion furnace. A sheet of thin asbestos around the furnace plenum or bonnet will do the trick. Also, plan some damper controls in the ducts before you insulate because after you insulate, the heating ducts will be much too large for the heating load of the rooms above.

By the way, because of fabricating methods and materials used in heating transfer systems, most of these systems leak air profusely. Tape all joints with duct tape before you add insulation.

Also, the vapor barrier of the insulation added to heating ducts should not be placed next to the duct itself. It should be placed to the outside.

You may wish to insulate the basement walls and take advantage of heat loss from ducts to warm your basement.

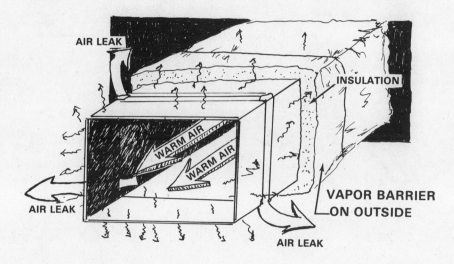

79

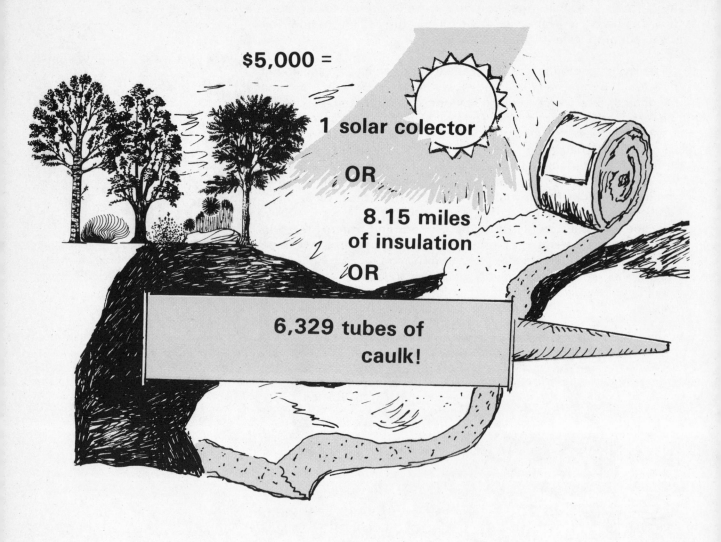

$5,000 =

1 solar colector

OR

8.15 miles
of insulation

OR

6,329 tubes of
caulk!

CHAPTER FOURTEEN
AIR INFILTRATION

The thunderous sound of the powerful hooves of a magnificent steed filled the Thermal Woods. To my astonishment, sitting on top of the speeding thoroughbred was a masked man, wearing a rhinestone cowboy outfit. His face was drawn tight with the effort . Instead of Colt 45's in his gun holsters, there were two silver-plated caulk guns. Two large sacks of caulk tubes filled his saddle bags. Rapidly, he disappeared over the horizon. Just at the edge of the Thermal Woods was an Indian. Cautiously I walked over to him. "Say," I asked "who was that masked man?" In a deep baritone voice he said, "Super Caulk!" I swear to this day I hear faint strains of *The William Tell Overture* coming from within the depths of the Thermal Woods

*　　　*　　　*　　　*　　　*

80

AIR INFILTRATION

Air infiltration is the secret of the Thermal Woods—infiltration and really knowing what is taking place thermally. At first, I felt very wise knowing it was really all that simple and not so expensive. However, my dreams of being the new Rockefeller of solar heat were smashed with this realization.

In preceding chapters, we discussed air infiltration and the costs of the thermal components that constitute our home. We have already mentioned the cost comparison of caulk but it's well worth the while to mention it again. With $5000, you can buy a backyard solar unit, or 8.15 miles of insulation, or 6329 tubes of caulk!

As the cold winter air penetrates all the cracks and crevices of your home, your heating bill will soar. To give you an idea of potential costs of heating resulting from air penetration, let's look at the effect of having one square foot of free open space exposed to the wind for one average heating season somewhere in Pennsylvania. Wind velocity in this dramatization will be assumed to be 10.56 mph, subject to a 5150 DD year.

Table 14-1. Costs of Heating Air Infiltration for One Heating Season in Columbus, OH

Area	Trans. Rate (U)	Elec. 1	Elec. 2	Fuel Oil (0.70)	Nat. Gas (0.70)
One square foot	522.28	$752.00	$375.00	$287.00	$203.00
One square inch	3.60	$ 5.18	$ 2.59	$ 1.98	$ 1.40

Air infiltration is often the direct result of not following through during the construction job. Poorly made window frames, improper setting of the window by the carpenter, poorly designed door thresholds, improper weather stripping, and again too little attention paid to detail when setting the door into the wall frame are some of the mistakes which are made.

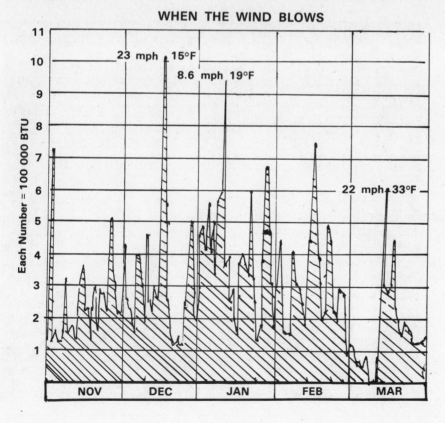

Air leaks through the siding into the wall cavities. This air leakage takes place through broken insulation board and through poorly cut electrical wire chases and plumbing chases. We pay dearly for heating cold air coming into the home. In addition, this cold air reduces the effectiveness of the insulation in the wall and consequently our heating bills soar ever higher. Air seeps into the attic area through electrical ceiling fixtures and through the attic access hole or door. It also seeps into the home through and around improperly fitted drywall. Window casements leak cold air into the basement cooling the floor above and wasting the heat given off by hot water tanks and heating ducts in the basement. Air seeping into the basement cools down floor members. Excessive air going up the chimneys of fireplaces and furnaces is replaced with cold air from outside.

Our tale sounds like a soap opera which might well be entitled *"As the Meter Turns!"* In most homes, both new and old, air infiltration could easily cause the largest chunk of the heating bill. Even in the so-called tight electric-heated homes, air infiltration will represent 40% to 60% of the total heating bill!

I have inspected many homes where the owners complained of very high heat bills. One couple had a heating bill (total electric bill actually) of $125.00 during the month of December, and their thermostat was set only at a chilly 60°F. Following my instructions, they covered the windows, sealed the electrical outlets, sealed the basement windows, and added insulation around the basement perimeter. They later told me their electric bill for the month of January was just $75.00, and this was with the thermostat set at 70°F, certainly a more comfortable temperature.

If all home builders and home owners would concentrate on reducing air infiltration and air exfiltration of the home they would enjoy more comfort and lower energy bills. In fact, the need for super insulators such as foam panel walls, 2 × 6 walls, and new truss (roof) designs would all be suspect.

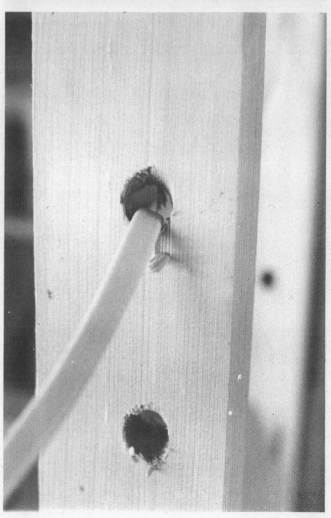

Woody Hayes, famous football coach of The Ohio State University, is famous for his fullback off-tackle play—a dull play but nevertheless effective. Why has Woody Hayes been running the off-tackle play for twenty years? He has found this play to be very effective and because it is effective he'll continue to use it over and over again. Woody Hayes' winning records prove he is not all wrong.

Dull and unexciting as it sounds to caulk and seal, keep at it. You will be amazed, as I was and some of my clients were, as to the number of heat leaks and air leaks which can be found in a home. Just when we thought we had the job right, we found more. Go over your home again and again.

AIR TURNS

Most heating companies evaluate heat loss caused by air infiltration according to *air turns* of the home. This arbitrary calculation is often one air turn per hour, which means that you are replacing the total amount of air in your home once an hour. I have not yet found a sound reason why this arbitrary calculation is thrown in at the end of heat loss calculations. Nevertheless, let's examine the cost of heating one or more air turns per hour in a region such as upper New Jersey. Keep in mind the fresh air intake is cold and has to be heated. These are approximate costs.

Table 14-2. Cost of Heating Air Leakage into a Home of 1040 ft² Floor Area

Air Turns/hr	Trans. Rate (U)	Elec. 1	Elec. 2	Fuel Oil (0.70)	Nat. Gas (0.70)
3	457.55	$658.88	$329.44	$251.65	$178.44
2	305.55	$439.99	$219.90	$168.00	$119.15
1	152.51	$219.61	$109.80	$ 83.88	$ 59.47
½	76.25	$109.80	$ 54.90	$ 41.93	$ 29.73
¼	34.55	$ 49.90	$ 24.95	$ 19.06	$ 13.51

The cost of heating three air turns per hour is still not as bad as the cost of heating one square foot area of free open space. So, we are paying for the cost of a combination of little air leaks. In our Work Section we show a method for estimating the air infiltration heating costs in your home. This economical take off will prove to you the cost of air leakage in the home.

An interesting paper has been written by G. T. Tamura, a research officer of the National Research Council of Canada. The paper is entitled "Measurement of Air Leakage Characteristics of House Enclosures." In his paper, Mr. Tamura describes his test procedure and his results. In his opening statement he says "The heat loss associated with air leakage through the enclosure of a typical detached house may be as much as 40 percent of the total heat loss." It should also be pointed out that some homes may even have heat loss cost higher than 40% due to air leakage.

Mr. Tamura tested six separate homes. All of these homes had storm windows and storm doors. One home had only 15% of air leakage through the windows and doors. The highest percentage of air leakage through the windows and doors was 24% in another of the six homes.

Two of the six homes had a brick-stucco combination on the exterior walls. In these homes, the exterior walls contributed only 15% to 21% to air leakage in the home. These same two homes showed 65% to 67% of air leakage through the ceilings!

Two other homes tested by Mr. Tamura had brick veneer siding. In these homes, the air leakage on the exterior walls averaged 65% to 42% There is a dramatic difference between brick and stucco sidings. In the all brick homes, 16% to 34% of the air leakage took place through the ceiling.

Another home tested had brick and asbestos shingles for exterior siding. The last home had brick veneer and aluminum siding. In the asbestos-sided home, 77% of its air leakage took place through the side walls. In the aluminum-sided home, 66% of its air leakage took place through the side walls. Both homes showed 8% to 11% of air leakage through the ceilings.

Although stucco appears to be the overall best anti-infiltration device, these tests cannot endorse stucco. What this test does show is that air leakage does occur in places other than through windows and doors. Sealing the home for air leakage is extremely important.

In the homes tested by Mr. Tamura, the volume of air turns per hour was rather high. Total air turns per hour was as low as 4.92 and as high as 9.13 turns per hour. These small air leaks must be detected and corrected. As you can see from our study here, it would be well worth the effort.

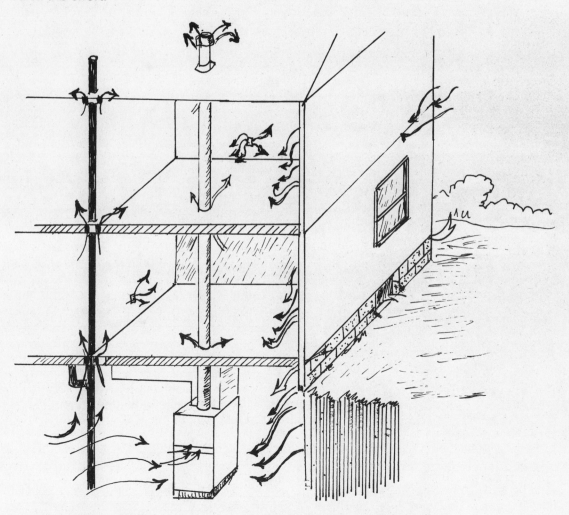

In gas-heated or fuel-oil heated homes, relying on natural infiltration to supply air for combustion can be costly. Instead, feed fresh air from the outside to the combustion chamber of the furnace with a separate fresh air duct.

We refer to air infiltration as convective losses while heat loss through solids (wood, brick, carpet, etc.) we refer to as conductive losses. In Appendix E, we demonstrate how to calculate the air turns per hour for your home. Also, in the Work Section, we demonstrate conductive losses. Practice our formula thoroughly because your greatest returns of low cost heating and comfort will come from correcting air leaks.

You will receive an unexpected bonus as you reduce the amount of air infiltration in the home. As you decrease air infiltration, the internal and external gains which we discuss and outline in the next chapter will further reduce your heating bill!

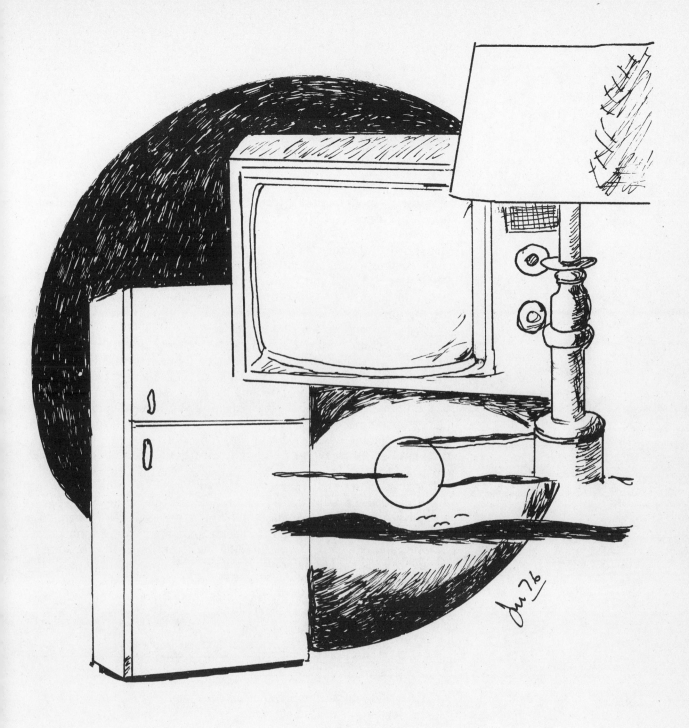

CHAPTER FIFTEEN

GAINS, GAINS, AND MORE GAINS

The first clue to heat gains is your electric bill exclusive of heating charges. Energy used for lighting, cooking, heating water and other functions of everyday living provides sources of heat gains.

Individuals contribute about 300 to 350 BTU per hour of body heat. This amounts to 7200 BTU per day and over a heating season a total of 1 800 000 BTU. Of course, the amount of heat loss from the body depends on size, nervous condition, and state of health. People are

considered a heat gain when it comes to heating economics. In the all electric home with resistance heat, this body heat could mean a contribution of $21.00 per heating season per person.

Electricity, when it is doing work such as operating a freezer or cooking your supper, will reject 3413 BTU/Kwh to the air in your home. So, as we are considering heat losses, we must also consider heat gains in the home.

So far, we have touched on solar heat contribution through windows, doors, and on side walls of a home. Solar gain is difficult to factor accurately into the heating load reduction of a home. The variables of sunshine hours, wind direction, and outside air temperatures all have a bearing on the net gain from solar heat.

During the heating months of October and November, the solar gain on the structure during the day is often more than enough to carry the house thermally through the solar night. During the months of December, January, and February, the solar gains on a home cannot be ignored. During March, April, and May, despite cold solar nights, the daytime heating load often goes to zero because of solar gains and internal gains on the home. Love that sun!

Heat rejection from the use of electricity takes place at the rate of 3413 BTU/Kwh. As you are using electric lights, washing clothes, or watching TV, the heat from these appliances is being rejected into your home. The air absorbs this heat energy and the heating requirements of the home are reduced accordingly. The actual heating load or loss of heat remains constant but because of internal gains and external gains the heating costs go down. The contribution of heat from electrical appliances on even a poorly insulated house will reduce heating costs 30% to 40%.

This revelation in the Thermal Woods startled me. Finding out about the value of these gains started me on a quest for a home designed to take advantage of thermal gains in the home. Interestingly enough, the internal gains can carry each home through the heating months of October and November without additional cost. Internal gains go on throughout the heating season and their contributions are rather high.

To demonstrate what internal gains can mean, let's look at the potential heat gains from appliances and solar gain for a family of five over a 250-heating-day season. These gains are in millions of BTUs.

Table 15-1. Potential Heat Gains in the Home

Source	Heat Gain	
Dishwasher	2.7	million BTU
Freezer (not frost-free)	3.9	million BTU
Cooking and baking	2.6	million BTU
Frost-free refrigerator	5.4	million BTU
Color television	1.1	million BTU
Black and White television	0.425	million BTU
Automatic washer	2.3	million BTU
Lights	3.4	million BTU
Clothes dryer	25.3	million BTU
Solar gain and body heat	27.8	million BTU

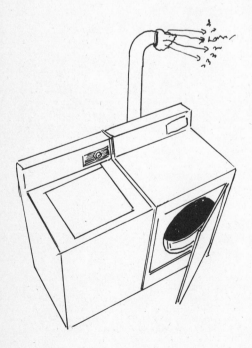

Without taking into consideration the potential heat gain from the clothes dryer (which is often vented outside), the potential heat gain for this family would be 84.14 million BTU per heating season. These gains will occur during the daylight hours because of the schedule of

88

the family's activities. With evening scheduling of appliance usage, these gains could carry over into part of the solar night.

According to Mr. E. R. Ambrose, author of the book *Heat Pumps and Electric Heating,* as one reduces air infiltration the reduction of heating costs will drop 35% over one heating season. Suppose we carry this notion one step further. Let's say that as we reduce air infiltration we will reduce heat loss costs. Then, heat recovery in the home should be substantial enough to carry much of the heating load over one heating season. The heating unit becomes a supplementary heating source instead of the "main" heating source of the home. By carefully finding heat leaks in the home or by designing a home for heat recovery, the fear of high heating bills should be laid to rest.

In Chapter 2 we examined two homes, one with insulation and another without insulation. We looked at the operational costs of the home for heating without plugging in any factor for the heat gains of the home. In Table 15-2, the annual heat loss for these two homes is converted into BTUs. This table represents the approximate loss of energy in BTUs for a heating season in Columbus, Ohio, and is a fair estimate of the heat loss but not of the heating cost. In the uninsulated home, we discover that the 84 million BTU heat recovery would be about 35% of the heat loss of the home. In actual field practice, the heating cost of the home would most likely be at least 35% less than our heating cost estimate. This figure holds true for almost every home in the country.

Table 15-2. Heat Loss of Uninsulated and Insulated Homes

Type	Trans. Rate (U_t)	Annual Heat Loss
Uninsulated House	1928.33	237 million BTU
Insulated House	445.52	55 million BTU

In the better insulated home, a paradox occurs. The potential heat gains of the home exceed the potential heat losses of the home. Yet, this home will still benefit with a 40% to 60% reduction of energy requirements for operating the heating unit in the home. We receive most of our heat gains during the day. In most well insulated homes the furnace functions during the night, not during the day.

In my own home, which is aptly named the Thermal House, this is demonstrated nicely. The Thermal House has a calculated heat transmission rate of 404, or a heat loss at 0°F of 28 280 BTU. The size of the home is 2800 square feet. A heat meter was installed in this home by the Columbus and Southern Ohio Electric Company and I installed some digital clocks to check out the heat pump and other items in the home. These were the results for the periods shown.

Table 15-3. Operational Costs of the Thermal House

Month	Master Meter	Heat Meter	House Use
September	1588 Kwh	0 Kwh	1588 Kwh
October	1190 Kwh	55 Kwh	1135 Kwh
November	2581 Kwh	177 Kwh	2404 Kwh
December	2917 Kwh	1091 Kwh	1826 Kwh
January	4376 Kwh	2471 Kwh	1905 Kwh
February	3715 Kwh	1917 Kwh	1798 Kwh
Total Kwh	16 367 Kwh	5711 Kwh	10 656 Kwh
Cost at $0.29/Kwh	$474.64	$165.62	$309.02

Electric meters and digital clocks were used in thermal studies on the author's home.

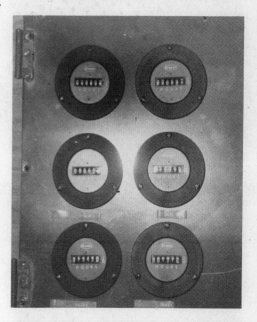

89

The Thermal House.

Interestingly enough, during the month of January we experienced very little solar heat gain because of constant cloud cover and cold temperatures. Out of thirty-one nights, the temperature never went above 32°F. During the day, the temperature went above 32°F on only fifteen of the thirty-one days. The highest temperature for the month was 49°F. This was for a period of only one hour. This month represented 41% of our annual heating bill.

December was just a little bit warmer than average and we had more sunshine than normal. October and November were normal for Ohio "Indian summer". The net heating bill from November through February represented only 35% of the total electric bill.

To recognize the total heat transmission rate (U_t) of any home, we have to factor in the conductive losses through the frames, ceilings, doors, etc., and the convective losses caused by air infiltration, etc. Because of the variable wind velocities and the normal use of doors, the heat loss caused by infiltration or convective losses is in a constant flux. During the heating months, we were able to estimate by meters the contribution of internal gains and factor in the approximate amount of air turns per hour on the average.

The representative months had a total DD of 2966 and our net consumption for heating was 5711 Kwh or very close to conductive losses only. During this same time span, we consumed another 7615 Kwh for

90

operating the home. (About 20% of the net operating cost for house operation was wasted to the outdoors because of the operation of a water pump in a well and the private aeration (sewage) plant.) The balance, converted into BTUs, amounts to 21 million BTUs which is almost equal to heat loss due to air infiltration into or out of our home. The convective losses of the home equaled a heat transmission rate of 300, two points above our conductive losses. This brought our gross to 598 Ut, not our calculated 404 Ut. The air infiltration load or heat loss due to air turns was carried entirely by the internal and external heating gains. This means over 50% of our entire heat loss was reduced by heat gains.

During the process of construction, careful inspection eliminated many of the potential heat leaks and air leaks in the home. However, our windows, as they were represented by the manufacturer, did not function properly as far as low air penetration is concerned. The infiltration of the windows at higher than "tested" wind velocities was the cause. On the average, we estimated air penetration of 10 cubic feet per minute over tested values. These windows have insulated glass panes, wood frames, and are supposedly tight in construction.

The front entry door is a door represented in the building trade as a "good" thermal door with good center core insulation and low air infiltration. In our case this description did not prove to be accurate. Ice formed at the bottom of the threshold because of air penetration. In addition, the weatherseal near the bottom and top allowed air to penetrate. Halfway through the month of February, I corrected these problems. The delay was caused by tests which were run on the windows.

Interestingly enough, a heat pump was installed as the supplementary heating system. During this heating period it was estimated the heat pump saved me about $68.00 over an electric furnace. The extra cost of the heat pump over a resistance furnace would take me about fifteen to sixteen years to get my investment back. Also, by getting a better seal on the windows with storm windows and by correcting the thermal leak on the front door, I feel I could have saved $60 to $70 during this test period. The savings achieved by reducing air leaks would match the savings resulting from the addition of the heat pump. Certainly, the heat pump can air condition the house during the summer but, frankly, except for a few nights, we do not really need air conditioning in Central Ohio.

Meanwhile, with the cooperation of a neighbor, we sealed off a home built in 1973 that did not have super insulation. By selectively insulating around the bandboard and part of the crawl space and by sealing electrical outlets and all potential heat leaks, this neighbor consumed only 8000 Kwh ($240.00 for the heating season) during the same heating period. His normal consumption for lights, etc., was exceptionally low (1000 Kwh/month) but, interestingly enough, his total electric bill almost duplicated the electric bill for the Thermal House. Frankly, this neighbor kept his thermostat set at 65°F which saved him about 8% to 10%, but even factoring in the thermostat setting, his performance was well below the average in our area.

A heat pump was installed as a supplementary source of heat in the author's home.

91

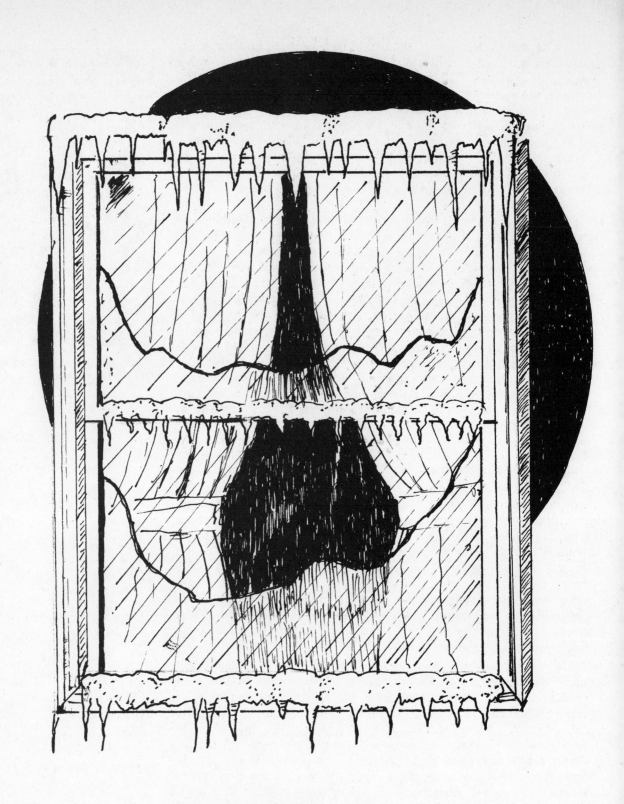

CHAPTER SIXTEEN
HUMIDITY AND ODOR

As we tighten up a home to save energy, are we causing potential problems such as humidity and odor build-up? Humidity will be the first problem we will address. Yes, it could be a problem if one does not understand some principles.

92

The capacity of air to hold water vapor depends on the temperature of the air. The lower the temperature, the lower is the capacity of air to hold water vapor. The point at which air temperature is low enough to cause water droplets to condense from moist air is called the dew point. If the frame of the window is metal and this frame has direct contact with freezing temperatures outside, you may witness both condensation and freezing of water on the window. Even windows with very thin thermal breaks such as vinyl will have frosting. Other than adding storm windows or completely replacing the window, there is little one can do to avoid this problem except add a vinyl shield on the inside of the window frame to prevent moist air from coming in direct contact with the frame.

Another suggestion is to protect the window frame with a thermal barrier or storm windows. In this way the temperature around the frame is kept in a higher range and thus prevents condensation or icing. This is why wood frame windows are slightly superior to aluminum frame windows which do not have an adequate thermal break. However, in severe weather conditions, such as $-20°F$, wood windows may frost as well.

Relative humidity percentage tells you the amount of moisture a given amount of air contains relative to the maximum amount of moisture that air can hold at a given temperature. A relative humidity rating of 40% at 70°F indicates that at 70°F the air contains 40% of the maximum amount of moisture it is capable of holding at that same temperature. As that same air is reduced in temperature, its relative humidity will climb even though no more moisture is added to the air.

Perm ratings are often stated in the building industry with little understanding of their meanings. *Perm ratings indicate the amount of moisture or water vapor that can pass through a material at a given temperature and at a given pressure per square foot.* The lower the perm rating of a given material, the lower the transmission of water vapor by that material. The need for using a material with a low perm number as a vapor barrier on the warm side of a wall, etc., is mandatory for today's energy problems.

The capacity of air to hold moisture is subject not only to temperature but also to pressure created by rapid movement of the water molecules. As the air temperature increases, so does the velocity of the water molecules in the air. If we have a high temperature and a high vapor resistance material, pressure can build up to phenomenal points. The pressure of water vapor trapped underneath roof shingles heated to high temperatures by radiation from the sun will reach pressures as high as 600 psi (pounds per square inch). The blistering of a low perm paint is caused by pressure exerted by water vapor on the paint's membrane.

We certainly do not want to see moisture building up on the inside of the wall. If it does, the insulation will become wet and lose its thermal qualities. Then, building board could begin to rot and vapor pressure could raise havoc with our exterior siding. Prevention is much better than any cure.

There are ways to assure that the potential problem of humidity and water vapor will be at a minimum. A chart in *Architectural Graphic Standards* published by John Wiley & Sons, Inc. of New York contains some perm ratings as established by the American Society of Heating, Refrigeration, Air Conditioning Engineers (ASHRAE).

Here are the most common materials used in construction and if one is not listed request the needed information from your supplier or directly from the manufacturer.

Table 16-1. Perm Ratings of Some Common Materials

Material	Perm Rating	Material	Perm Rating
Brick	0.8 to 1.1	Plywood Ex. Glue	0.7
Drywall	50.0	Plywood Int. Glue	1.9
Kraft Paper	1.8	Insulation Board	50-90
Vinyl (4-mil)	0.08	Poly Foam	1.2
Fiberglass	20.0	Aluminum Foil	0.0
Paint (2 coats)	3.0	Roof Shingles	0.24

The lower the perm number, the greater is the resistance of the material to the passage of water vapor. An ideal ratio of perm ratings is at least five to one from the inside to the outside. Let's say we have a wall section like this:

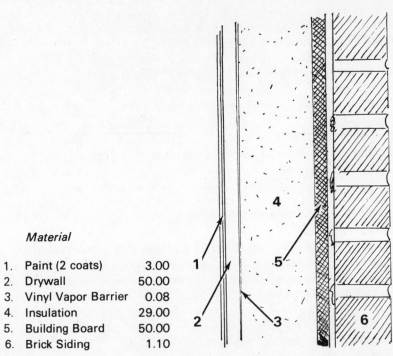

Material

1.	Paint (2 coats)	3.00
2.	Drywall	50.00
3.	Vinyl Vapor Barrier	0.08
4.	Insulation	29.00
5.	Building Board	50.00
6.	Brick Siding	1.10

The lowest perm number is from the vinyl (4-mil) vapor barrier right next to the drywall and before the insulation. The paint and the drywall will allow moisture to penetrate to the vinyl, but the vinyl will pass very little of the moisture beyond that point. Since the thermal qualities of the paint and drywall are low it is most likely the temperature of the vinyl is about room temperature and no moisture should form at this point.

As the vinyl allows moisture to pass through, the insulation and then the building board with their high perm ratings, will allow this moisture to literally pass right on through. The brick, however, has a low perm number. Thus, it may be possible to have condensation on the inside of the brick because of low temperature on brick. For this reason, "weep holes" are installed in brick walls to allow an escape for this moisture. Aluminum siding is designed so it can "breathe" and allow water vapor and condensation to escape. As we know, this breathing will add to our heating problem; however, venting is very important. Otherwise, we may have wet insulation and condensation problems.

The attic presents an unusual problem. As indicated by their perm ratings, the ceiling drywall and insulation allow rapid transmission of moist air to the attic. If the attic is undervented, this moisture will

Weep holes in a brick wall.

94

 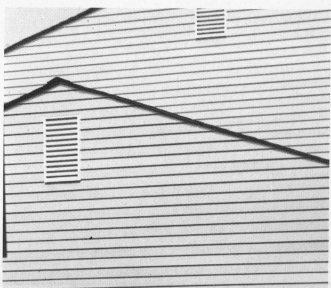

condense on the underside of the roof as temperatures go down at night. If the attic is overvented (as is too often the case), the amount of vapor escaping from the home during the winter months will cause the humidity level of the home to be low. Excessively low humidity will cause health problems such as dryness of the nasal and throat passages, be conducive to high static electricity levels, and cost you money in heating. The molecules of the water vapor absorb large quantities of energy. As the vapor passes through the walls and the ceiling of your home, so does your heat.

High moisture areas such as bathrooms, especially showers, should be vented directly to the outside instead of to the attic area. If your laundry area is small, an exterior vent might be in order. Venting the dryer to the outside will rid you of some moisture, however, you will also blow out some precious heat. If you fear that moisture from your dryer will be a problem, by-pass a couple of sections of water lines past the blower outlet and the moisture in the dryer air will condense on the pipes. As it condenses, you will get the benefit of heat from the dryer.

In my home, the walls in the basement were insulated, a vinyl vapor barrier was placed over the insulation, and the water lines were insulated. The dryer blows directly into the laundry room. A dehumidifier in the laundry room is set at 60%. I want to capture that 34 million BTU from the dryer over a heating season and not send it to the outdoors.

Some people recommend correcting a humidity problem in the home by opening the door or by leaving the vent open in the fireplace. There is really little need for this in the winter unless your problem is out of control. If there is a condensation problem, someone did not do his homework on establishing the proper perm ratings on the walls and ceilings. If you have a problem, turn the fan on the furnace to continuance and let it run until the moisture escapes through the attic ceiling and out through the vents of the roof. That's a lot cheaper than opening doors. Then search for and correct the problem.

Condensation of moisture or ice build-up usually indicates thermal weakness, not necessarily humidity problems. Occasional moisture on the windows will do little, if any, harm to the home. Most of the time, this moisture build-up indicates air infiltration as well. Seal off the air flow. Correct thermal weaknesses (See Work Section). It has been sug-

gested that storm windows steam up, but I have yet to see this happen. Should this be your problem, some warm air must be leaking from the inside window to the outside storm window.

An attorney friend has a home with paint blisters on his outside siding. This problem was corrected by adding a couple of coats of oil paint inside with a lower perm rating than the perm rating of the outside paint. In this way, the transfer of water vapor was reduced to the point where the outside paint could let water vapor pass through without condensation. Often what many people think are humidity problems are really thermal leaks caused by air infiltration or by a thermal weakness some place in the wall section. The ideal humidity level in a home is about 40%. Humidifiers cost very little and can be added to most heating systems by the owner. Check with a reliable firm and inquire about cost. The more automatic the controls, the less room there is for error.

There are a variety of sources of moisture in the home. Some of these are listed in Table 16-2.

Table 16-2. Moisture from Various Sources*

Source	Amount
Cooking	5.66 lb/day
Washing and drying of clothes in the home	30.75 lb
Bathing—showers,	0.5 lb each
baths	1.2 lb each
Human body	5.7 lb each/day

*Ambrose, E.R., *Heat Pumps and Electric Heating.* New York: John Wiley & Sons, Inc., 1968.

As the difference from the inside temperature to the outside temperature increases, the flow of moisture from the inside to the outside will be greater. The reason is that the warmer air inside has more pressure per square foot than the colder outside air.

ODOR

Odors within a tight home are another source of fear for some people. Odors are possible where there is little air movement within the house, such as in a home heated with a straight resistance baseboard as opposed to a forced air system.

Let's consider some of the sources of odors and corrections. Body odor is corrected by soap and water. Kitchen odors, other than cooking, can be eliminated through cleanliness. If you are going to let trash and garbage sit for days there is nothing we can do to help you. Cooking odors can be kept to a minimum with a vent fan over the stove. Vent fans over stoves should not be vented to the outside. A charcoal filter stove hood and quick and orderly clean-up around the stove after cooking will cure most odor problems here.

Most bathroom odors also disappear as soap and water are used. Toilets with self ventilation, as manufactured by American Standards, will resolve obvious odor problems without expensive outside venting.

If you plan to or are lucky enough to have an extremely tight home with minimum air leakage, a fresh air inlet could be added to the furnace.

96

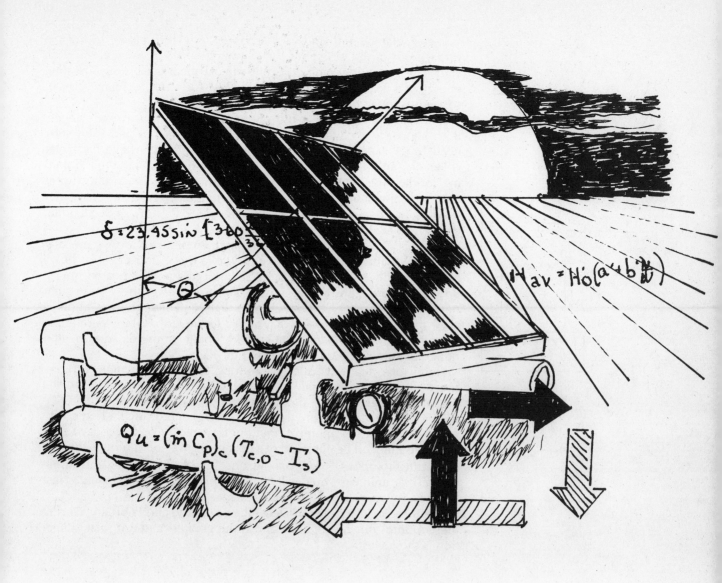

CHAPTER SEVENTEEN
SOLAR HEATED HOMES

As we begin our discussion of solar heated homes, we realize that we are truly advancing into the Space Age. Sunlight is captured on the roof and piped into the home. With a tiny little fan we can circulate solar heated air throughout the home—free heat—thumbing our nose at the utility man!

The search for the technology and methods to design a solar heated home is what really started me, a country builder, on the journey through the Thermal Woods. To this quest for knowledge of solar heated homes, I owe all my findings.

The technology level of this country is such that successful solar heated homes are here now. There are about 1000 to 1500 solar heated or solar boosted homes in this country now. The number of new solar heated homes will climb as the public becomes bitten by the solar heat bug.

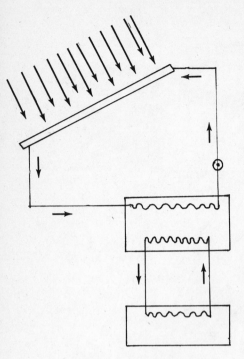

These solar heated units are accomplishing the feat of taking the furnace out of the basement and putting it on the roof or in the back yard. The sole underlying objective of solar heat is to reduce heating energy of a given home. They can do this. You can buy many types of solar units today but there is a catch—price.

Solar collection and the use of solar energy is not a new science. Both Leonardo da Vinci and Aristotle were aware of and used solar heat. Israel, Japan, Chile, and many other countries have had solar collectors and heat transfer systems for some time. Some homes in Florida, Arizona, and California use solar heat for heating water and, in a few cases, for heating of the home. In Chile, a solar water distiller has been in use since the late 1800s. It is my understanding that this solar still is functional to this day.

The U.S. Government is spending large amounts of money on solar heat. Newspapers all over the country love the sound of "solar heat" and will gladly give you free press is you build a solar heated house. Books by the dozens telling about solar heat are on the market right now. However, some of the books are slightly slanted by the authors to favor the solar unit they just happened to "invent." Many people are jamming the U. S. Patent Office with applications for solar heated homes or some type of solar assisted device.

These solar heat advocates are serious. So, let's treat them with respect but at the same time let's be practical. On page 89, we showed the operational costs of the Thermal House for the winter of 1975-1976. For a heating season, the total cost of heating such a home with electricity and a heat pump, should not exceed $205.00 at today's cost. If we used fuel oil heat instead of a heat pump we could reduce the cost of heating to about $89.00 per heating season. In heating this home with a solar unit, we would still need our present heating unit as a "just in case" measure. The "just in case" measure is for the normal cycle of the three cold months of December, January, and February. During these months our heating demand is the greatest and our solar collection is the lowest.

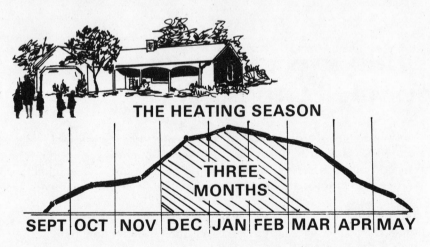

THE HEATING SEASON

THREE MONTHS

SEPT | OCT | NOV | DEC | JAN | FEB | MAR | APR | MAY

The proposed solar collector would have to be large enough to compensate for heat loss from the collector to the sky, the heat loss of the transfer system and storage unit, and the heat loss of the home itself. We would also have to allow for a little extra needed on days when solar heat collection would be zero.

During the heating month of January, 1976, we had only 8% of possible sunshine in our area. The cost of heating the Thermal House during January, 1976, was about $68.00, or 41% of the annual heating bill. A solar collector system could have carried very little of this heating bill because we experienced only 8% of normal sunshine.

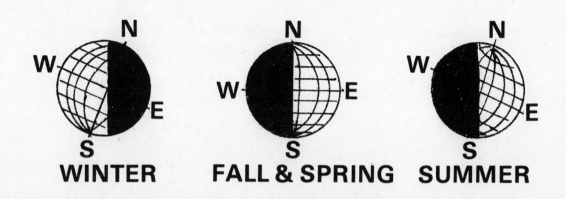

WINTER   FALL & SPRING   SUMMER

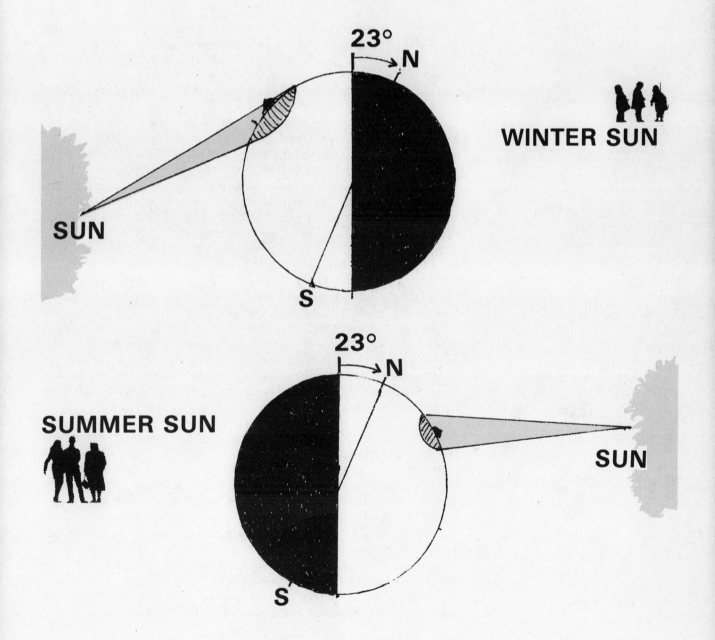

23°

WINTER SUN

SUN

SUMMER SUN

SUN

Let's suppose that, in the near future, a reliable solar collector which has automatic controls, a ten-year guarantee (which I doubt), proper storage, and transfer system is designed. Let's also pretend this proposed solar unit could carry the ENTIRE heating load of a Thermal House or your home after thermal corrections. Frankly, a solar system like this would cost well over $15 000 on today's market but let's be fair and say we can buy such a unit in our choice of colors, for a mere $7500. Assuming our potential cost of heating would be $150 to $160 per heating season, how long would it take us to recover our investment in the proposed solar heating system? The payback period in years for different systems is given in Table 17-1.

Table 17-1. Payback for a Solar Heating Unit

	Elec. 1	Elec. 2	Fuel Oil (0.70)	Nat. Gas (0.70)
Payback period (years)	46.8	93.78	140	150+

Note the numbers in Table 17-1 have not been adjusted for interest on money, breakage, repairs, replacements, and operational costs. Enough said? Some people may argue that we may not have fuel in the future for heating. That remains to be demonstrated.

What about a cheaper or lower cost backyard solar furnace? Such units are available for the mere price of $2000 plus rocks, delivery, setup, and fans which could raise the installed price to $3000. The unit has an upper potential of collecting and storing 158 000 BTU per day. Normal collection and storage losses will diminish this collection. If we assume this backyard collector will carry the entire heating load (which both we and the manufacturers know is not a reasonable assumption), the payback period could be about one-half of the payback we demonstrated on the Thermal House. This period would be longer in the "average" heat-leaking home.

One seller of such a solar unit told me of the dramatic savings (about 50%) that one family experienced by using a solar unit in the backyard. On investigating this claim, it was discovered that ample new insulation had been added to the home before the solar unit was hooked up. So walk carefully and investigate, friend.

Keep in mind that $2000 will buy enough insulation to completely fill one and one-half homes from floor to ceiling, and from wall to wall. In this case, the only heating source required would be body heat.

So, while the politicians in Washington are "researching" facts about solar heat, we might as well be beating the heating game right now by adding insulation.

SOLAR HEAT TODAY!

In almost every chapter we have discussed how you already benefit from solar heat in your present home. The secret of solar heat capture is to reduce thermal leaks so the sun will continue to decrease your heating bill even more.

Solar REJECTION during the summer cooling months is another objective. Solar heat will cause the attic temperature to rise during the solar day and thus will result in heat gains during most of the solar night. A simple, but effective, solution to this problem is an automatic thermostat-controlled roof fan. This fan will reject the solar heat gains and keep the attic temperature low during the day.

100

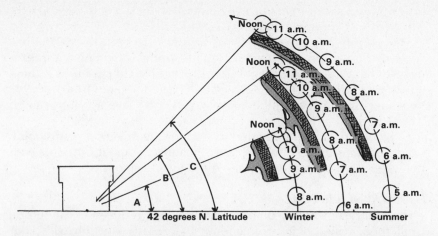

As the sun arcs through the sky we discover less potential heat in the winter due to the angle of the sun to the horizon and six hours less of sunlight.

The solar gains on the roof and also on windows facing east and west will often represent 40% of your heat gains during the summer months. Film which will reflect about 90% of the solar rays from these windows is manufactured by 3M and similar companies. The insulation added for stopping heat leaks during the winter months, along with a roof fan and solar rejection film, will lower your costs of cooling considerably.

ANOTHER CASE

As you reduce the heat loss of your home, you will also certainly reduce the cost of a solar collector system needed to heat your home. As you reduce the heat loss, you will also lower heating bills. With the lower heating dollars, it would be difficult to justify the high cost of most solar collector systems, especially when you consider potential problems like freezing of solar collectors and heat transfer lines during cold winter days and nights.

During my study period, I was shown a seemingly inexpensive solar collector designed to lower the cost of heating hot water in the home. This unit was small enough to be placed on the roof. It also contained automatic controls. The suggested purchase price, INSTALLED, was only $440 (to a builder). Its suggested retail price was $1000. To top the cake, the supplier said his company was selling his unit to an agency of the U.S. Government. Frankly, I was even more impressed when he showed me certified tests indicating that this unit could reduce hot water bills in a home by 50% or more. If this were the case, one could retire his present hot water system in an all electric home in four to five years. I investigated.

His claims were true! A fifty percent reduction was actually possible with his unit. However, the small print on the literature gave his game away. The literature suggested that to operate his solar collector properly, the home owner should turn the thermostat on the hot water tank down to 110°F, a temperature 50° lower than the average factory setting of 160°F. With a screw driver, not with a solar collector, were most of the savings achieved.

Unfortunately, this is still not the end of this tale. I further inquired of the manufacturer's representative how they solved the problem of freeze-ups during the cold winter months. With his system this could be a real problem because they were pumping water directly from the hot water tank to the roof. According to him, this problem had been

101

solved by using thermocouples to sense when the water in the collector was near or at freezing temperatures of 32°F.

My curiosity was at a peak. What happens? Do you have a thermal cover or do you use antifreeze? How do you actually prevent freeze-up? Simple. When the collector senses freezing temperatures it sucks up hot water from the hot water tank and keeps the pipes from freezing. Very successful, he continued—we have yet to have a failure caused by freeze-up.

As you can imagine, I decided to stop my investigation at this point. I did not want to be responsible for heating the great outdoors with hot water from my hot water tank during winter months.

FOREWARNED IS FOREARMED!

Hopefully, the cost of solar heat units will be reduced in the future. Until then, you can get tremendous heat cost reduction with your present home with very few insulation dollars.

By establishing a firm heat transmission rate (U_t) of your home and factoring in the fuel cost factor, you will get an idea of potential cost of heating for a given season. This dollar estimate, or BTU consumption estimate, will give you a guide line as to economics of a solar unit.

The formula for calculating heat loss in BTUs in a heating season or for whatever time span you select is: $(DD \times 24) \times U_t = BTU$ consumption. In Appendix C, we give you a guide for solar collector systems.

Should you still decide that you want to try a solar heating system, be sure to correct all thermal leaks and establish a firm convection cost (air infiltration) before designing or installing this solar heat system.

CHAPTER EIGHTEEN
THE HEATING OF WATER

Recently, I read in a newspaper about the great dissatisfaction of a European motel owner with American tourists. His dissatisfaction was not with manners, method of payment, or philosophy. Instead, he was concerned with the fact that Americans used so much water that his septic tanks would back up! Americans, thanks to the soap manufacturers, are obsessed with cleanliness—and should be. I, too, am indoctrinated, just as you are.

Water heating cost can be considered in terms of three factors: amount of hot water used, temperatures, and heat loss from the hot water system. The amount of hot water used can really be cited as a status symbol. The more money a person earns, the more hot water a person tends to use. Water flows at the rate of about ½ gallon per minute in a ½" water line at a water pressure of 60 pounds per square inch. Thus, the use of water can be considered as a function of time. The longer you stay in the shower, the more hot water you will

103

use. Table 18-1 lists approximate rates of water usage for various functions requiring hot water.

Table 18-1. Water Usage for Various Functions

Function	Amount of Water
Shower	10 gallons/shower
Bath	10 gallons/bath
Automatic clothes washer	15 gallons/load
Automatic dishwasher	15 gallons/load
Washing hands or shaving	½ gallon/usage
Testing water for temperature	½ to 2 gallons/test

At first glance, all the figures seem harmless until we examine water usage in terms of time. Table 18-2 shows what the annual usage of hot water would look like for a family of five.

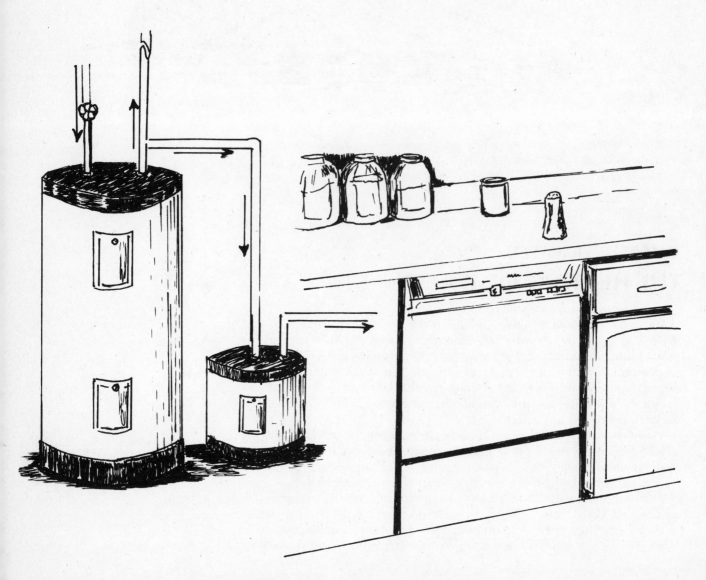

Table 18-2. Annual Water Usage

Function	Annual Water Use
Showers	4680 gallons/yr
Baths	4680 gallons/yr
Automatic clothes washer	10 000 gallons/yr
Automatic dishwasher	6000 gallons/yr
Washing hands or shaving	1000 gallons/yr
Testing water for temperature	730 gallons/yr

This is a grand total of 27 090 gallons per year. That is enough to fill a swimming pool 8 ft × 40 ft × 84 ft. On a monthly basis, the average use of hot water would be about 2257 gallons per month.

For our calculations in this chapter, we will assume the average usage of hot water is 2500 gallons per month or 30 000 gallons per year. The temperature of the water is important because the higher the water temperature, the more energy we will consume. Most hot water tanks are set at 165°F in the factory. The thermostat which controls the temperature of the water in a hot water tank is no different in principle than the thermostat used in your heating system. When the temperature falls below 165°F, the thermostat mechanisms are activated and energy is used to heat the water to the desired temperature setting.

Recall that one BTU of energy is required to raise the temperature of one pound of water by one Fahrenheit degree. A gallon of water weighs about 8.33 pounds. Thus, it takes 8.33 BTU to raise the temperature of one gallon of water by one Fahrenheit degree.

The temperature of the inlet side of your hot water tank is about 55°F. This temperature is very close to ground temperature. Suppose we want to raise the temperature of one gallon of water from 55°F to 165°F, a temperature difference of 105°. How much energy would be required? It would take (105 × 8.33) or 874.65 BTU per gallon of water to raise its temperature from 55°F to 165°F. Also, there would be heat losses from the hot water tank and the hot water lines to consider. Our annual usage of 30 000 gallons of water would require at least 26.23 million BTU. After allowing for tank losses and line losses, this figure could be as high as 30.17 million BTU. In dollars this would mean $353.00 for electricity at 4¢ per Kwh; $94.28 for fuel

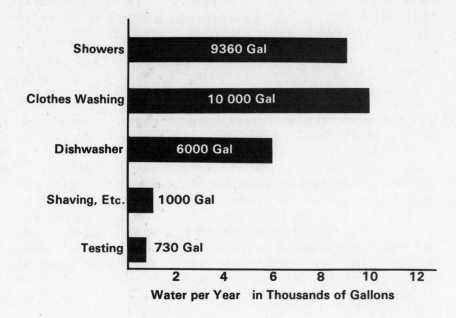

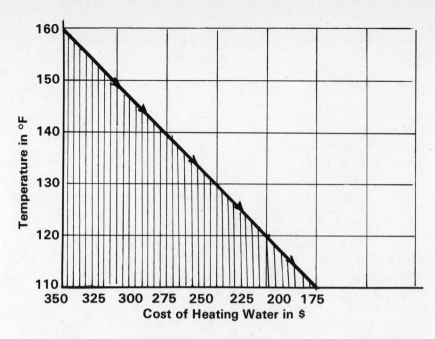

As the temperature setting of the hot water tank is reduced, the cost of heating is reduced accordingly.

oil at 45¢ per gallon; and $88.09 for natural gas at $2.20 per 1000 units.

As you can see from this example, natural gas and fuel oil are bargains compared to electricity. Let's carry this one step further and see how many dollars one would spend per year as we turn the water temperature down.

Table 18-3. Estimated Cost of Heating 30 000 Gallons of Water for One Year

Temperature Setting	Electricity	Fuel Oil	Natural Gas
160°F	$344.00	$102.25	$95.70
150°F	$328.61	$97.11	$91.21
140°F	$279.30	$82.28	$77.52
130°F	$246.16	$73.29	$66.44
120°F	$213.42	$63.29	$59.23
110°F	$180.68	$53.58	$50.15

These figures do not take into consideration the efficiency of the hot water heating exchanger. Because of soot (carbon) build-up on the heat exchanger, these costs could rise about 40% for fuel oil and natural gas. Mineral deposits on electric heaters in electric hot water tanks will increase the cost of heating water with electricity. We did consider waste of heat radiating from the hot and cold water lines near the hot water tank.

Heat loss from the water lines close to the hot water tank can be controlled. In a test I set up, I reduced the dollar cost of heating water by 12% just by insulating all the water lines close to the water tank. You can do this too. By feeling the water lines until you find where the temperature in the line is close to body temperature, you will see how many feet of pipe need insulation. In this figure, you can see how to determine where the thermostat control is and what water lines need to be insulated.

106

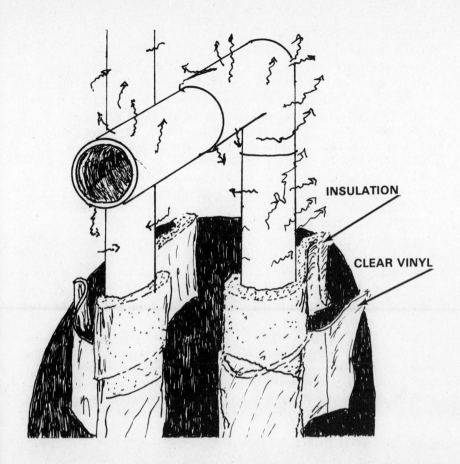

INSULATION

CLEAR VINYL

The need for washing clothes in hot water is greatly reduced with the new cold water detergents available. While some clothes demand warm water, certainly not all of them do. Most clothes washers have an automatic temperature setting for going from hot to cold wash cycle. It may be advisable to contact your appliance dealer or manufacturer for instructions on setting your washer to cold water cycle.

By reducing the amount of water used and by setting the thermostat on the hot water tank lower, you will be able to save many dollars per year. For those of you who are not mechanically inclined, or do not understand how to reset this thermostat, contact a reliable individual to help you. If you have an electric hot water tank and you fear electricity, turn the main switch off before resetting the thermostat. A reliable electrician can set the thermostat back for you in very little time. In fact, it can be done with a screw driver.

Most automatic dishwasher manufacturers recommend that you use water no lower in temperature than 140°F. This temperature insures that chances of spotting of glassware are greatly reduced. Possibly, a soap manufacturer can step in and market a soap to insure no spotting with water at 110°F.

Home owners with natural gas hot water heaters could save about 75 000 cubic feet of natural gas per year by just turning the temperature setting from 160°F to 140°F. Considering the millions of homes using natural gas, you can see that the savings would be quite large. Insulating water lines and not using hot water for clothes washing should save another 85 000 cubic feet of natural gas per year per family of five.

In all-electric homes as well as in smaller well-insulated, fuel-oil and natural-gas heated homes, many families were surprised to discover their hot water usage and resulting heating cost was as much as the cost of heating a home.

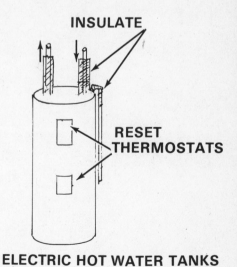

INSULATE

RESET THERMOSTATS

ELECTRIC HOT WATER TANKS

SOLAR COLLECTOR SYSTEMS FOR HOT WATER

Solar hot water systems could provide a savings for the family. However, the economics are only in the favor of the all-electric home. A solar collector with an area of about 60 square feet could contribute significantly to savings in heating over a year's time. Heating or pre-heating of hot water is actually the only and best place for solar heat at this time. Interestingly enough, if the market were large enough, an inexpensive solar collector with a tempering tank could be installed for about $750. Since the sun shines profusely during spring, summer, and autumn, with such a system you could probably realize savings of from 60% to 80% of dollars spent for heating water. Using our base cost of $750, we would get our return on heating water with solar heat in about 4.4 years for electricity, in about 14 years for fuel oil, and in about 15.8 years for natural gas. As you can see the economics are in the favor of the electric hot water tank.

An ideal solar hot water system would have low cost antifreeze safeguards during the cold winter months. Solar technology will definitely advance and if the market increases, then reliable, low cost units may appear.

In this chapter, you have seen that great savings can be realized by reducing hot water consumption as much as possible, by reducing water temperature, and by insulating hot and cold water lines near the water tanks. Look and investigate solar collector systems before installing. Be sure to investigate the entire solar collection system!

THINK ABOUT SOLAR HEAT

108

CHAPTER NINETEEN
FIREPLACES

Fire has long fascinated mankind. The dancing flames, the warmth from the hearth, and the snug feeling of heat from an open, controlled fire are all inviting. The wonder of it all after playing in the snow or coming in from an ice skating party attracts everyone. Just to sit near a fire and watch TV adds immeasurable comfort and pleasure to life.

Within the Thermal Woods, is the fireplace a friend or foe? Is it really a heat saver or is it a hidden enemy not unlike the Horse of Troy? In reality, it is both friend and foe. While we are burning wood in our fireplace, heat is being added to our home. When the fire is out, heat is being lost from our home. With the average flue-closing system (damper), warm air will be sucked up the stack and lost to the outdoors. This heat waste could add as much as 25% to our heating bill!

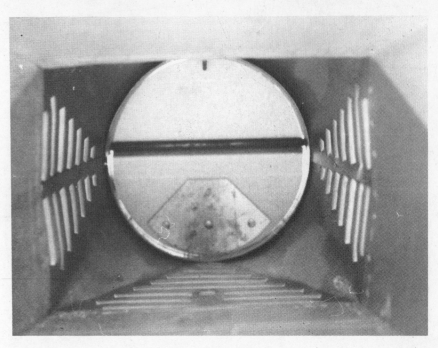

This fireplace damper may be a source of considerable heat loss.

The dampers in most fireplaces are poor fitting. Also, while the fire is dying out we cannot really close the damper. Instead, we wait until the next day to close it. Often we forget and this next day stretches into more days and our heating bill climbs. A glass fire screen will certainly help us. When we go to bed at night, we can close this glass fire screen and let the fire die out by itself. With this type of screen we do not have to be overly concerned about closing the damper the next day. In fact, we could leave the damper open as long as the fire screen is closed tightly.

Each species of wood we burn has its own BTU rating. For an average, let's establish the BTU rating of wood as 5482 BTU/pound. Combustion is a chemical process. The heat released during the combustion of wood is released when oxygen from the air and carbon from the wood combine to form carbon dioxide. As a fire burns in the closed confines of the modern home, toxic gases may be introduced into the home. The chimney is designed to rid the house of these gases as fast as possible. Elimination of these toxic gases is necessary for our safety. However, it has been established over and over again that in this process, 80% of heat from combustion goes right up the stack. Therefore, of the 5482 BTU released during the combustion of one pound of wood, only 1096 BTU are available for heating our home.

Wood needs oxygen for combustion. This oxygen comes from the air around us and is often introduced into the room by way of cracks and crevices under doors, windows, etc. To sustain combustion we need about 390 cubic feet of fresh air per minute.* This amount is for a fireplace with only a front opening. For fireplace units with side openings

---

*From a formula established by Robert B. Martin, AIA, Lincoln City Oregon. This formula is included in the appendix.

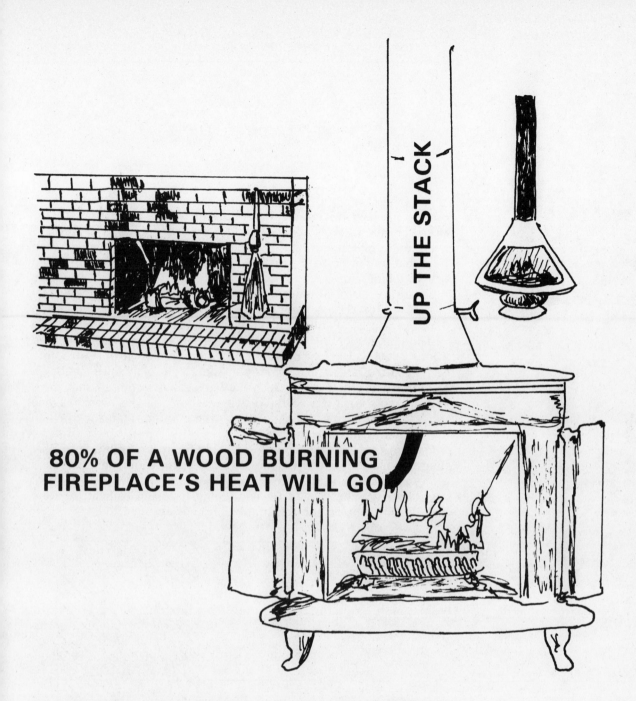

80% OF A WOOD BURNING
FIREPLACE'S HEAT WILL GO
UP THE STACK

or double openings, much more air is required to support combustion.

We have seen that we benefit from only 20% of the maximum heat from each pound of wood and that for combustion this wood needs fresh air from outside. How many pounds of wood do we need just to keep a room at constant temperature on a cold winter night? First, we must know outside temperatures. Table 19-1 lists the number of pounds of wood we must burn per hour just to maintain room temperature of 70°F at various outside temperatures.

To raise the air temperature of the room by one Fahrenheit degree, wood must be burned faster than the pounds per hour rating for a given outside temperature. If the fire is left unattended, cold air can enter from the outside at the rate of 390 cubic feet per minute. If the outside air temperature drops from 10°F to 0°F, you will have a temperature reduction in the room. Your thermostat senses this temperature reduction and on goes the furnace. The solution to this problem is to have

Table 19-1. Pounds of Wood Required to Maintain an Inside Temperature of 70°F at Various Outside Temperatures

Outside Temperature	Pounds/hour
40°F	9.78 lb
30°F	13.69 lb
20°F	17.60 lb
10°F	21.52 lb
5°F	23.47 lb
0°F	25.43 lb

outside air feed directly to the fireplace! In this way, the warm air already in the room is not required for combustion and the fireplace will radiate 1096 BTU/hr/lb of wood burned. The fireplace will then be a real source of heat. Also, less wood will be required to maintain proper temperatures in the room.

Before we go on to another use of the fireplace, let's look at that air turnover of 390 cubic feet per minute in a room 12 feet × 14 feet with 8 foot ceilings. The volume of air in such a room is 1344 cubic feet. To sustain combustion in our fireplace for a period of one hour, we need about 21 600 cubic feet of air. In other words, the air in this room is turning at the rate of 16.07 times per hour. Now, maybe we can begin to understand the need of tall, wing-back chairs in the colonial days. The air movement was so rapid that the drafts in the room became more than noticeable. The drawing in of cold outside air made the hind part colder than the front part.

One heat-saving device being marketed today is a hollow grate that holds the burning wood. Air is circulated from the room into the hollow grate and back into the room again. The manufacturer claims a heat recovery of about 28 000 BTU per hour. This claim of heat recovery can be substantiated and this simple device is effective.

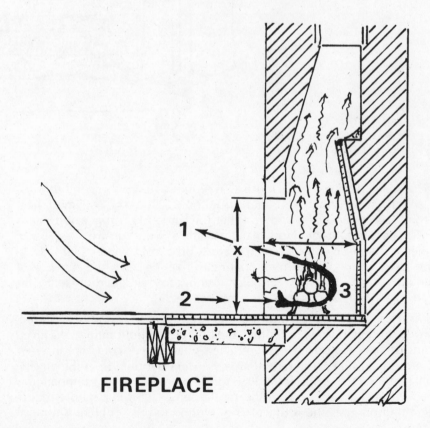

FIREPLACE

112

From all weakness comes some strength. The weakness of the modern fireplace is the amount of heat that goes up the stack. Let's look again at the amount of wood we burn by the pound and compare the number of useable BTUs radiated with those that go up the chimney.

Table 19-2. Average Number of BTUs Lost in a Fireplace per Pound of Wood Burned

Pounds of Wood/hr	Usable BTUs Radiated	BTUs up the Chimney
9.78	10 689	53 445
13.69	14 963	74 815
17.60	19 236	96 184
21.52	23 521	117 606
23.47	25 652	128 263
25.43	27 794	138 974

In order to raise the temperature of 82 gallons of water (average daily consumption) from 55°F to 140°F, about 58 060 BTU are required. If we had a heat exchanger that could capture just thirty percent of the stack's loss when we are burning wood at the rate of 13.69 pounds an hour, we could have our water heated for us in about three hours!

In fact, if you had a cabin in the woods with a heat exchanger in the fireplace and a large thermal storage unit, you could have heat all night long even when the fire is out. The heat exchangers and the technology are here already. Check your plumbing supply or industrial suppliers for the latest information on heat exchange systems available in your area. Should you decide to install one of these systems, be sure to add a safety valve to prevent a pressure burst of pipes and exchangers.

Available on today's market is a heat exchanger that fits on some fireplace chimneys. This heat exchanger has a fan which will blow normally wasted heat into the house. This device can also be fitted on fuel-oil and natural gas furnaces.

The major problem of solar heat boosting on cloudy days could be solved with heat recovery from the fireplace. This might be a real and practical solution to a tricky heating problem in some areas of our country.

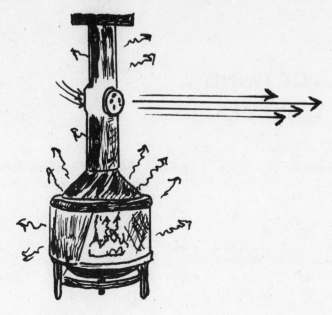

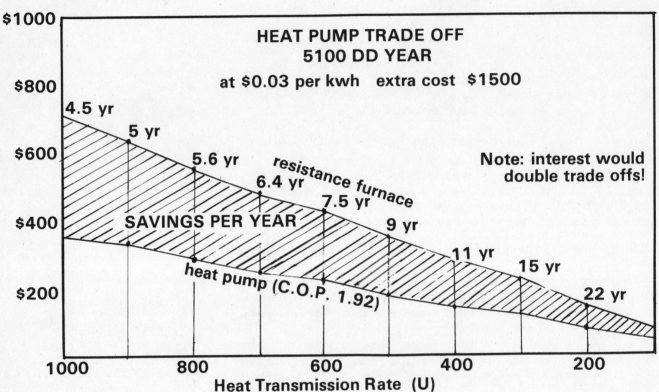

HEAT PUMP TRADE OFF
5100 DD YEAR
at $0.03 per kwh   extra cost $1500

Note: interest would double trade offs!

4.5 yr
5 yr
5.6 yr
6.4 yr
7.5 yr
9 yr
11 yr
15 yr
22 yr

resistance furnace

SAVINGS PER YEAR

heat pump (C.O.P. 1.92)

Heat Transmission Rate (U)

CHAPTER TWENTY
HEAT PUMPS

The rush is on. Many home owners with all-electric homes are running to buy a heat pump. The advertisements assure us of saving 40% to 50%. Are the savings really that high? Is the overall investment of $1100 to $1500 really worth it?

Before we can answer that question, we must find out how a heat pump functions and then compare its performance with the performance of a straight resistance electric heating system. You lucky people who heat your homes with fuel oil and natural gas can zip on to the next chapter because the heat pump does not apply to you. The heat pump is only for the all-electric heated homes.

114

A heat pump is simply a compressor with two heat exchangers. By compressing a fluid, we can extract heat from the fluid. By expanding the same fluid, we can absorb heat with the fluid.

By blowing air over a heat exchanger with a fan, we can extract heat from the outside air and move it or "pump" the heat indoors to another heat exchanger. By blowing air over the indoor heat exchanger, we can then move the heated air to various rooms within the home.

On all heat pumps we have a fixed amount of air blowing over the outside heat exchanger. Actually, this is one of the limiting features of the heat pump. The other limitation is the temperature of the outside air. As the outside air becomes colder, there is less heat for the heat pump to extract per cubic foot of air.

We can demonstrate this very readily by calculating heat output of a heat pump at various temperatures. Results of these calculations are given in Table 20-1. These figures were calculated from various tables published by General Electric. According to tests which I ran in my own house, these calculated figures appear to be very representative of actual performance.

Table 20-1. **Heat Output of a Two-Ton Heat Pump***
at Various Temperatures

Outside Air Temperature	Output BTU/hr	Kwh/Use	C.O.P. at Temp.
62°F	26 400	3.6	2.2
52°F	25 500	3.4	2.19
32°F	18 300	3.0	1.79
17°F	13 000	2.7	1.41
7°F	10 600	2.5	1.24
–18°F	6 600	2.0	–0.04

*One ton = 12 000 BTU

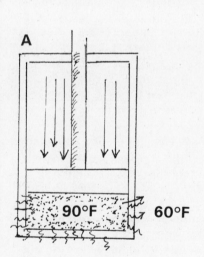

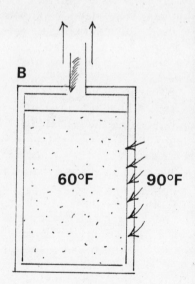

A. As molecules of a fluid are compressed, the probability of molecular collision is increased, thereby causing a rapid transfer of heat and a rise of temperature in the fluid.

B. Subject to temperature differences an expansion or increase in air volume we can obtain a rapid transfer of heat to a fluid.

115

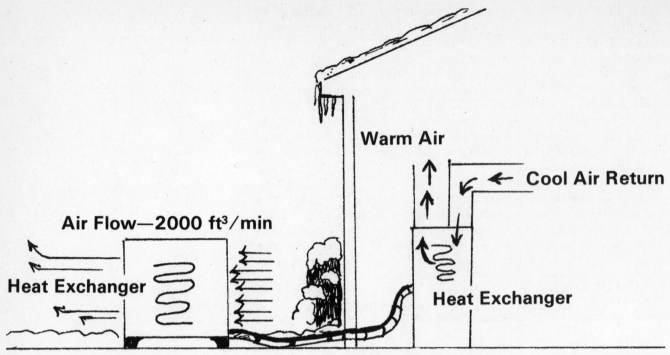

Warm Air

Cool Air Return

Air Flow—2000 ft³/min

Heat Exchanger

Heat Exchanger

Winter Cycle of Heat Pump
A set rate outside air is blown over a heat exchanger and heat is absorbed by a fluid. The fluid is transferred to an inside heat exchanger. Return air is passed over the interior heat exchanger and warm air is sent through the heat transfer system.

Recall that C.O.P. is known as the coefficient of operation performance factor. Note that we labeled the C.O.P. of the heat pump in our table for each temperature drop. If you multiply the C.O.P. by the number of Kwh needed to operate the heat pump, you would have the equivalent Kwh required to yield the same amount of BTUs in a straight resistance electric furnace. C.O.P. is a comparison of the heat yield of the heat pump with the heat yield of the straight resistance heating system.

The –0.04 Kwh at –10°F tells us that we could have used a straight resistance heating unit at a lower cost to generate 6600 BTU. The BTU output of one Kwh is 3413 BTU. The compressor used 2.0 Kwh to generate 6600 BTU while straight resistance heating system would have generated 6822 BTU with 2 Kwh.

This table also shows that as the outside air temperature drops, the heat or BTU output drops on the heat pump. If we installed a two-ton heat pump in a home which experiences a 32 000 BTU heat loss at 7°F, the heat pump could not carry the heating load. We would be short 21 400 BTU per hour. Certainly the interior temperature of the home would become colder as the outside temperature stayed at 7°F or became lower. On the modern heat pump, strip resistance heating elements are installed on the air handler inside the home. When the outside temperature drops, these heating strips act as a booster for the heat pump.

By adding a larger compressor, one would not need the services of the seemingly more expensive straight resistance heating strips when the outside temperature drops. A five ton heat pump would yield 23 800 BTU per hour at 7°F. This value is closer to our 32 000 BTU heat loss of the home. However, we can see that the larger compressor is also

116

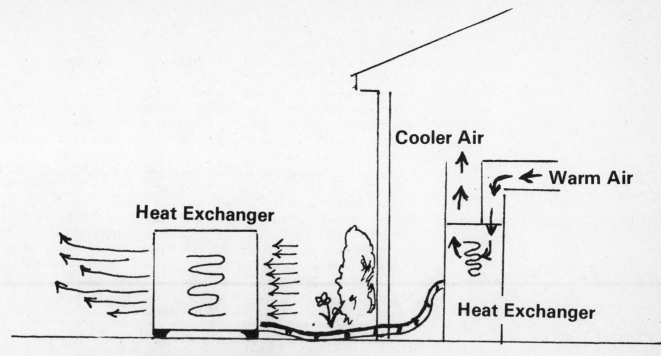

Summer Cycle of Heat Pump
Warm air from the house is passed over interior heat exchanger and heat is absorbed by a fluid. The fluid is pumped to an exterior heat exchanger and heat is rejected to the outside.

falling short of producing our needed heat. Thus, the addition of a larger compressor may not be the proper solution.

How many hours are really cold during the winter heating season? Let's look at Table 20-2 which contains some values for an average midwestern town.

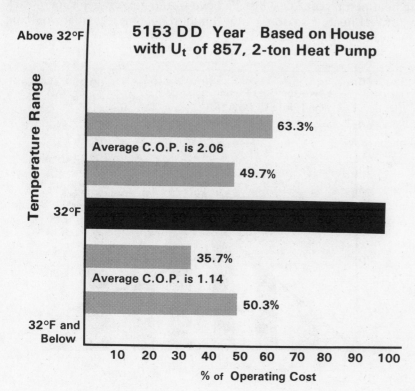

5153 DD Year   Based on House with U_t of 857, 2-ton Heat Pump

Above 32°F

Temperature Range

63.3%

Average C.O.P. is 2.06

49.7%

32°F

35.7%

Average C.O.P. is 1.14

50.3%

32°F and Below

% of Operating Cost: 10 20 30 40 50 60 70 80 90 100

Table 20-2.   Temperature Information for an Average Midwestern Town

Temperature	DD Year	% of Total Year
62°F to 37°F	3261	63.28%
32°F	772	15.00%
27°F	502	9.77%
22°F	280	5.45%
17°F	169	3.25%
12°F	94	1.80%
below 12°F	75	1.45%

Despite the fact that most of the temperatures were above 32°F, one can see that 50.3% of operating costs were on temperatures below 32°F.

117

Looks good so far, right? If we assume that this particular heat pump is able to handle all the temperatures above 32°F without any aid from its backup electric resistance unit, the heat pump should perform well. This graph also points out the small amount of time during one heating season in this 5153 DD region (comparable to Cleveland, Ohio) when the winter temperatures really get cold—below 22°F.

To save you from the chore of going through each temperature range, which is the only true way to calculate the anticipated efficiency of the heat pump, let me quickly give you an example of how to estimate the efficiency of a heat pump.

Let's judge the operational cost of two homes WITHOUT calculating heat gains. To begin, let's assume the two homes are exactly alike except for the heat loss of the two structures. Suppose the first house has a heat transmission rate (U_t) of 750 and the other house has a heat transmission rate (U_t) of 295. To make the comparison, let us estimate the Kwh it would take to heat each individual home using straight resistance heating or a heat pump. Our figures are given in Table 20-3.

Table 20-3. Cost of Heating Two Homes with a Straight Resistance Furnace and with a Heat Pump

	Type of Heating System	No. of Kwh/ Heating Season	C.O.P.
House with U_t 750	Straight resistance	31 125 Kwh	2.19
	Heat pump	14 215 Kwh	
House with U_t 295	Straight resistance	7427 Kwh	1.85
	Heat pump	4019 Kwh	

For the first house, we found the C.O.P. by dividing 32 125 by 14 215. The resulting C.O.P. of 2.19 means we have cut our heating cost in half. At $0.04 per Kwh, this would be a savings of about $676.40 per year. If the heat pump cost $1500 installed, we would get our investment back in just 2.21 heating seasons. After the third heating season, it would be like money in the bank.

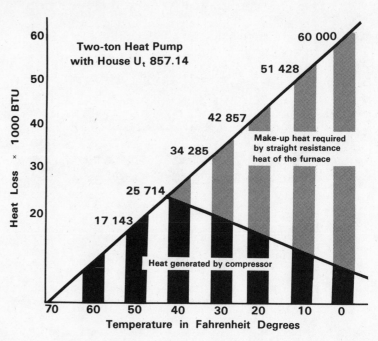

The Efficiency of the heat pump is very dependent upon outside air temperatures and total heat loss of the house.

118

On the second home, we found that the savings per year at $0.04 per Kwh is only about $136. At this rate, it would take 11 years to get your investment of $1500 back! In real life, the payback would actually take longer because of heat gains. As the heat loss is reduced, heat gains could diminish our heating bill by 50%. This reduction in heating cost would increase our payback period of the heat pump on the second house. In fact, it would double our payback period to 22 years! In addition, as with a solar heat collector, we would also have to factor in interest and repairs.

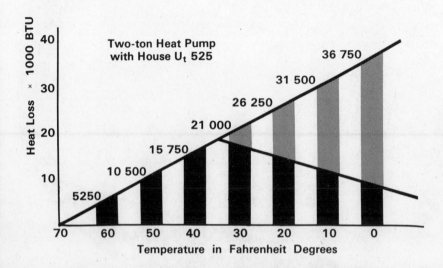

As heat loss decreases the compressor can carry more of the heating load without the aid of strip or resistance heaters.

Although the heat output of the compressor is not greater—due to the lower heat loss of the house— the heat pump is more efficient.

So, whether or not you can save money with a heat pump depends directly upon the size of heat loss you have in your home! The greater the heat loss, the better is the chance of the heat pump working in your favor. The lower the heat loss, the lower is the chance of the heat pump paying good dividends for you. In fact, families installing heat pumps who never had air conditioning before would find that their dollar outlay in one year could actually increase because the heat pump would automatically add air conditioning costs to their home. A heat-pump fault which cannot be ignored is the low temperature of the air delivered to the rooms of your home. Its temperature is lower than resistance heat—about 85°F for air from the heat pump and about 95°F or more from resistance heat furnaces. Take your choice, but I find this lower air temperature unsatisfactory.

To summarize, you should concentrate on reducing heat loss with insulation and air sealing BEFORE even thinking about a heat pump. The lesson should be very clear—insulate, seal, and maybe—just maybe—think about a heat pump.

119

CHAPTER TWENTY-ONE
BESIDES HEATING COSTS

Certainly we could not have covered every possible detail and problem with the heating of a home but some of the effort you put in the Work Section should help.

It has amazed me how many home owners could run off the actual amount of electrical costs they have experienced in the past few years. At coffee klatches, at lunches, at restaurants, and elsewhere, the cost of heating has often been the center of conversation. Yet, regardless of what type of heating system you may have, you are faced with the cost of operating lights, refrigerators, and all the other electric appliances in the home. If your electric bill is about $50.00 per month without heat, this means you are spending about $600 per year just for operating electric appliances and other nonheating functions. In fact, even with the prospect of high summer rates forcing home owners who heat with natural gas or fuel oil to reduce the consumption of electricity for air conditioning, your summer electric rates will be higher than winter rates.

120

A partial list of the average cost of operating various appliances for the period of one year is given in Table 21-1. These costs are estimated and are subject to brand, insulation, maintenance and amount of use. Your local electric company can give you a more accurate idea of what your costs are in Kwh. I have compiled this chart from information given to me by the Columbus and Southern Ohio Electric Company.

Table 21-1. Average Cost of Operating Various Appliances

Appliance	Cost per Year
Electric blanket	$5.26
Clothes dryer	$101.00
Dehumidifier	$18.00
Dishwasher	$14.68
Attic fan	$10.90
Freezer (15 cubic feet)	$68.74
Electric oven (40 hr/month)	$23.45
Refrigerator-freezer (frost-free)	$120.00
Refrigerator (12 cubic feet, not frost-free)	$37.87
TV, black and white	$9.12
TV, solid-state black and white	$6.33
TV, color tube type	$34.56
TV, color solid-state	23.04
Washing machine	$21.12

Keep in mind that we calculated these at $0.04 per Kwh. In Florida, where electricity is very expensive, these costs will certainly be higher. In some areas the cost may be lower. However, the real question is—do you really need the electric appliance? If you do, fine, but remember this, each electric appliance contributes to the cost of operating a home.

For example, I investigated the cost of operating a freezer chest for a year. I did some calculating and discovered it would really be impossible for me to save money with the freezer. In fact, in some cases, my food costs were actually increased by the freezer because of high operational costs. An even more startling revelation is the cost of operating a frost-free refrigerator.

AUTOMATIC NIGHT-TIME TEMPERATURE SET-BACKS

Night-time or automatic temperature set-back devices are operated by a clock. With a preset clock, your thermostat can be turned down and then back up automatically for a predetermined period of time. Such a device will certainly save you money. In fact, tests have been made to determine the amount of money such a device will save you. Mathematically, you can estimate this savings.

Over a heating season (average 250 days), we would be setting the thermostat back five degrees for one-third of a 24-hour period. Thus, your furnace will operate fewer hours and you will save money.

Despite all the old wive's tales about using more energy to reheat the house at higher temperatures after the setback period, these devices will save you about 5% to 8% of your heating dollars during the heating season. The installed price of such automatic thermostat set-backs will average about $40 to $60 (not including wiring). In homes with large heat losses (before thermal correction), there may be enough of a savings in the first year to retire the installed cost of the set-back device! As you reduce the heat loss of your home, retirement of the installed price takes longer.

To conserve energy in public buildings such as schools or in buildings owned by the private sector that are not in use 50% to 60% of the time, such a device would really be helpful in reducing energy. In homes where families are gone most of the day, the thermostat set-back would certainly save our supply of fuel and give our fuel resources a longer life span. This judgment call is up to you.

AIR CONDITIONING

We have touched on air conditioning for summer months throughout this book. An air conditioner rejects heat from inside the home to the outside. An air conditioner also acts as a dehumidifier to keep you comfortable in the home.

Since most electric companies recognize that the majority of energy peaks occur during the summer months, they have and will probably continue to increase summer electric rates to discourage energy consumption. The electric companies will tell you (truthfully) that their generators often run at less than 75% of capacity during the winter heating months. During the summer months, because of the added load of air conditioners, their generators are much too small to handle present loads—much less future summer electric loads.

Heat rejection is very important during the summer. As you reduce air infiltration and heat leaks for heating months, you will also reduce cooling loads during the summer months. At this point in our discussion, you may want to review the chapters on solar heat, ceilings, and windows because the solar gains on your home during the summer months will often represent 40% to 50% of your cooling load.

Let me suggest some energy saving procedures for those of you with air conditioners. Keep your storm windows on during the summer. Add solar rejection film or awnings, etc., on the east and west windows, especially the west windows, because this is the area where the interior temperature will really climb in your home. The reason for this temperature rise is that the sun has all day to heat your home and the afternoon sun will increase the temperatures very rapidly because of this preheating during the morning and early afternoon hours.

Ventilate your attic. During the solar night use window fans to move the cooler solar night air into the home. Close the windows the next day to capture this cooler air. By following our instructions of moisture rejection during summer months, all high moisture-laden air from your dryer and baths and especially the laundry area will be vented during the summer months and your home will be more comfortable.

IS THERE REALLY AN ENERGY SHORTAGE?

I really cannot tell you if there is an energy shortage and I doubt if anybody else can really give you a clear, accurate picture. The use of

122

energy per person is higher in the United States than in any other place in the world. We are highly mobile and industrial, and we are used to low energy prices.

At the rate our energy dollars are leaving this country, we will most likely be headed for more serious economic problems in the future. The unbalanced payment of money, be it goods, technology, or cash, is certainly tipping the scales against our country.

There are millions of homes in this country. If we directed our efforts toward reducing the energy requirements of each home by 50%, we would most likely reduce the total energy consumption in this country by about 10%.

Saving energy in the home is a step in the right direction, but not the total answer. Restaurants, giant energy-wasting shopping malls with heating curtains, etc., schools, government buildings, business offices, and factories all use great quantities of energy and most likely could achieve the highest energy reduction by thermal correction. When considering the large number of homes and other types of buildings, factories, and people in this country, the energy savings potential becomes staggering.

Let's reduce this to a one-on-one situation. In the Work Section, you can find out how to solve your energy problem and the high heating and operating cost yourself. There is really no reason why, with intelligent application of thermal correction, we can't turn the whole energy picture around. If, and it's a big IF, millions of families reduce energy costs, we will find that natural gas companies, oil companies, and electric companies will encourage us to use more energy for their revenue needs. If, as a collective group, we allow indiscriminate taxation of utility companies and indiscriminate and unfair regulations by the government bodies, we will most likely continue to see higher and higher utility bills.

Most utility companies are plagued by regulation and extremely high taxation. These two factors contribute greatly to the economics of our energy problem. I am just a country builder who tried to save money and I am glad to share this information with you. With just a little effort, each uf us should be able to live more comfortably in our homes and enjoy life.

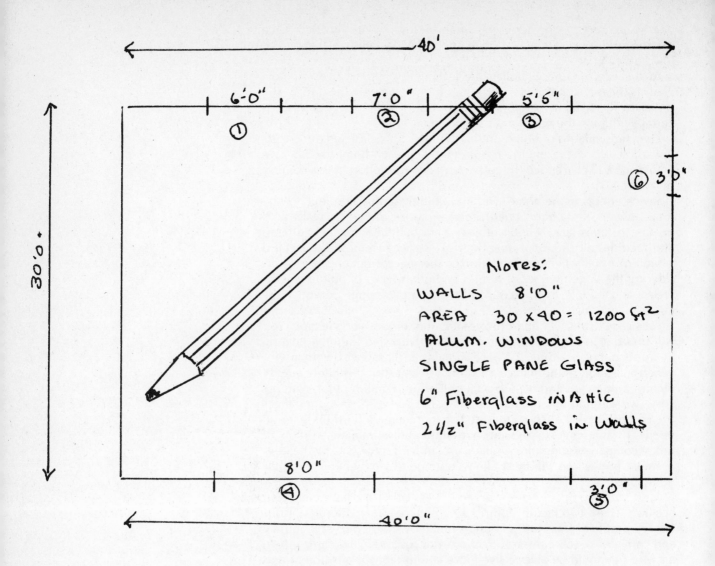

Notes:
WALLS 8'0"
AREA 30 x 40 = 1200 ft²
ALUM. WINDOWS
SINGLE PANE GLASS
6" Fiberglass IN ATTIC
2½" Fiberglass in Walls

CHAPTER TWENTY-TWO
PRACTICAL STEPS TO REDUCING HEATING COSTS

Throughout this book, we have constantly pointed out to you that the integrity of any thermal barrier is subject to air leaks in the home. Some of these air leaks could have been the direct result of poor workmanship while the house was being built or shrinkage of lumber components as the house aged.

Presenting this book to the wider audience of existing home owners, and not only to owners of newly constructed homes, creates the problem of instructing each and every home owner exactly what to do in his own home. To do proper justice to the various methods of construction and to cover each and every possible detail in the millions of homes in this country would require another book on HOW TO DO carpentry, plumbing, etc., in the home. However, throughout this book we have pointed out to you potential heat leaks that may occur in your home. With a work list or inspection list of possible heat leaks we can at best guide you in your search. Common sense, through inspection, and of course, our arithmetic approach to heat loss will keep you on the right track. Before we start outlining our inspection list and using arithmetic to find trade-offs, let's discuss different types of homes and insulation. Then let's quickly review some practical steps to reducing energy costs.

TYPES OF HOMES

There are only four basic types of homes. The rest are combinations of these four basic types. The four classifications are Ranch, Split-Level, Bi-Level and Two Story. As you start your journey through your home, first arm yourself with a pencil and paper. Better yet, arm yourself with the Inspection Sheets found in the Work Section. The other tools you will need are a 50-foot measuring tape, a 10-foot measuring tape, and a flashlight. You may also need a ladder to get into the attic.

RANCH
Ranch style homes are the easiest to check for thermal leaks because there are only two levels to be concerned with. We will need to know the size of the crawl space, basement, or slab and the outside walls. (See of the Work section for detailed instructions for finding each area.) The size of the foundation will often give us the size of floor area and ceiling. Be sure to consider the wall between the living area and an attached garage as an exterior wall.

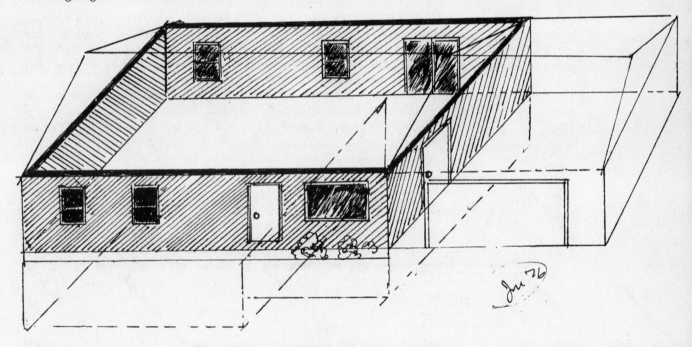

SPLIT LEVELS
Split-level homes must be examined very carefully when searching for thermal leaks. You may be dealing with as many as four to five levels by the time you consider the basement area. At least half of some interior walls will be exposed to the outside and the other half may act as a curtain wall for an adjoining roof. Some split-levels may have a garage inside the structure and bedrooms or other rooms above it. In this case, the ceiling of the garage is a source of heat loss for the rooms above. Be sure to check for uninsulated heating ducts in the garage area.

125

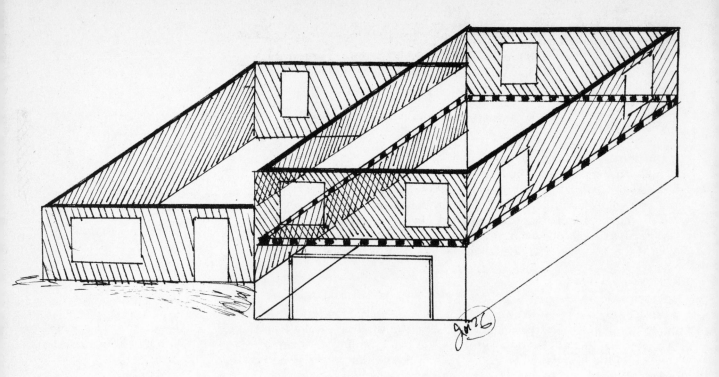

BI-LEVELS

Bi-level homes are, in effect, a raised ranch. What would normally constitute a basement in the ranch home is raised three to four feet out of the ground for a bi-level. In inspecting a bi-level home, you should pay special attention to a knee wall in the lower level. Part of the knee wall will be lumber and part will be masonry.

Be sure to consider a wall which partitions the living area from an attached garage as an outside wall. The ceiling of the garage in most bi-levels must be considered as a heat loss area if there are heated rooms above.

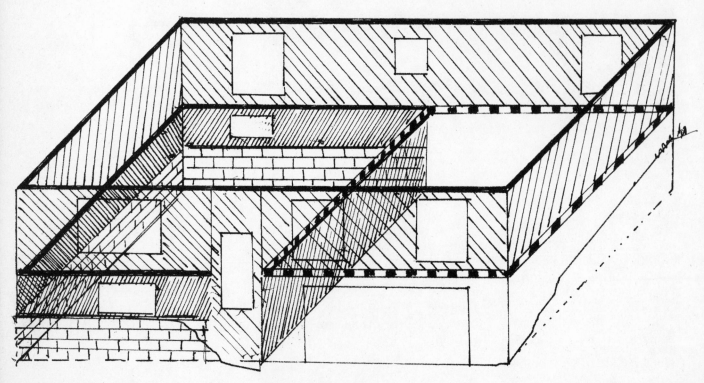

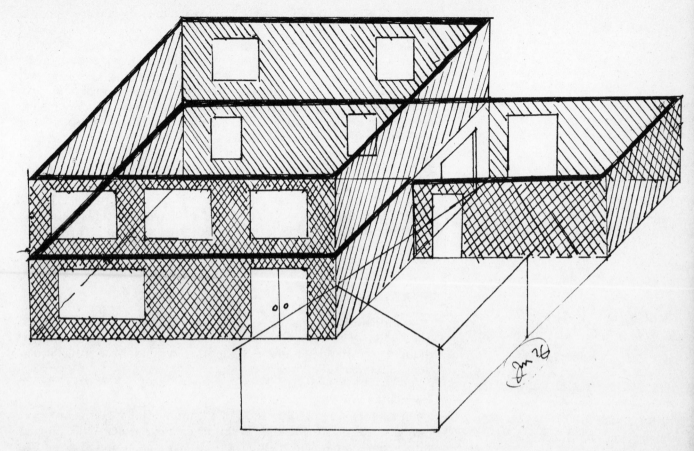

TWO STORIES

Cape Cods are two-story houses with bedrooms directly under the roof. The wide walls of bedrooms in Cape Cods may be only three to four feet high. These wide walls are considered outside walls even though there may be a crawl space beside them. The outside walls of a two story will be the primary sources of thermal losses of the house.

In a two-story, you may have less roof area per square foot of living area than in a ranch. Be sure you consider the thermal losses through the ring or bandboard, as well as through partition walls next to an unheated area.

TAKING MEASUREMENTS

Be reasonably accurate. Instead of recording your final measurements in fractions, convert them into decimals for easier calculations. For example, ½ inch can also be expressed as 0.5 inch. Round fractions and decimals accompanying large numbers to the nearest whole number. For example, 1107.4 inches can be rounded to 1107 inches.

DRAWINGS

Certainly, you need not be an architect. With the help of graph paper you will be able to make a reasonably accurate drawing of your home.

It will be well worth your while to take a little time and care in preparing your drawings because these drawings will be a primary tool in determining the best way to save your heating dollars.

Our Inspection Sheets will cover each and every area that you must examine in your home and will tell you what to look for. You may then apply these inspection sheets to your home and then combine them for a total picture of your individual house.

127

HOW MUCH MONEY SHOULD YOU SPEND?

The amount of money you spend will depend on your budget. In general, the more you insulate the more dollars you will save on heating costs; however, you must realize that there is a limit. Our main goal is to seal off air infiltration in order to make use of internal heat gains and reduce our heating costs. Get a good measure of the conductance rate of the house **before** you make a major investment in something like a heat pump or even in a solar heat unit. Be sure you factor in heat gains!

You will want to spend whatever is necessary to reduce major thermal leaks in such areas as ceilings and sidewalls. You will also want to spend the required amount to seal off air infiltration. This is a must. Remember, **you** are the one who will have to decide how to allocate the dollars you have to spend between money to be invested in saving fuel and money to be spent for comfort.

INSULATION

To insulate is to create a thermal barrier that delays heat transfer. The choice of what type of insulation you use is your decision but we thought you would like to know about a few of the acceptable insulations being marketed today.

FIBERGLASS

On each package of insulation, the R rating of that particular thickness of insulation is marked on the bag. Some insulation is shipped with vapor barriers on them. The most common vapor barrier is a treated kraft paper. This type of insulation is designed to fit between studs that are 16 inches on center or 24 inches on center. There are tabs on either side of the paper to facilitate stapling the insulation to the studs.

In the field the tabs are often stapled to the sides of studs to make the job easier for the drywall installer. These tabs will overlap on the studs and cause ridges on the face of the stud. These ridges will make it impossible to apply drywall smoothly.

Major insulation manufacturers recommend that the tabs be stapled to the side of the studs to make the job easier on the drywall installer. However, installing kraft paper-backed insulation in this manner will decrease the total thermal resistance value of the insulation. Air pockets will be formed in the cavity area. Because there are other methods, I feel that in new construction and in many existing homes the consumer should stay away from using kraft paper-backed fiberglass insulation.

Friction-fit insulation comes in two widths. One is for placing in studs 16 inches on center and the other for cavities 24 inches on center. This insulation does not have a vapor barrier but this problem will be corrected by stapling vinyl sheet **over** the insulation and the studs.
Besides, in the tighter home the need for a superior vapor barrier is mandatory. Vinyl sheets are far superior to kraft paper as a vapor barrier. Another alternative is to use drywall with an aluminum foil backing on it. This method is "pooh-pawed" as too expensive. The cost is small compared to the results it will give because with it you can glue and nail the drywall onto the face of the studs and thus achieve a superior vapor barrier.

In areas such as floor cavities friction-fit insulation can be installed in floor spaces with greater ease and less work than kraft paper-backed

insulation. Wire, straps, or wood strapping can be used to prevent the insulation from falling to the floor. Also, on floors the insulation should be **placed next to the floor** as shown in the diagram.

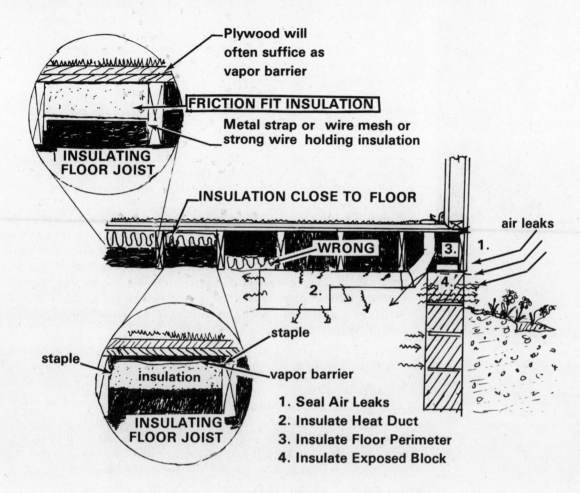

Plywood will often suffice as vapor barrier

FRICTION FIT INSULATION

Metal strap or wire mesh or strong wire holding insulation

INSULATING FLOOR JOIST

INSULATION CLOSE TO FLOOR

WRONG

air leaks

staple

staple

insulation

vapor barrier

INSULATING FLOOR JOIST

1. Seal Air Leaks
2. Insulate Heat Duct
3. Insulate Floor Perimeter
4. Insulate Exposed Block

CELLULOSE

Cellulose can be used inside walls. In most cases this installation job should be done by a professional if the home owner does not have the required skills. Holes will have to be drilled on the exterior siding to allow insulation to be blown into the wall cavity.

Blowing insulation like cellulose into the attic could be an easy and rewarding project for the home owner. Be sure to protect each and every light fixture and furnace flue with asbestos before adding insulation and, of course, seal off air leaks.

Wet application of cellulose could be used in the basement on the basement walls and between floor joists. Vinyl adhesive solidifies the cellulose into a complete blanket. With this method you can seal most air leaks as the insulation is "blown" onto the wall.

FOAMS

Solid foam boards can be used in the home. However, I must caution you that a complete fire retardant seal over the insulation is mandatory. Wet application of foam calls for a certain amount of skill in handling the equipment required for the job. Unless one becomes thoroughly familiar with the method of application, I recommend you hire a professional for the job.

CAULK

Sealing air leaks is the key to getting a low heating bill. If you feel the handling of a caulk gun could be too messy use rope caulk and/or duct seal. This compound will adhere to most materials when applied with proper pressure but will not stick all over your hands, etc.

The secret in using a caulk gun is to carry a rag to wipe the nozzle of the caulk gun as you use it. Be careful not to over-cut the nozzle tube because this will allow large quantities of caulk to come out of the tube. Use a smooth, even action with the caulk gun at a slow pace. This technique will provide you with the best results. Use the right caulk for the right job. Remember, the low-cost caulk will certainly fill the cavity; however, it may also dry and have to be replaced shortly.

Stop before you fill any crack over ½ inch with caulk. Instead, stuff the crack with oakum, rolled insulation or any other vermin and insect proof material, and then add a seal of caulk to assure the crack is sealed tightly.

Removing door casings, window casings, and woodwork may or may not prove necessary for you in correcting thermal air leaks. If you want to tackle this job, first gently pry the casing loose until the nails are exposed in the casing. A small magnet will help you find nails. Once the nails are found, use a nail set and drive the nails all the way through the casing. After the casing is replaced, the nail holes can be filled with putty sticks available in a wide variety of colors in most building supply stores or hardware stores.

Openings to be sealed with caulk must be free from frost, moisture, dirt, rust, and loose caulk, putty, or mortar.

LATEX CAULK

Latex caulk provides a tough, non-staining, non-bleeding, durable compound which bonds to most building materials. It needs no priming, withstands year-round exposure from below $0°F$ to $180°F$, and may be applied on damp surfaces. It can be used to fill cracks between wall, woodwork, baseboards, doors and window frames.

BUTYL CAULK (RUBBER BASE)

Butyl caulk bonds to wood, metal, masonry, tile, or glass. It remains flexible and withstands expansion and contraction caused by temperature variation from below $0°F$ to $212°F$. It is ideal for use around windows, doors, sinks, tubs, chimneys, flashing gutters, sky lights, boats and other areas where a waterproof rubber sealant is desired.

OIL-BASE CAULK

Oil-base caulk provides a temporary seal for wind drafts, etc. It is limited in use with some materials. It has a tendency to dry and crack and is often difficult to work with and smooth on properly. It is the least expensive type of caulk on the market.

SILICONE CAULK

Silicone caulk provides a tough, rubber-like seal when it cures. It resists mildew, can be cleaned up with water before it cures, and is easy to smooth. Silicone caulk provides an excellent bonding to most building materials because of maximum water resistance. Plastic, metal, and ceramic tile may be set with this material. It is one of the most expensive materials for caulking on the market, but excellent.

130

INSULATING HEATING DUCTS AND WATER LINES

Tape all air leaks on heating ducts first. Then add insulation. The insulation can be held in place by wires wrapped around the ducts. On heating ducts, the vapor barrier (preferably aluminum foil or treated kraft paper) must be placed on the outside and away from the heating ducts. DO NOT crush the insulation while applying it to the heat ducts.

Water lines do not require a thick insulation. You can purchase kits for this purpose in stores. A very inexpensive method is to make strips of insulation from larger insulation batts. Be sure the insulation is wrapped with a vapor barrier, either aluminum foil or vinyl.

STORM WINDOWS AND STORM DOORS

If you want to tackle the job of installing storm windows and doors yourself, follow detailed instructions given with each window or door by the manufacturer. Seal the edges of the storm doors and windows to assure a tight fit. On storm windows, the bottom flange has vent holes to allow rain water to escape. Whatever you do, DO NOT seal these vent holes or you will have rain water coming in the house via the windows!

WEATHER SEALING DOORS AND WINDOWS

When installing weatherseals, follow the outlined instructions given in the package by the manufacturer. The secret of getting a good weather seal is taking your time. Do not rush the job. Patience will pay.

The job of weather sealing doors and windows can be done easily with purchased foam strips with a sticky tape on one side.

ELECTRICAL OUTLETS

Caution—never place oversized light bulbs in any light fixture. These bulbs are rated by Underwriters Laboratory as to their capacity, and oversizing could cause a fire hazard.

If you have any fear of electricity, by all means turn the electric power off. Use only insulated screwdrivers (plastic handles) and be sure that you do not have metal touching metal. To seal around light fixtures, you may need oakum or fiberglass rope (make your own). Use only caulk that will not cause a chemical reaction with the plastic insulation cover used in modern homes. Seal tightly, take your time. Make sure you seal from the basement and attic.

PLUMBING

Seal from the basement and the attic. Large wads of fiberglass insulation will do the trick here. Use caulk around the packed insulation to assure that air leakage is stopped. Again, take your time and do a good job.

FIREPLACES

Unless you are skilled and knowledgeable, do not attempt to add heat exchangers for hot water systems or to add air ducts from the outside by yourself. Get a firm contract price from a skilled workman on these projects.

FURNACES AND HEATING SYSTEMS

On older homes, the economics of adding a new furnace and partial heat transfer system may or may not be on your side after thermal corrections. Hire a professional to do the job but be sure he understands the heat loss calculations of this book. To make the chore less formidable to your heating contractor, just tell him "Manual 'J' has H.T.M." (heat transfer multipliers) in the last section that can be calculated by the same method we are employing. Our method calls for closer inspection and eliminates error-producing "rules of thumb" used in the industry. Be in no hurry and weigh all the possibilities.

Your local gas company will be very helpful in telling you the proper sized fresh air feed you need for your furnace. A barometric damper control on the fresh air duct, although expensive, will insure against down-drafts into the home. Again, unless you know the job from top to bottom BEFORE you start, hire a furnace company to do the job for you.

An electrically controlled attic fan calls for a wire to be run to the fan and this means putting a hole in the roof. Have a skilled electrician run the wire to the fan. Be sure that the hole which is made in the roof is no larger than necessary. In each package that the fan comes in, there are detailed instructions on how to do the job. Follow the instructions carefully so you do not create a roof leak.

VENTING BATHS AND LAUNDRY AREAS

The vinyl-covered hose used for venting dryers can be used to vent fans in the baths and laundry areas to the outside. Currently, most vent fans call for three-inch duct but the vent hose is four inches. You will need an adaptor for the job. You can use metal ducts but the vinyl duct is much easier to use. MAKE THE JOB AS EASY AS POSSIBLE. If possible, vent to an outside gable instead of through the roof. There is less chance for a roof leak this way.

DO IT YOURSELF MANUALS

Many excellent do-it-yourself manuals are available at book stores and libraries. Some of the better ones have many good graphics and pictures which explain tools, nails, electrical work, plumbing, and carpentry in the home. The cost of these manuals may seem high but the most rewarding project is one well done by yourself . . . at a much lower cost than a professional will charge. You may have noticed the slow thorough way in which professionals work. This is not because they wish to charge you more for the extra time. They know from experience that one mistake caused by haste has cost them many a day's wages in replacement and call-backs for servicing an error.

Take your time. Think out your project. Heed the old saying used in the carpentry industry . . . "MEASURE TWICE—CUT ONCE."

WORK SECTION

Part One of the Work Section provides you with separate check lists for examining various components and sections of your home. Very simply, you are looking for two basic items—air leaks and lack of insulation. Keep in mind that these check lists are designed to serve only as guidelines and are by no means designed to be complete enough to cover every detail in the great variety of homes across this country.

These check lists can be used in examining homes under construction as well as older homes. Careful checking and rechecking during the construction process and a little extra time spent on thermal corrections will pay great dividends in the long run.

Part Two of the Work Section provides you with an arithmetic approach to examining heat losses and economics in the home. Those of you who want to pursue the arithmetic will find it very rewarding.

You may wish to complete only the check lists in Part One or you may wish to go on to complete the arithmetic approach in Part Two. In both cases, you must realize that thoroughness is the key to obtaining the maximum savings and to beating the heating game.

PART ONE
CHECK LISTS

BASEMENT

Caution: *As you seal the basement air leaks in homes which are heated with fuel oil, natural gas, or propane, fresh air may have to be fed to the furnace.*

Inspection   Correction
Date   Date

_____ _____ Basement windows.
   a. Look for air leaks around the sash. Seal with oakum, insulation, and/or caulk.
   b. Consider using storm windows or window well covers. If your budget is low, tape heavy pieces of newspaper or plastic over the windows to seal them off for the winter season.

_____ _____ Bandboard or ring.
   a. Get up on a ladder and look for air leaks around the floor perimeter. Seal off any leaks from the inside of the home with caulk.
   b. Add the required insulation and be sure that the vapor barrier is facing the floor system above and not the basement side below.

_____ _____ Basement Ceiling.
   a. Seal all holes around electrical, plumbing, and heating ducts which penetrate the floor system.
   b. If you plan to use the basement for storage only, insulate the basement ceiling with friction-fit or kraft paper insulation. The vapor barrier should face the floor above.

_____ _____ Basement walls.
   If you plan to use the basement for living area, then insulate the walls by furring or building a false wall. Be sure to have a vinyl vapor barrier facing the warm side of the basement wall.

136

_____ _____ Access panels to crawl spaces.
Seal air leaks around these panels with the
appropriate materials.

_____ _____ Water lines, heat ducts, and furnaces.
See check lists on pages 144, 145, and 150.

_____ _____ Furnaces in the basement.
See check list on page 145.

CRAWL SPACE

_____ _____ BEFORE ADDING INSULATION, seal off all potential air leaks caused by plumbing, heating, and electrical ducts.

_____ _____ Floor.
The floor of the crawl space should be covered with visqueen (vinyl sheet). Be sure that the joints overlap and are sealed.

_____ _____ Sidewalls.
Economics may indicate that insulation should be added to the side walls of the crawl space.

_____ _____ Bandboard or ring.
If the crawl space is large, consider adding insulation around the bandboard and then insulate the ceiling of the crawl space for at least two feet in from the perimeter.

_____ _____ Vents.
Vents to the crawl space should be sealed off during the winter months and opened during the summer months. Most vents are opened or closed with a special mechanism. You can stuff insulation or newspaper into the vent to assure tightness temporarily. See Appendix F for information concerning proper venting.

_____ _____ Heating ducts.
All heating ducts in the crawl space should be sealed for air leaks with duct tape and then insulated.

138

SLABS

Inspection Correction
Date   Date

_____ _____ Check the perimeter of the slab where the outside wall rests on the floor. You will most likely find air leaks. Seal these leaks from the inside with caulk. In rooms which have wall to wall carpeting, you should work carefully on only a small section at a time.

_____ _____ Install carpet in rooms which are not now carpeted.

_____ _____ If you already have carpet on the floor and your floor is still cold, consider having a carpet company pull up your carpet long enough to install a double layer of foam carpet pad under the carpet for insulation value.

_____ _____ Dig a ditch around the perimeter of the home and add two inches of Styrofoam® to the foundation walls. Dow Chemical Company manufactures a paint which you can use to decorate the exposed foam.

_____ _____ Dirt has excellent insulation value. Grade as high as practical.

_____ _____ On new construction, you may want to insulate the entire slab with one inch of foam in the center and two inches of foam at the perimeter.

_____ _____ Check for potential air leaks under your siding from the outside. Seal these leaks with the appropriate caulk.

139

EXTERIOR WALLS

Exterior walls are those walls exposed to the outside cold. These walls include garage partition walls, knee walls, and attic partition walls.

Inspection Correction
Date   Date

_____ _____ To discover the amount and type of insulation in the wall, remove some electrical wall covers or remove some of the baseboard and probe into the wall system. If there is no insulation in the wall, add some. You can do the job yourself or you can get someone to do the job for you. Get estimates from three or four reliable companies. *Be sure to find out who is responsible for repair work.*

_____ _____ Seal off air leaks coming under the wall section by pulling back small sections of carpeting and caulking around the baseboard.

_____ _____ Seal around all electrical wall switches and outlet boxes, especially in walls having exterior lights and outside waterproof outlets. Seal small cracks with caulk or duct seal. Seal larger cracks with oakum, or stuff insulation into the crack.

_____ _____ Seal all holes leading into electric boxes with caulk or duct seal.

_____ _____ Install waterproof, plastic, electric covers on inside electric outlets.

_____ _____ Windows, doors, and sliding glass doors. See pages 146, 147, and 148.

——— ——— New construction.

a. Seal all air leaks and repair damaged insulboard BEFORE adding insulation.

b. Caulk each and every hole made by electrical and plumbing ducts. There should be no heating ducts in the outside walls unless the heating ducts are fully insulated, even if this requires that the heating ducts be boxed in.

c. Place exterior lights on overhangs rather than on the side-walls, or use underground wiring to yard lights. Place a piece of secured plywood in the cavity area on the inside so the electrical outlet can be surface mounted to the house.

d. Great care should be taken in inspecting all outside material. Add caulk wherever necessary.

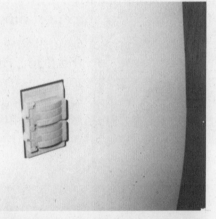

WOOD FLOOR SYSTEMS

_____ _____ Floors over basements should be considered in the heat loss of the basement.
  a. If you use the basement for storage only, insulate the basement ceiling under the wood floor.
  b. If you plan to use the basement for activities other than storage, insulate the floor for at least two feet in from the perimeter.
  c. Regardless of the basement use, insulate the bandboard (ring).

_____ _____ Floors over garages and crawl spaces should in most every case be insulated.

_____ _____ Check for and seal all air leaks around plumbing, heating, and electrical ducts which penetrate the floor system.

_____ _____ Consider installing carpet with a double layer of foam padding in cold rooms.

_____ _____ Overhangs or garrisons should be insulated. If you have carpet on the floor, remove the carpet, drill holes in the floor over the garrison, and blow in liquid foam insulation, loose fiberglass fill, or loose cellulose.

142

CEILINGS AND ATTICS

_____ _____ Light fixtures in ceilings should be sealed with caulk or duct seal. Stuff holes with fiberglass "rope."

_____ _____ Seal off all holes around electrical wires, plumbing, and heating ducts before adding insulation. Even if you already have insulation in the attic, you should seal off these holes. Take your time and be sure to stand on a board that is strong enough to hold you so that you do not fall through the ceiling.

_____ _____ Heating ducts in the attic should all be insulated.

_____ _____ Look for daylight in the roof and around roof edges. Seal these holes.

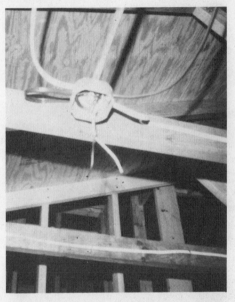

_____ _____ Seal around the chimney. *CAUTION: Seal around the chimney with asbestos only.*

_____ _____ Insulate the gable ends with R-7 to R-11 insulation to prevent heat gains during the summer and heat losses in the winter.

_____ _____ Check your venting system by checking numbers in Appendix G. If it seems necessary, add an electric vent fan. Be sure to follow the manufacturer's specifications for installation.

_____ _____ Add insulation as required to the ceiling. Use the math as outlined in Part Two of the Work Section, to determine the optimum amount for your area of the country. *Overinsulating the ceiling does not pay, regardless of propaganda to the contrary.* Either rent a machine and blow the desired insulation into the area yourself, or have the work done by a professional.

143

HEATING DUCTS

Inspection Correction
Date   Date

_____ _____ Seal off all air leaks in the ducting system with heating duct tape.

_____ _____ Before adding insulation to the heating ducts, consider adding dampers to the duct system.

_____ _____ If there are a number of ducts in the garage ceiling, take off a piece of ceiling and find out if the ducts are adequately insulated. The cost of adding new drywall will average only about $0.25 per square foot in most areas and the benefits will be highly rewarding. See Chapter 13 on heat transfer systems.

_____ _____ When installing insulation on heating ducts, the vapor barrier must be placed on the cold side (the outside) of the heating ducts. (Most insulation is installed with the vapor barrier facing the warm side; however, on heating ducts the vapor barrier must be placed toward the outside.)

_____ _____ Wrap insulation around the heat ducts and secure it in place with wire or tape.

FURNACES

Inspection Date	Correction Date	
_____	_____	Keep the air filter very clean during the heating season.
_____	_____	Clean the furnace and have it checked during the off season.
_____	_____	In very old homes, consider installing a new heating unit to replace the monster you may now have in your basement. A new heating system is a major expense and should be thoroughly investigated before any investment is made.
_____	_____	Install a heat recovery fan in your chimney stack and utilize heat that normally goes up the chimney to heat your basement or crawl space. Be sure that this heat recovery unit is installed according to the manufacturer's specifications.

145

WINDOWS

Inspection Correction
Date   Date

_____ _____ Check for air leakage around sashes, frames, and trim. Seal these leaks with weather stripping or caulk, or by covering the window with plastic sheets.

_____ _____ Consider installing storm windows to give more thermal protection and to reduce air penetration.

_____ _____ If air leakage is great around the window, remove the window trim and add insulation around the window frame.

_____ _____ In rooms which are not used during the heating season, add a well-fitted foam panel to the window.

_____ _____ If there are too many windows on the north side of the house, consider removing some of them.

_____ _____ Work the arithmetic in Part Two of the Work Section, also, examine the solar gain calculations in Appendix C.

EXTERIOR DOORS

Inspection   Correction
Date   Date

_____ _____ Weather stripping should be checked each heating season and be replaced if neccessary.

_____ _____ Thresholds should be checked and corrected for air leakage each heating season.

_____ _____ Consider adding storm panels on hollow or solid wood doors which are exposed to the most severe weather conditions.

_____ _____ Consider the door between the living area and the attached garage as an outside door. Correct this door for air leaks in the same way you would correct any other exterior door.

_____ _____ Consider side lights and transoms as windows and correct them for air leakage accordingly.

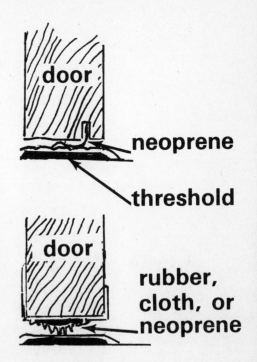

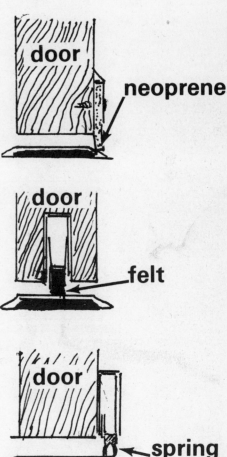

147

SLIDING GLASS DOORS

*Inspection   Correction
Date   Date*

_____ _____ Check for air leakage around sashes, frames, and trim. Seal these leaks with weather stripping or caulk, or by covering the doors with plastic sheets.

_____ _____ If air leakage is great around the door, remove the door trim and add insulation around the door frame.

_____ _____ Consider removing sliding glass doors on the north side of the house.

_____ _____ Work the arithmetic in Part Two of the Work Section; also, examine solar gain calculations in Appendix C.

FIREPLACES

Inspection Date *Correction Date*

_____ _____ Add a door or glass screen to the opening of the fireplace to prevent air from leaking up and past the damper control of the fireplace.

_____ _____ Have a professional add air vents to the fireplace firebox to utilize fresh air from the outside for combustion. Make covers for these vents so they can be closed when not in use. The area of the vents should be twice the cross sectional area of the stack or chimney. See Appendix H for math.

_____ _____ Add a heat recovery grate to the fire box. This type of grate can be purchased in fireplace departments or in stores which specialize in fireplace equipment.

_____ _____ If you want to add a fireplace, consider installing a wood-burning stove for high efficiency and add a fan heat recovery unit to the chimney so you can not only enjoy the fireplace but also use less wood.

149

HOT WATER TANK

Inspection   Correction
   Date   Date

_____ _____ On electric hot water tanks, turn both thermostats (top and bottom) down to at least 140°F.

[OR]

_____ _____ Add a twenty gallon hot water tank to feed the dishwasher at 140°F and turn the main tank thermostat down to 110°F.

_____ _____ On fire combustion hot water tanks, you can turn the thermostats or water temperature regulator to 140°F. The economics of adding another hot water tank for the dishwasher alone is questionable.

_____ _____ If you are going to purchase a new dishwasher, consider the type that preheats water to 140°F or 150°F before it will operate. In this case, the main hot water tank can then be turned down to 110°F. This holds true for electric hot water tanks only.

_____ _____ Insulate hot water lines and cold water lines near the hot water tank. *Caution: Do not foul up the pressure relief valve on top of the hot water tank.*

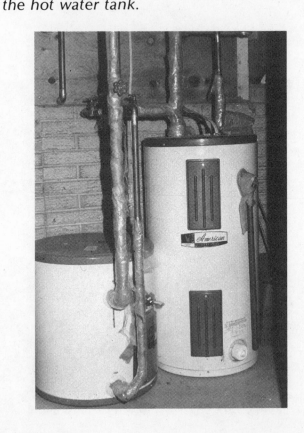

150

APPLIANCES

Inspection Date   *Correction Date*

_____ _____ If you use your electric oven a lot, consider the purchase of a microwave oven. If you have a stove which uses natural gas, the purchase of a microwave oven would be for convenience and not for economics.

_____ _____ Allow the dishes in the dishwasher to dry with only the fan operating and with the electric resistance heater turned off. This feature is often called an energy saver on dishwashers.

_____ _____ In the washing machine, use a detergent that will allow you to use cold water for washing clothes. The dollar savings will amount to the dollars needed to heat the hot water (which amounts to 15 gallons per load).

_____ _____ Clothes dryers should be vented to the outside in summer months and vented inside during the winter.

_____ _____ Frost-free refrigerators have an energy saver switch that lessens the dollars of operation during the low humidity months of winter. Use it.

_____ _____ When purchasing major appliances, check and compare the energy efficiency rates (EER) of the various models to be sure you are getting the model with the best operating performance. In comparing models of like capacity, the model with the highest EER will give you the best operating performance for the least amount of dollars.

151

PART TWO
CALCULATIONS

SECTION A

FUEL COST FACTORS

In this section, we will show you how to calculate your fuel cost factor. Next, we will show you how to determine the conductive heat losses of your home component by component; the windows, doors, the walls, ceilings, floors, and basements. Finally, we will show you how to calculate air infiltration and the number of air turns per hour in your home.

Armed with the U values of the components of your home and your fuel cost factor, you will be able to calculate heat loss under a variety of conditions before and after thermal corrections. With this knowledge you will be able to make intelligent decisions as to the best way you can save heating dollars and beat the heating game.

FUEL COST FACTOR FOR PORTION OF YOUR HOME EXPOSED TO OUTSIDE AIR

Find the DD year for your city in Appendix K. If your city is not listed in Appendix K, use the value listed for the city nearest your community and which is most representative of the climate in your area. Enter this value in line 1 of Table A-1.

TABLE A-1

1. DD year for your city .... _____

2. Unit cost of your heating fuel .... _____

3. C.O.P. of your heating unit .... _____

4. BTU rating of fuel .... _____

Your heating bill will tell you how much you are paying per unit of fuel. Find your unit cost of fuel on your heating bill and enter this value below and also in line 2 of Table A-1.

$$\text{Electricity} = \underline{\hspace{3cm}}/Kwh$$
$$\text{Natural gas} = \underline{\hspace{3cm}}/m.c.f. \text{ (1000 cubic feet)}$$
$$\text{Fuel oil} = \underline{\hspace{3cm}}/gallon$$
$$\text{Other} = \underline{\hspace{3cm}}/Unit$$

Find the C.O.P. of your heating unit and enter this value on line 3 of Table A-1. If you do not know the C.O.P. of your furnace, you may have to call your local heating man. For the price of a service call, most heating companies will test your furnace for efficiency. Ideally, you should get the C.O.P. value for your heating unit from your service man when he does your annual furnace cleaning and checking. Remember, the newer and the better the working order and condition of your furnace, the higher its C.O.P. and consequently, the lower your heating costs under a given set of conditions. The C.O.P. value for your unit will probably fall somewhere in the range given below:

Type of Heating Unit	C.O.P.
Electricity	
Straight resistance—baseboard	about 1.00
Electric furnace	0.86—0.95
Heat pump	1.3—3.2
Fuel oil-fired furnace	0.40—0.80
Gas-fired furnace	0.40—0.80

From the following list, select the appropriate BTU rating of fuel and enter this value on line 4 of Table A-1.

Fuel	BTU Rating of Fuel
Elec. 1 (baseboard and elec. furnace)	3413 BTU/Kwh
Elec. 2 (heat pump)	6826 BTU/Kwh
Natural gas	1 000 000 BTU/Unit
Fuel oil	144 000 BTU/Gallon
Wood	5400 BTU/Pound

Calculate the fuel cost factor for components exposed to the outside air by substituting the values entered in Table A-1 into the following equation:

$$\text{Annual fuel cost factor} = \frac{\text{DD year for your city} \times 24}{\text{BTU rating of fuel} \times \text{C.O.P.}} \times \text{Unit cost of fuel}$$

(for home exposed to outside air)

$$= \frac{? \times 24}{? \times ?} \times ?$$

$$= \underline{\hspace{3cm}}$$

Enter your Annual fuel cost factor for the home exposed to outside air in Section A of Worksheet One, page 189.

153

FUEL COST FACTOR FOR PORTION OF YOUR HOME EXPOSED TO CONSTANT GROUND TEMPERATURE

The heating season begins the first day your furnace begins operation (usually September or October) and extends through the winter until the last day of operation (probably April or May). In Ohio, the number of heating days averages about 250. You can find the average number of heating days for your area by writing to

National Climatic Center
Federal Building
Ashville, North Carolina 28011

Enter the number of heating days in your area in Table A-2.

Table A-2.

1. Number of heating Days in your area .... _____
2. Base temperature of your home .... _____
3. Ground temperature .... _____
4. DD of home exposed to ground temperature ...... _____
5. DD year of the ground .... _____

Enter the base temperature of your home in Table A-2. Recall that the base temperature of the home is usually defined as 65°F. If you have a temperature setting which is above or below 70°F, add or subtract the difference between 70°F and your home temperature to or from the defined base temperature of 65°F and record this value in line 2 instead.

Enter the temperature of the ground in line 3 of Table A-2 (Recall that in most areas the base temperature of the ground is established as 55°F.).

Subtract the ground temperature (line 3) from your home temperature (line 2). This temperature difference gives the value of a heating degree day. Enter the DD value in line 4 of Table A-2.

To find the DD year of the ground, multiply the number of heating days in your area (Table A-2, line 1) by the temperature difference for your DD year of the ground (line 4). Enter your DD year of the ground in line 5 of Table A-2.

Calculate the fuel cost factor for components exposed to the constant temperature of the ground by substituting the DD year of the ground (Table A-2, line 5), the BTU rating of the fuel (Table A-1, line 4), and the C.O.P. of your furnace (Table A-1, line 3) in the following equation:

$$\text{Annual fuel cost factor} = \frac{\text{DD year of ground} \times 24}{\text{BTU rating of fuel} \times \text{C.O.P.}} \times \text{Unit cost of fuel}$$

(for home exposed to constant ground temperature)

Enter your annual fuel cost factor for the portion of your home exposed to constant ground temperature in Section A of Worksheet One, page **189.**

154

SECTION B
U VALUES FOR YOUR HOME

In Section B, you will perform a number of measurements and calculations in order to determine the U values of various areas in your home. Finally, you will add your individual U values together to determine the U_t of your home.

WINDOWS

You will calculate the total heat loss rate of each of the windows in each room of your home in place. As you calculate the U_t of each window in a given room, enter each window U_t value in a table like Table B-1. Also, note and record the direction of each window as you study it—north, south, east, or west. When you have studied ALL of the windows in a certain room, you will add up their individual U_t values to find the U_t of all of the windows in that room. Let us begin our study of windows with your living room windows.

(a) Number each of the windows in your living room. Begin your measurements with window #1. The accompanying diagram will help you in your measurements. To make your calculations easier, record fractions as decimals. For example, 5½ feet should be recorded as 5.5 feet. (For your convenience, sheets of graph paper have been included at the back of this book.) Measure the parts of window #1 listed in lines 1 through 5 of Table B-1 and enter your measurements in Table B-1.

Table B-1. Data for Living Room Window #1

(1) width of window frame ("A")	_____ ft
(2) height of wall ("B")	_____ ft
(3) height of window frame ("C")	_____ ft
(4) width of glass area alone	_____ ft
(5) height of glass area alone	_____ ft
(6) area of glass alone	_____ ft²
(7) lineal footage of window	_____ ft
(8) total area of wall and window	_____ ft²
(9) total window area	_____ ft²
(10) area of wall alone	_____ ft²
(11) area of lumber only	_____ ft²
(12) U of lumber	_____
(13) area of cavity alone	_____ ft²
(14) U of cavity area only	_____
(15) U of glass alone	_____
(16) area of frame alone	_____ ft²
(17) U of frame alone	_____

155

(b) Calculate the area of the glass alone by multiplying the width of glass alone (line 4 of Table B-1) by the height of the glass alone (line 5 of Table B-1). Record the area of the glass itself in line 6 of Table B-1.

(c) To find the linal footage of the window, add 0.66 ft to the width of the window frame recorded in line 1 of Table B-1. Record the lineal footage of the window in Table B-1.

(d) To determine the conductance rate of the lumber in the wall, first find the total area of the wall and window by multiplying the lineal footage of the window (line 7 of Table B-1) by the height of the wall (line 2 of Table B-1). Record this value in line 8.

Next, find the total window area by multiplying the width of the window frame (line 1) by the height of the window frame (line 3). Record the total window area in line 9.

To find the area of the wall alone, subtract the window area (line 9) from the total area of the wall and window. Record the wall area alone in line 10.

Calculate the area of the lumber only by multiplying the net wall area (line 10) by 0.35. We are assuming that 35% of the wall is wood.) Record the area of the lumber in line 11.

To find the U of the lumber, multiply the net area of the lumber (line 11) by one of the U/ft^2 values given here (either 0.148 for regular construction, or 0.081 for foam on exterior). Record the U of the lumber on line 12 of Table B-1 and also on line 1 of Table B-2.

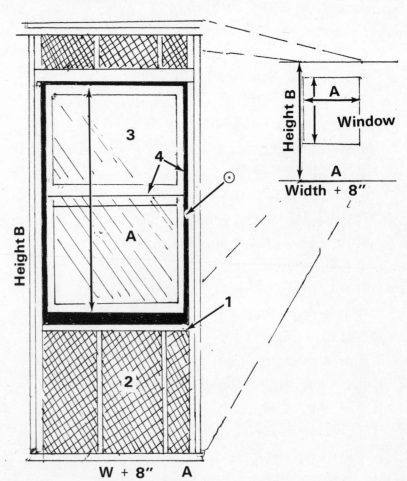

Heat loss of this window is subject to total area of (W + 8") × Height which includes:
1. Framing material
2. Insulation
3. Glass in window
4. Frame of window

*This dark area often is uninsulated!

156

Table B-2. U_t of Living Room Window #1

(1) U of lumber alone _____

(2) U of cavity alone _____

(3) U of glass alone _____

(4) U of window frame _____

U_t of window #1 _____

(e) In finding the conductance rate of the cavity area, we must first find the net cavity area. To find the area of the cavity only, multiply the net area of the wall (line 10 of Table B-1) by 0.65. (We are assuming that 65% of the wall area is cavity.) Record the area of the cavity alone in line 13 of Table B-1.

Next, select from this list the appropriate U/ft^2 for your wall cavity:

Amount and Type of Insulation	U/ft^2
0″ insulation	0.189
2″ fiberglass	0.110
3.5″ fiberglass	0.072
3.5″ cellulose	0.061
3.5″ fiberglass + 1″ foam	0.055
3.5″ foam	0.058

Finally, to calculate the U of the cavity alone, multiply the net cavity area (line 13) by the U/ft^2 which you selected from the list just presented. Record your calculated value for the U of the cavity area on line 14 of Table B-1 and also on line 2 of Table B-2.

(f) To find the conductance rate of the window glass, first select the appropriate U/ft^2 from the list below.

Window type	U/ft^2 (without storms)	U/ft^2 (with storms)
Single pane	1.13	0.383
or		
Insulated with:		
3/16″ air space	0.69	0.315
1/4″ air space	0.68	0.306
1/2″ air space	0.58	0.290

Next, calculate the U of the window glass alone by multiplying the area of the glass alone (line 6 of Table B-1) by the U/ft^2 which you just selected. Record your calculated U for glass alone on line 15 of Table B-1 and also on line 3 of Table B-2.

(g) Before you can calculate the U of the window frame, you must first find the area of the frame alone by subtracting the area of the glass (line 6 of Table B-1) from the total window area (line 9). Record the area of the window frame alone on line 16.

Next, select the appropriate U/ft^2 for the frame material from the list below:

Material	U/ft^2 (without storms)	U/ft^2 (with storms)
Aluminum	1.21	0.390
Vinyl aluminum	1.17	0.389
Wood (1" thick)	0.68	0.314

Calculate the U of the window frame by multiplying the area of the window frame alone (line 16) by the U/ft^2 value which you just selected. Enter your calculated U for the window frame alone on line 17 of Table B-1 and also on line 4 of Table B-2.

(h) At last, you are ready to calculate the U_t of the window. To do so, simply add the values in Table B-2. The sum of these U values is the U_t of your window. Record the U_t of #1 in line 1 of Table B-3.

Repeat the whole procedure for each window in your living room and record your data for each window in tables like Table B-1 and B-2. Enter the U_t for all of the other living room windows in Table B-3.

When you have completed your study of all of your living room windows and have entered the U_t, the lineal footage, and the direction for each window in Table B-3, add the values in Table B-3 to find the U_t and the total lineal footage for all of the living room windows. Enter these totals in Table B-4.

Table B-3. Ut for all Living Room Windows

	U_t	Lineal Footage	Direction
Window #1	_____	_____	_____
Window #2	_____	_____	_____
Window #3	_____	_____	_____
Window # 4	_____	_____	_____
Window #5	_____	_____	_____
Total	_____	_____	_____

Be sure to study all of the windows* in all rooms of your home in the manner described here for the living room. Enter your room window totals on the appropriate lines of Table B-4.

*Note: Basement windows will be treated separately in the section on basements.

Table B-4. U_t for All Windows and Total Lineal Footage of All Windows in Your Home

Room	U_t	Total Lineal Footage
(1) living room		
(2) dining room		
(3) family room		
(4) bedroom #1		
(5) bedroom #2		
(6) bedroom #3		
(7) bedroom #4		
(8) bedroom #5		
(9) bath #1		
(10) bath #2		
(11) bath #3		
(12) kitchen		
(13) laundry room		
(14) other		
(15) other		
Total		

Finally, enter the U_t of all windows and the total lineal footage of all windows in line (1) of Section B of Worksheet One, page 189.

An interesting project is to multiply the U_t of a window by your fuel cost factor to get the potential heating cost of this window. Later we will show you how to calculate the potential gain of the window due to solar heat. Also, if you do not have storm windows, you may wish to multiply the U_t of a window without storms and with storms by your fuel cost factor to get a heating cost comparison.

U_t OF DOORS IN PLACE

The only doors we are concerned with in this part are the exterior doors. Remember that the door between the living area and an attached garage must be treated as an exterior door. (Sliding glass doors are treated separately in the next part.)

(a) Number each of the exterior doors in your home beginning with your front door. Make the measurements listed on lines 1 through 3 of Table B-5. (The accompanying diagram can be used as a guide in taking these measurements.)

Table B-5. Data for Front Door

(1) width of door ("A") _____ ft

(2) height of wall ("B") _____ ft

(3) height of door ("C") _____ ft

(4) lineal footage of door _____ ft

(5) total area of door and wall _____ ft^2

(6) area of the door _____ ft^2

(7) area of wall alone _____ ft^2

(8) area of lumber alone in wall _____ ft^2

(9) U of lumber area alone in wall _____

(10) area of wall cavity alone _____ ft^2

(11) U of wall cavity alone _____

(12) area of door alone _____ ft^2

(13) U of door alone _____

(14) area of door window alone (if any) _____ ft^2

(15) U of door window alone (if any) _____

(b) To find the lineal footage of this door, add 0.66 ft to the width of the door (line 1). Record the lineal footage in line 4 of Table B-5.

(c) In finding the conductance rate of the lumber in the wall, you must first find the total area of the door and the wall around the door. To do this, multiply the height of the wall (line 2) by the lineal footage of the door (line 4). Record this value in line 5.

Next, find the total area of the door by multiplying the width of the door (line 1) by the height of the door (line 3). Record the area of the door on line 6.

You can now find the net area of the wall by subtracting the area of the door (line 6) from the total area of the door and wall (line 5). Record the area of the wall alone on line 7.

To find the area of the lumber in the wall only, multiply the area of the wall alone (line 7) by 0.75 (Here we are assuming that 75% of the wall area alone is lumber.) Record the area of lumber alone in the wall on line 8.

160

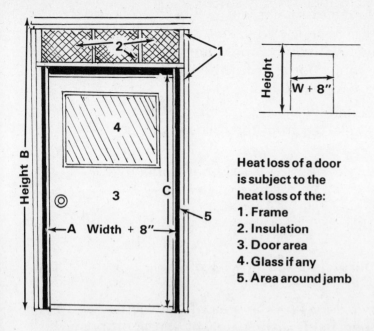

Heat loss of a door
is subject to the
heat loss of the:
1. Frame
2. Insulation
3. Door area
4. Glass if any
5. Area around jamb

Choose the appropriate U/ft^2 given here (either U/ft^2 for regular construction = 0.148, or U/ft^2 for foam on exterior = 0.081) and multiply this number by the net lumber area (line 8) to find the U of the lumber area alone of the wall. Record this value in line 9 of Table B-5 and also in line 1 of Table B-6.

Table B-6. U_t of Front Door

(1) U of lumber alone in wall _____

(2) U of cavity alone in wall _____

(3) U of door alone _____

(4) U of door window (if any) _____

(d) The conductance rate of the cavity area alone can easily be calculated. First, find the area of the cavity of the wall by multiplying the area of the wall alone (line 7) by 0.25. (We are assuming that 25% of the net wall area is cavity.) Record the area of the wall cavity alone in line 10 of Table B-5.

You can now calculate the conductance value (U) of the wall cavity alone by multiplying the area of the wall cavity alone (line 10) by the appropriate U/ft^2 selected from the list given here.

Amount and type of insulation	U/ft^2
0" insulation	0.189
2" fiberglass	0.110
3.5" fiberglass	0.072
3.5" cellulose	0.061
3.5" fiberglass + 1" foam	0.055
3.5" foam	0.058

Record the U of the net cavity area on line 11 of Table B-5 and also on line 2 of Table B-6.

161

(e) Next, we want to find the conductance rate of the door. To do this, we must first find the area of the door itself by multiplying the width of the door (line 1 of Table B-5) by the height of the door (line 3). (If the door contains a window, be sure to correct your door area for the window area.) Enter the area of the door alone on line 12 of Table B-5.

To calculate the conductance rate of the door, multiply the area of the door alone by the appropriate U/ft^2 selected from the following list:

Door type	U/ft^2 (without storms)	U/ft^2 (with storms)
hollow core	1.87	0.442
solid wood door	0.34	0.214
steel door/foam center	0.181	0.131

Record the U value for the door alone on line 13 of Table B-5 and also on line 3 of Table B-6.

(f) If there is a window in your door find the area of the window and enter it on line 14 of Table B-5. Then multiply this area by the appropriate U/ft^2 as given in the preceding section titled WINDOWS. Enter the conductance rate of the door window alone on line 15 of Table B-5 and also on line 4 of Table B-6.

Recall that transoms and side lights should already have been treated as windows and entered separately in the preceding section on windows.

(g) Find the U_t of the door in place by adding the values in Table B-6. Record the U_t of this door in place and its lineal footage on line 1 of Table B-7.

Table B-7. U_t of All Exterior Doors in Your Home

	U_t	Total Lineal Footage
(1) Door #1 (front door)	_____	_____
(2) Door #2	_____	_____
(3) Door #3	_____	_____
(4) Door #4	_____	_____
(5) Door #5	_____	_____
Total	_____	_____

Study all of the exterior doors in your home in the step-by-step manner we have just described for the front door and enter your data in tables similar to Table B-5 and B-6. As you complete your study for each door, enter the U_t for the door in place and its lineal footage in Table B-7.

When you have completed your study of all exterior doors add the values in Table B-7 and record the resulting U_t for all doors and the lineal footage for all doors on line 2 of Section B of Worksheet One, page 189.

You may want to apply your fuel cost factor to the U_t of the various doors to study their heating costs under a variety of conditions as well as with and without storm doors.

U_t OF SLIDING GLASS DOORS

To find the conductance rate of your sliding glass doors, follow the outline given below. (The accompanying guide can be used to guide you in your measurements.)

(1) Number each set of sliding glass doors in your home. For sliding glass door #1, make the measurements needed for lines 1 through 3 of Table B-8.

Table B-8. Data for Sliding Door #1

(1) width of door ("A")   _____ ft

(2) height of wall ("B")   _____ ft

(3) height of door ("C")   _____ ft

(4) width of glass alone   _____ ft

(5) height of glass alone   _____ ft

(6) area of the glass alone   _____ ft^2

(7) lineal footage of door   _____ ft

(8) area of wall and door   _____ ft^2

(9) area of door alone   _____ ft^2

(10) area of wall alone   _____ ft^2

(11) area of lumber only in wall   _____ ft^2

(12) U of lumber only in wall   _____

(13) area of cavity alone   _____ ft^2

(14) U of cavity alone in wall   _____

(15) U of glass alone   _____

(16) area of frame   _____ ft^2

(17) U of frame   _____

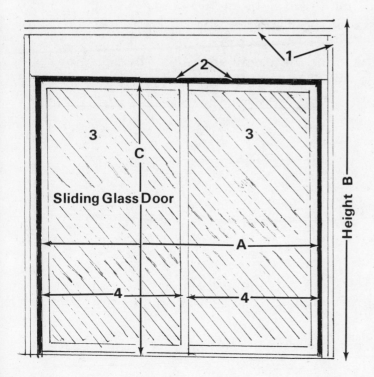

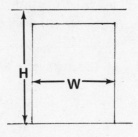

Heat loss of a
sliding glass door
is subject to:
1. Framing
2. Insulation (if any)
3. Glass area
4. Glass frame area

163

(b) Calculate the area of the glass alone by multiplying the width of the glass alone by the height of the glass alone. Record the area of the glass in Table B-8.

(c) Find the lineal footage of the sliding glass door by adding 0.66 ft to the width of the glass door (line 1). Record the lineal footage of the sliding glass door in Table B-8 and also in Table B-10. Also note in Table B-10 the direction which the door faces.

(d) In finding the conductance rate of lumber in the wall, first find the total area of the wall and the door by multiplying the lineal footage of the door by the height of the wall. Enter the total area of the wall and the door in Table B-8.

Next, find the area of the door alone by multiplying the door width by the door height. Enter this value in Table B-8.

Find the area of the wall alone by subtracting the area of the door alone from the area of the wall with the door. Enter this value in Table B-8.

To find the area of lumber alone in the wall, multiply the area of the wall by 0.80. (We are assuming that 80% of the wall is lumber only.) Enter this value in Table B-8.

To calculate the U of the lumber only in the wall, select one of the following U/ft^2 values (0.148 for regular construction, or 0.081 for 1" foam on exterior) and multiply this number by the area of the lumber. Enter this value on line 12 of Table B-8 and also on line 1 of Table B-9.

Table B-9. U_t of Sliding Glass Door #1

(1) U of lumber alone in wall   _____

(2) U of cavity alone in wall   _____

(3) U of glass alone in door   _____

(4) U of frame alone   _____

     Total   _____

(e) In calculating the U of the cavity alone, you must first find the net cavity area. Find the net cavity area by multiplying the net wall area (line 10) by 0.20. (Here we are assuming that 20% of the wall area alone is cavity.) Record the net cavity area in Table B-8.

Begin your calculation of the U of the cavity area alone by selecting the appropriate U/ft^2 from the following list:

Amount and type of insulation	U/ft^2
0"	0.189
2" fiberglass	0.110
3.5" fiberglass	0.072
3.5" cellulose	0.061
3.5" fiberglass + 1" foam	0.055
3.5" foam	0.058

Multiply this value by the area of the cavity alone to find the U of the cavity area alone. Enter this U value on line 14 of Table B-8 and also on line 2 of Table B-9.

(f) Find the conducatance rate of the glass alone by multiplying the area of the glass alone (line 6) by the appropriate U/ft^2 given here:

164

Type of glass	U/ft^2
single pane glass	1.13
3/16" insulated glass	0.69
1/4" insulated glass	0.68
1/2" insulated glass	0.58

Record the U for the glass alone on line 15 of Table B-8 and also on line 3 of Table B-9.

(g) In finding the conductance rate of the frame, you must first find the area of the frame. This can easily be done by subtracting the area of the glass alone from the area of the door. Record this value in Table B-8.

To find the U of the frame, multiply the area of the frame by the appropriate U/ft^2 chose from the following list

Type of frame	U/ft^2
aluminum	1.21
vinyl over aluminum	1.17
wood (1" thick)	0.68

Enter the U of the frame on line 17 of Table B-8 and also on line 4 of Table B-9.

(h) To find the U_t of the sliding glass door, add the values in Table B-9. Record this value on line 1 of Table B-10.

Table B-10. U_t of all Sliding Glass Doors

	U_t	Total lineal footage	Direction
(1) Sliding Glass Door #1			
(2) Sliding Glass Door #2			
(3) Sliding Glass Door #3			

Study all of the sliding glass doors in your home in the step-by-step manner we have just described for the first sliding glass door and enter your data in Tables similar to Tables B-8 and B-9. As you complete your study for each sliding glass door, enter the Ut for the door, its lineal footage, and the direction which it faces in Table B-10.

When you have completed your study of all sliding glass doors, add the values in Table B-10 and record the resulting Ut for all sliding glass doors in your home and the total lineal footage for all sliding glass doors on line 3 of Section B of Worksheet One, page 189.

You may want to use your fuel cost factor here to discover the annual potential heating cost of one sliding door.

In the case of windows, doors and sliding glass doors we have not even attempted to factor in air infiltration because we will treat air infiltration as one massive problem. Even many of the air tests made by manufacturers can only be relied on for the particular window tested. Often field applications will destroy some of the seals the manufacturer relied upon for his testing. Nevertheless, air penetration is expensive and should be guarded against on doors, windows and sliding glass doors.

165

EXTERIOR WALLS

There is a slight difference between the conductance rate of stucco, aluminum, and brick siding. Our U values used below do not reflect the difference. If you want to be more exact, deduct 0.45 per ft^2 from the U if you have stucco, and add 0.15 per ft^2 to the U if you have brick siding.

(a) Measure the lineal footage of each exterior wall, add all of these measurements together, and record the total in line 1 of Table B-11.

(b) Add together all the lineal footage of windows, doors, and sliding glass doors. (You can find these values in earlier tables in this part of the Work Section which you have already completed.) Record this value in line 2 of Table B-11.

(c) Find the net exterior wall area in your home by subtracting line 2 from line 1 in Table B-11. Record this value on line 3 of the table.

Table B-11. Data for Exterior Walls

(1) total lineal footage of walls _____ ft

(2) total lineal footage of windows, doors,
and sliding glass doors _____ ft

(3) total net exterior wall footage _____ ft

(4) height of wall _____ ft

(5) gross wall area _____ ft^2

(6) net lumber area in wall _____ ft^2

(7) U of net lumber area in wall _____

(8) net cavity area in wall _____ ft^2

(9) U of net cavity area _____

(d) In finding the U of lumber in the exterior wall (based on 16″ on center studs), first measure and record the height of the wall. Next find and record the gross wall area (in ft^2) by multiplying the net lineal footage by the height of the wall.

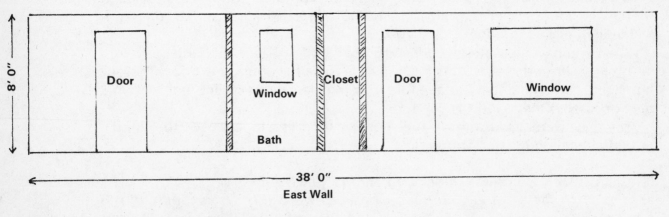

East Wall

The heat loss of this east wall is subject to the heat loss of:
Two doors
Two windows
The area of studs and lumber in the wall
The area of insulation between the studs
Air infiltration through cracks and crevices

166

To find the net lumber area in the wall, multiply the gross wall area by 0.106. (Here we are assuming that 10.6% of the wall is lumber only.) Record this value.

Finally, find the U of the net lumber area by multiplying the net lumber area in the wall by the appropriate U/ft^2 (0.148 for regular construction, and 0.081 for 1" foam on exterior) and record this value on line 7 of the table.

(e) In calculating the U of the cavity area of the wall, first multiply the gross wall area by 0.894. (Here we are assuming that 89.4% of the gross wall area is cavity.) Record this value.

Next find the U of the net cavity area by multiplying the net cavity area by the appropriate U/ft^2 from this list:

Amount and type of insulation	U/ft^2
0"	0.189
2" fiberglass	0.110
3.5" fiberglass	0.072
3.5" cellulose	0.061
3.5" fiberglass + 1" foam	0.055
3.5" foam	0.058

Record this value on line 9 of the table.

(f) Find the total U of the wall by adding the U of the net lumber area (line 7) and the U of the net cavity of the wall (line 9). Record this value in table B-11 and also on line 4 of Section B in Part Two of the Work Section, page 189.

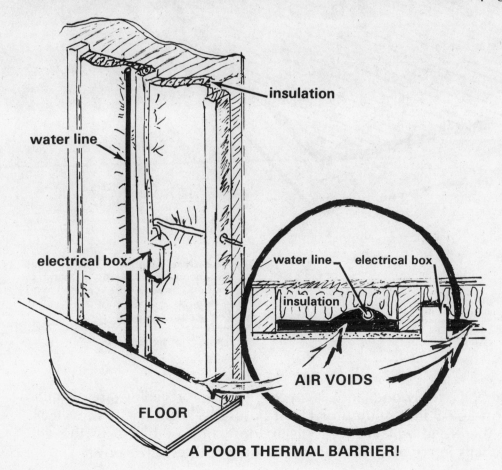

A POOR THERMAL BARRIER!

167

CEILINGS

Be sure to take into account the trap door or access panel going into the attic area. Measurement is simple for ceilings. Measure the length and width of the floor area below the attic. By multiplying the length times width you can find the gross ceiling area.

Use the following equations to find the U of the net lumber area in the ceiling and the U of the net cavity area:

$$U \text{ of net wood} = 0.106 \times \text{gross area} \times U/ft^2$$
$$U \text{ of net cavity} = 0.894 \times \text{gross area} \times U/ft^2$$

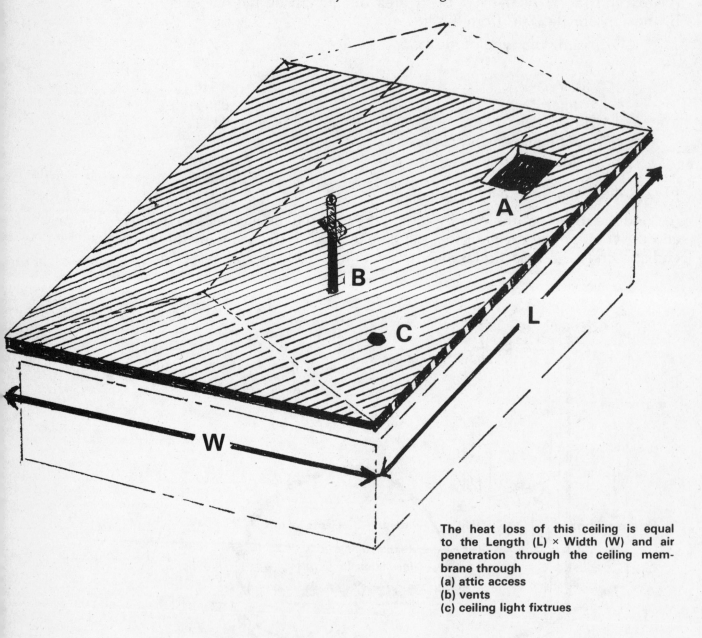

The heat loss of this ceiling is equal to the Length (L) × Width (W) and air penetration through the ceiling membrane through
(a) attic access
(b) vents
(c) ceiling light fixtrues

Add the total U for wood and cavity to get U_t for ceiling area. Record this value on line 5 in Section B or Part Two of the Work Section, page 189. The U_t of the wood will change only if loose fiber is blown in the attic. If you have batts in the attic, then the U of the wood remains constant.

168

Cavity	Fiberglass R 2.7/inch	Cellulose R 3.5/inch
4" fill	.081 ft^2	.064
6" fill	.056 ft^2	.044
8" fill	.043 ft^2	.033
10" fill	.035 ft^2	.027
Wood		
4" fill	.174 ft^2	.174
6" fill	.089 ft^2	0.78
8" fill	.06 ft^2	.05
10" fill	.045 ft^2	.037

The rating of loose fiberglass is 2.70 per inch of thickness. In many cases especially older homes, the rating per inch of thickness is as low as 2.20 per inch of thickness. The Ut is assuming the triangular correction for a 4/12 pitch roof as pointed out in Chapter 9. Once you have established U_t, just for fun throw some numbers around your fuel factor and see how many dollars you can save by adding insulation.

CONCRETE SLABS

At this time we are interested in slabs under heated areas or in the interior of the house. Basement floors will be treated separately and garage slabs should be ignored.

(1) Measure the length and width of the slab. Use the accompanying diagram as a guide. Record as required, such as A-1, A-2, A-3, etc. It would pay for you to make a diagram if your slab home is irregular in shape.

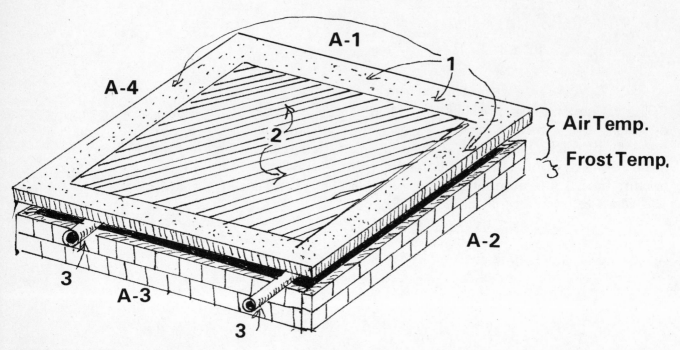

Heat loss of a slab is subject to:
1. Edge losses that are subject to exterior air temperatures (A) and (B) frost temperatures
2. Center losses subject to ground temperatures
3. Duct losses are subject to:
Ground temperature (55°F) or the entire spectrum of air temperatures, depending on location

Table B-12. Data for Slabs

(1) length of A-1	_____ ft
(2) length of A-2	_____ ft
(3) (length of A-3)	_____ ft
(4) (length of A-4)	_____ ft
(5) area of slab exposed to outside temperature	_____ ft²
(6) U of slab edge	_____
(7) area of slab center	_____ ft²
(8) U of slab center	_____
(9) total U of slab	_____

170

(b) In calculating the U of edge loss, any part of the slab that is exposed to the exterior usually is calculated two feet back. So we must find the AREA of the slab exposed to the outside air temperatures. In some cases the slab edge will be next to a basement wall or crawl space wall. This area should be treated as a center of slab.

Add the lineal footage of edge and multiply by 2 to get the area of slab exposed to outside air temperatures.

Select the appropriate U/ft^2 and multiply it by the area of the edge of the slab to find the U of the edge of the slab.

These Us will apply for both edge and center losses

Area	U
no insulation and no carpet	0.57
no insulation and carpet	0.235
one inch foam at edge and carpet	0.102
two inch foam at edge and carpet	0.65

In calculating the U of the slab center, discover the entire area of the slab (A-1 × A-2). Then subtract the area of slab edge from the entire area of the slab to find the area of the slab center.

Find the U of the slab center by multiplying the area of the slab center by the appropriate U/ft^2, and record this value in the table.

To find the total U of the slab, add the U of the slab center to the U of the slab edge. Record this value on line 9 of Table B-12 and also on line 6 of the Worksheet for Part Two of the Work Section, page 189.

Since the slab center is not exposed to outside temperatures, the heat transfer is subject to a predictable 2500 DD year. In most cases, we can divide the U of our slab by 2 and multiply by our fuel heating cost factor to find the heating cost of the slab.

171

WOOD FLOORS

For floor systems, edge heat losses are higher than the center heat losses. (We already know that the same is true for slabs.) However, because of air infiltration, the center of the floor is most likely not losing the same amount of heat as the edges are. This is the drawback over slabs but wood floors are, in most cases, easy to add insulation to. Also, in making calculations on wood floors, you must take into consideration the heat loss of the crawl space or the basement under the floor. You can by-pass this calculation if you plan to insulate the foundation area.

(a) Measure and record the length and width of the floor area.

Table B-13. Data on Wood Floors

(1) length of floor	_____	ft
(2) width of floor	_____	ft
(3) total area of floor	_____	ft^2
(4) area of lumber only	_____	ft^2
(5) U of lumber only	_____	
(6) area of cavity	_____	ft^2
(7) U of cavity only	_____	
(8) total U of wood floor	_____	

(b) Follow the same procedure you have used earlier in this section in the process of calculating the U of the net lumber area and the net cavity area. From the following list, select the appropriate U values to use in your calculations.

Floor Systems Assuming 2 × 8 Floor Joists

Floor	*U/ft^2*
Wood - without carpet	0.084
with carpet	0.071
Cavity - zero insulation	0.177
4" fiberglass	0.060
6" fiberglass	0.046
8" fiberglass	0.037

In your U calculations, use the following equations. (Here we are assuming that 10% of the total floor area is lumber only.)

$$U \text{ of lumber} = 0.10 \times \text{total floor area} \times U/\text{ft}^2 \text{ of lumber}$$

$$U \text{ of cavity} = 0.90 \times \text{total floor area} \times U/\text{ft}^2 \text{ of cavity}$$

Record these U values in your table above.

172

(c) Finally, find the total U of the wood floor by adding together the U of the lumber alone and the U of the cavity alone. Record this value on line 8 of Table B-13 and also on line 7 of the Worksheet for Section B of Part Two of the Work Section, page 189.

Note: After you get U_t of floor, use your fuel factor and see how much the heat loss of the floor is as compared to the ceiling in your home. You, as I was, will be surprised.

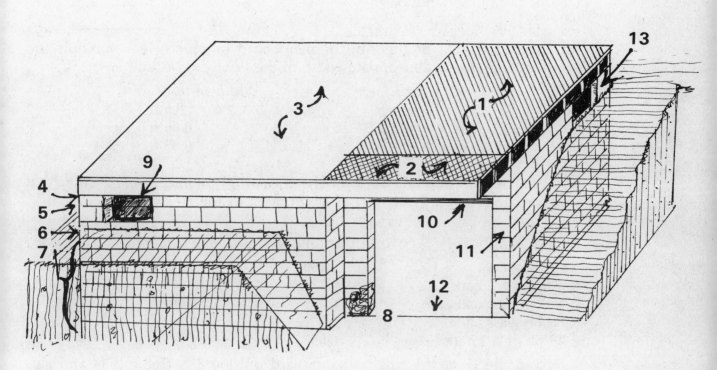

Heat loss of a floor would be subject to:
1. area over garage
2. overhang or garrison
3. area over basement

Basement heat loss would be subject to:
4. air penetration under deck
5. block above grade
6. block at frost line
7. block below grade
8. floor
9. windows

Garage heat loss is subject to:
10. air penetration through floor
11. blocks above and below grade
12. floors
13. windows

173

RINGS AND BANDBOARDS

If you have already calculated heat loss of the floor over the basement or crawl space, do not calculate heat loss of bandboard. Slab homes do not have a ring or bandboard; however, if you have a two-story or split-level home, be sure to calculate this area.

(a) Add up the measurements of outside wall area, where applicable for the bandboard to find the total lineal footage.

Table B-14. Data on Rings and Bandboards

(1) lineal footage of ring or bandboard   _____ ft

(2) area of ring or bandboard   _____ ft²

(3) U of ring or bandboard   _____

(b) To get the area of the ring or bandboard in square feet, multiply the lineal footage by the appropriate width of the floor joist listed here.

Type of floor joist	Width of floor joist
$2' \times 6'$	0.5 ft
$2' \times 8'$	0.66 ft
$2' \times 10'$	0.83 ft

(c) Select the appropriate U from the following list and calculate the total U of the bandboard by multiplying this number by the area of the bandboard.

U/ft^2

Ring or Bandboard	No Insulation Board	Insulation Board	Foam board
no insulation	0.289	0.209	0.110
R-4 fiberglass batts	0.134	0.113	0.076
R-6 fiberglass batts	0.105	0.092	0.066
R-8 fiberglass batts	0.069	0.063	0.049
R-19 fiberglass batts	0.057	0.042	0.035

Record the U of the ring or bandboard on line 3 of Table B-14 and also on line 8 in Section B of the Worksheet for Part Two of the Work Section, page 189.

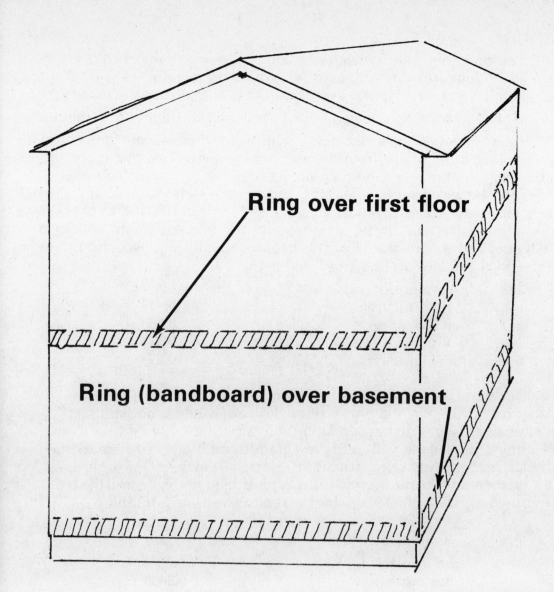

Ring over first floor

Ring (bandboard) over basement

BASEMENTS

The portion of your house below grade will not be subject to the normal DD year for your area. Instead, because ground temperature is fairly constant throughout the country, we will use a 2500 DD year to anticipate heating cost.

(a) Measure and record the data needed for lines 1 through 4 of Table B-15.

(b) Calculate and record the net area (exclusive of windows) out of the ground. Examine each side of the foundation because there may be more blocks out of the ground on one side than on another.

From the list given here, select the appropriate U/ft^2 value to use in your calculation of the U of the wall above ground. Calculate the U of the wall above ground by multiplying the net area of the basement wall by this U/ft^2 value, and record the U of the basement wall above ground on line 6 of Table B-15 and also on line 1 of Table B-16.

Amount of insulation	U/ft^2
no insulation	0.413
R-4 insulation	0.155
R-6 insulation	0.118
R-8 insulation	0.095

(c) Calculate and record the area of the block wall below grade. (To do this, find the area of the entire masonry wall exclusive of windows and subtract from this value the area of the foundation above ground.)

Determine the U of the wall area below grade by multiplying the area of the wall below grade by the appropriate U/ft^2 selected from the following list. (The insulation value of the ground is already included here.) Record the U of the wall below grade on line 9 of Table B-15 and also on line 2 of Table B-16.

Amount of insulation	U/ft^2
no insulation	0.057
R-4 insulation	0.0466
R-6 insulation	0.0426
R-8 insulation	0.0393

(d) To find the conductance rate of the basement floor, you must first calculate the area of the basement floor. Then multiply the area of the basement floor by the appropriate U/ft^2 for the basement floor (U/ft^2 of uncarpeted basement is 0.57, and the U/ft^2 of carpeted basement is 0.24) to find the U of the basement floor. Record this value on line 3 of Table B-15 and also on line 11 of Table B-16.

(e) Find the U value of the basement windows by following the procedure outlined for windows in an earlier part of this Work Section, page 155. In your calculations on basement windows select appropriate U values from the lists given here.

Glass		Frame	
Type	U/ft^2	Type	U/ft^2
single pane	1.13	metal	1.21
single/storm	0.383	metal/storm	0.390
insul. glass	0.68	wood	0.68

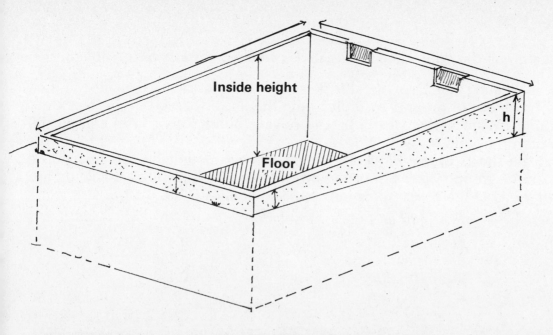

Inside height

h

Floor

Record the U of the basement windows on line 12 of Table B-15 and also on line 4 of Table B-16.

(f) Find the total U of your basement by adding the U values in Table B-16. Record the U of the basement in the worksheet for Section B of Part Two of the Work Section, page 189.

Table B-15. Data for Basements

(1) height of interior basement wall	_____ ft
(2) length of foundation	_____ ft
(3) width of foundation	_____ ft
(4) height (average) of foundation out of ground	_____ ft
(5) net area of basement wall out of ground (exclusive of windows)	_____ ft^2
(6) U of net area of basement wall out of ground	_____
(7) area of entire basement walls (exclusive of windows)	_____ ft^2
(8) area of basement walls below ground	_____ ft^2
(9) U of basement wall below ground	_____
(10) area of basement floor	_____ ft^2
(11) U of basement floor	_____
(12) U of basement windows and frames	_____

Table B-16. U_t of Basement

(1) U of basement wall out of ground	_____
(2) U of basement wall below ground	_____
(3) U of basement floor	_____
(4) U of basement windows and frames	_____
U_t of basement	_____

177

CRAWL SPACE

(a) Measure and record the data needed for lines 1 through 6 of Table B-17.

(b) In calculating the U of the block above ground, first calculate the area of the block out of ground by multiplying the lineal footage of the block out of ground by the height of the block above ground. Record the area of the block out of ground in Table B-17.

Calculate the U of the block above ground by multiplying the area of the block above ground by the appropriate U/ft^2 selected from the following list. Record the U of the block above ground on line 8 of Table B-17.

Type and amount of insulation	U/ft^2
no insulation	0.413
R-4 insulation	0.155
R-6 insulation	0.118
R-8 insulation	0.095

(c) In finding the U of the block below ground, first find the area of the block below ground. The area of the block below ground can be found by multiplying the lineal footage of the wall by the total height of the wall, and by subtracting the area of the wall above ground from the total area of the wall. Record the area of the wall below ground in Table B-17.

Finally, calculate the U of the crawl space wall below ground by multiplying the area of the wall below ground by the appropriate value selected from the following list. Record this value on line 11 of Table B-17.

Amount and type of insulation	U/ft^2
no insulation	0.057
R-4 insulation	0.046
R-6 insulation	0.426
R-8 insulation	0.0393

(d) To find the U of the floor of the crawl space, first calculate and record the area of the crawl space floor. Then calculate the U of the crawl space floor by multiplying the area of the floor by the appropriate U/ft^2 selected from this list. Record the U of the crawl space floor on line 13 of Table B-17.

Type of floor	U/ft^2
bare ground	1.06
vinyl cover	1.06
2" concrete	0.74
1" foam (R-4)	0.202

(e) Find the U of the whole crawl space by adding lines 8, 11, and 13 of Table B-17. Record this value on line 14 of Table B-17 and also on line 10 of Section B of the Worksheet for Part Two of the Work Section, page 189.

Table B-17. Data for Crawl Spaces

(1) length of portion of block walls exposed to outside air   _____ ft

(2) width of portion of block walls exposed to outside air   _____ ft

(3) height of portion of block walls exposed to outside air   _____ ft

(4) total height of block wall inside crawl space   _____ ft

(5) width of crawl space floor   _____ ft

(6) length of crawl space floor   _____ ft

(7) area of block out of ground   _____ ft^2

(8) U of block above ground   _____

(9) total area of wall   _____ ft^2

(10) area of wall below ground   _____ ft^2

(11) U of wall below ground   _____

(12) area of crawl space floor   _____ ft^2

(13) U of floor of crawl space   _____

(14) U_t of the crawl space (wall above ground, wall below ground, and floor)   _____

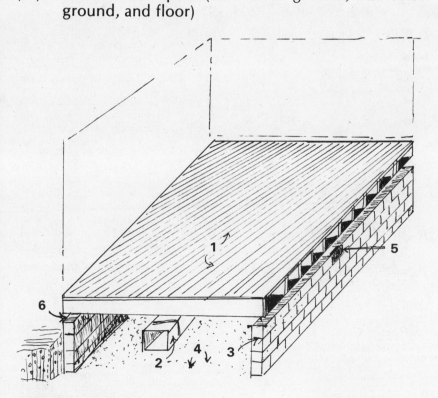

Uninsulated Floor. Heat Loss of Crawl Space is subject to:
1. Heat loss of floor
2. Heat loss of ducts
3. Heat loss of block wall
4. Heat loss to ground
5. Air flow through vents
6. Air flow under floor

Insulated Floor
Heat loss of floor would be subject to:
1. Heat gain of duct
2. Heat loss of block wall
3. Heat loss to ground
4. Air flow through vents
5. Air flow under floor

179

AREAS PARTLY BELOW GRADE AND KNEEWALLS

This discussion is divided into two separate parts. The first part covers masonry above and below grade. In some homes, the masonry walls may extend above grade and be finished on the inside with paneling or drywall. If this is the case, there is no need to continue with the rest of this exercise.

Kneewalls are the subject of the second part. Kneewalls could be found as shown in the diagram and also in cape cod homes as well as in some split level homes where the wall is not normal height. For calculation on kneewalls, use the second half of the following discussion.

MASONRY ABOVE AND BELOW GRADE

(a) Treat the masonry walls as outlined in the section on basements. Find the U of the masonry above grade and the U of the masonry below grade and record these values in lines 1 and 2 of Table B-18.

(b) The U of the floor is treated in two parts. Here we must consider the U of the carpeted portion of the floor and the U of the uncarpeted portion of the floor.

Begin by calculating the area of the entire floor. Next calculate the area of the carpeted floor. Finally, find the area of the carpeted floor from the total floor area. Record all of these values in Table B-18.

Table B-18.   Data for Masonry Above and Below Grade

(1) U of masonry above ground   _____

(2) U of masonry below ground   _____

(3) area of floor   _____ ft^2

(4) area of carpeted floor   _____ ft^2

(5) area of uncarpeted floor   _____ ft^2

(6) U of carpeted floor   _____

(7) U of uncarpeted floor   _____

(8) U of masonry above and below ground   _____

(c) Calculate the U of the floor with carpet and the U of the floor without carpet. Multiply the area of the floor portion under study by the appropriate U value selected from figures given here. Record the U of carpeted floor on line 6 of Table B-18, and the U of the uncarpeted floor on line 7 of the same table.

Types of floor	U/ft^2 with carpet and pad	U/ft^2 bare concrete/tile
no insulation	0.261	0.71
R-4 insulation	0.127	0.184
R-8 insulation	0.084	0.106

(d) Finally, find the U of all of the masonry above and below grade by adding lines 1, 2, 6, and 7 of Table B-18. Record this value on line 8 of Table B-18 and also on line 11a of Section B of the Worksheet for Part Two of the Work Section, page 189.

180

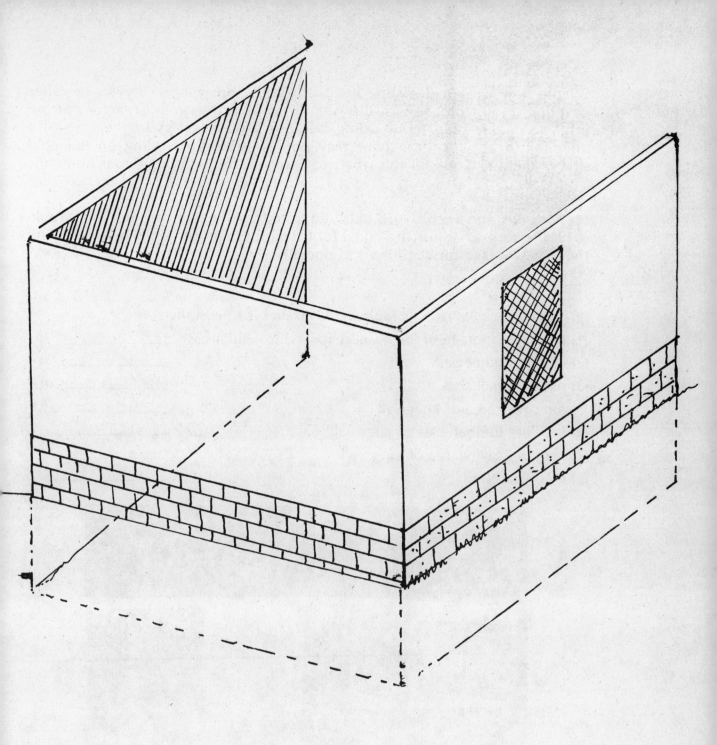

KNEEWALLS

Note how we are depicting kneewalls with and without drywall or other covering on just one side of the wall. In some cases we must factor out the insulation value of exterior siding because sometimes, as in the case of a kneewall in an attic loft, there may not be drywall or siding on the cold side of the wall. Look for this when you are searching through your home for heat leaks.

(a) Measure and record the data requested for lines 1 through 5 of Table B-19. (Be sure to adjust the lineal foot measurement for walls by subtracting the lineal footage for windows and doors.)

Table B-19. Data for Kneewalls

(1) net lineal footage of kneewalls exposed to cold areas _____ ft

(2) height of kneewall _____ ft

(3) net kneewall area _____ ft^2

(5) net cavity area of kneewall _____ ft^2

(6) U of net lumber area of kneewall _____

(7) U of net cavity area of kneewall _____

(8) **U_t of kneewall** _____

182

(b) Calculate the net wall area by multiplying the net lineal footage of the kneewall by the height of the kneewall.

(c) In calculating the U of the kneewall, we must consider the lumber portion of the kneewall separately from the cavity portion of the kneewall. In doing so, select the appropriate decimal from the following list to use in your calculations.

Height of kneewall	lumber	cavity
two feet	0.117	0.883
three feet	0.120	0.880
four feet	0.114	0.886

Record the net area of the lumber and the net area of the cavity in the kneewall in Table B-19.

(d) Using the information provided in the following list of types of walls and U/ft^2 for lumber and cavity, calculate the U of the net lumber area and the U of the net cavity area. Record these values in Table B-19.

Exterior siding	U/ft^2 lumber	U/ft^2 cavity
drywall one side	0.26	0.66
drywall both sides	0.25	0.272
drywall and exterior, insu. board	0.148	0.189
Insulation		
3.5" fiberglass	0.148	0.07
3.5" cellulose	0.148	0.058
3.5" fiberglass + 1"foam	0.081	0.055

(e) Finally, find the U of the kneewall by adding lines 6 and 7 of Table B-19. Record the U of the kneewall on line 8 of Table B-19, and also on line 11b of Section B of the Worksheet for Part Two of the Work Section, page 189.

SECTION C
CONVECTIVE HEAT LOSS

CALCULATION OF CONVECTIVE HEAT LOSS

(a) Look in Appendix K and find the average DD for January in a city nearest you. Record this value on line 1 of the worksheet for Section C of Part Two of the Work Section, page 190.

(b) Get out your electric and fuel bills for the month of january. Find the number of units you used during that month and record these values in Table C-1 on page 190. Examples of these units are gallons of fuel oil, 1000 cubic feet of natural gas, or the number of Kwh of electricity used. Heat available from these energy sources is as follows:

FUEL OIL—One gallon = 101 000 BTU when there is a heat loss up the chimney (stack) of 30%.

NATURAL GAS—One thousand cubic feet of natural gas (mcf) = 750 000 BTU when 25% of the heat produced is going up the chimney.

ELECTRIC—For straight resistance electric heating, 3413 BTU are available per Kwh and the conversion to heat is 100%

HEAT PUMPS—To delete and separate the elctrical consumption of the heat pump, factor out the electricity consumed in the non-heating or non-air-conditioning month. The balance would then be multiplied by 5460 BTU per Kwh (an average of 1.6 C.O.P. for the month of January). In very cold regions, the C.O.P. would be much lower and in warm areas the C.O.P. would be higher.

(c) Turn to Worksheet One for Part Two of the Work Section and find the U(conductive) of your home in Section B. Record the U(conductive) in Table C-1.

(d) Find the number of BTUs obtained from electricity during January and record this value in Table C-1.

No. of BTUs from electricity = No. of Kwh's × 3413

(e) Find the number of BTUs obtained from other fuel during January and record this value on Table C-1.

No. of BTUs from other fuel = No. of units of fuel × fuel rating (in BTU)

(f) Find the number of BTUs obtained from people in the home during the month of January. (Recall that in 24 hours, one person generates 7200 BTU in the home.) Record this value in Table C-1.

No. of BTUs from people = No. of people × 7200 × 31 days in January

(g) Estimate the solar gain in BTUs in your home and record this value in Table C-1. (See Appendix C for solar gain information.) Record your value for solar gains in Table C-1.

(h) Calculate the total amount of heat (in BTU) available in the home during January by adding together lines 5, 6, 7, and 8 of Table C-1. Record the total on line 9 of this table.

184

(i) Find the U(convective) of your home by performing the following calculation:

$$U(convective) = \frac{total\ BTUs\ available}{24 \times DD\ January} - U(conductive)$$

AIR TURNS PER HOUR

U(convective) CALCULATION

(a) Let us discover what the U(convective) of one air turn per hour is or would be in your home. One air turn means that the entire air in your home changes once per hour. As the cold air comes in the home it would normally be heated by your furnace. So the idea is to reduce the cost of heating this cold air during the heating season.

$$\frac{square\ footage\ of\ home \times wall\ height}{60} \times 1.1 = U(convective)$$

Using the above equation, calculate the U(convective) of one air turn per hour in your home. Record this value in Table C-1.

(b) Divide the U per one air turn per hour into the U(convective) to get the air turns per hour. Record this value in Table C-1.

If you multiply the U for one air turn per hour by the fuel cost factor, you can find out what one air turn per hour is costing you for one heating season. Ideally, we want to reduce the number of air turns to less than one. In most homes the air turns per hour value is much higher than one.

EXAMPLE

Let's assume there is a family of four living in Newark, New Jersey. This family owns a 1500 square foot home that has eight foot high walls. The DD of one January was 945 normally, and solar gain on the structure is minimal during the month of January. They consumed 2500 Kwh of electricity for TV, etc., and 23 mcf (1000 cubic feet) of natural gas in their furnace. U(conductive) of their home is 450.

(a) Find the U of air infiltration

$$
\begin{aligned}
2500\ Kwh \times 3413 &= 8\ 532\ 500\ BTU \\
23\ mcf\ of\ nat.\ gas \times 750\ 000 &= 17\ 250\ 000\ BTU \\
4\ people \times 7200 \times 31\ days &= 892\ 800\ BTU \\
(solar\ gain\ negligible) &= \\
\hline
&\ 26\ 675\ 300\ BTU
\end{aligned}
$$

$$
\begin{aligned}
U(convective) &= \frac{26\ 675\ 300}{24 \times 945} - 450 \\
&= 1176 - 450 \\
&= 726
\end{aligned}
$$

185

(b) Next find the U(*convective*) of one air turn per hour

$$U \text{ of one air turn per hour} = \frac{1500 \times 8}{60} \times 1.1 = 220$$

(c) Find the number of air turns per hour

$$\frac{726}{220} = 3.3 \text{ air turns per hour}$$

Work Sheet number three will show you how to use the U(*conductive*) and U of air infiltration to get economical trade-offs, furnace sizing, etc.

U_t (*convective*) × Fuel cost factor = Heating cost per year for air infiltration!

SECTION D
TRADES, HEAT LOSS, ETC.

HEAT LOSS OF YOUR HOME IN BTUs

(Record all of your data in Worksheet Three on page 191.) By adding up the U*(conductive)* and U*(conductive)*, you can find the U*(total)* of your home. By multiplying the Ut by the temperature setting of your thermostat, you will get the heat loss for one hour when it is 0° outside. By checking our weather data, you will see what the average low temperature is in your area. Subtract this low temperature from your thermostat setting (normally 70°F) and multiply the difference by U_t.

EXAMPLE

Low temperature average 5 degrees, thermostat setting 70°F, U_t of the home of 850

$$(70° - 5°) \times 850 = 55\ 250 \text{ BTU per hour}$$

Discover the original estimated Ut of the home estimated by the furnace installer by dividing the temperature difference (low average outside temperature by inside temperature) into the net output of the furnace.

EXAMPLE

$$70° - 5° = 65°$$
$$\text{Furnace output} = 75\ 000 \text{ BTU/hr:}$$

$$U_t = \frac{75\ 000}{65} = 1153.84$$

CORRECTING FUEL COST FACTOR FOR INTERNAL AND EXTERNAL HEATING GAINS

As we have mentioned before the cost of heating is subject to heat gains internally and externally. This method will give you a better estimate of heat contribution for one heating season. (Record your data in Table D-2.)

(a) You will need the actual amount of fuel consumed for heating for one heating season and then factor out the amount used for heating water and cooking.

(b) You will also need the actual DD year for your area for the time span being calculated. Write to NOAA.

(c) Also you will need the Ut of your home.

$$\text{Estimated fuel for heating season} = \frac{DD \times 24 \times U_t}{\text{fuel in BTUs} \times \text{C.O.P.}}$$

Divide the actual amount of fuel used over one heating season by the calculated amount in C-1. This gives you the percentage of net fuel consumption.

EXAMPLE

U_t = 850   Fuel consumed for heating = 600 gallons of fuel oil.
DD year is 5150

$$\frac{5150 \times 24 \times 850}{144\ 000} = 729.59 \text{ gallons}$$

$\frac{600}{729.59}$ = 0.82 or 82% which means we have had an 18% contribution of heat gains over one heating season.

Therefore, in economical tradeoffs we can reduce our fuel cost factor by at least 18% for one heating season, for net fuel cost.

Since the heat gains will remain constant as we reduce the U_t or heat loss of the home, the percentage of heat contributions to heating costs will naturally increase. Our cost of heating will also decrease.

ECONOMICAL TRADE-OFFS

First calculate the corrected fuel cost factor as already outlined. If you want to, you may use the uncorrected fuel cost factor only if you understand that this will give you the upper limitations of heating costs.

From Worksheet One and Two of Part Two of the Work Section, rewrite your U_t and then multiply by your fuel cost factor. Your dollar figures separately will tell you where your heating dollars are going.

Next impose some corrections of the thermal leaks by adding insulation into the wall area. In Appendix N, we show you how to calculate the U combination of materials that are on the market. These new corrections will then constitute the thermal correction. Factor the new U_t by the fuel cost factor and this will give you estimated heating costs for one heating season. Deduct the cost of the old insulation versus the cost of the thermal correction and this will give you the savings for one normal heating season. Get a cost estimate for one heating season and divide by savings to get payback period.

EXAMPLE

This home has 2000 square foot ceiling with four inches of loose fiberglass insulation rated at R-2.20 per inch. The heat supply is electricity, with a fuel cost factor of $1.05.

U_t of 2000 square foot ceiling = 199.99

U_t after adding four inches = 110.99

Cost of heating:

199.99 × $1.05 = $209.99 per heating season

110.99 × $1.05 = $116.54 per heating season

Savings = $93.45

If the cost of adding four inches of insulation was $385.00, then the payback in this case would take about 4.119 years. We got this answer by dividing our annual savings into the estimated cost of making the thermal improvement.

If the air turn/hour calculation showed that you had an air turn of 1.0 or greater per hour, your greatest reduction and best payback should occur by reducing air infiltration.

188

WORK SHEET ONE

CONDUCTIVE LOSSES OF YOUR HOME

Use this sheet to record your fuel cost factors, and U values for windows, doors, etc., as determined in the preceding pages of Part Two of the Work Section. The methodology used for windows and doors is by lineal footage so that we can estimate the heat loss of the wood in the wall.

Section A. Fuel Cost Factors
(1) Fuel cost factor for portion of your home
    exposed to outside air   _____

(2) Fuel cost factor for portion of your home exposed
    to constant ground temperature   _____

Section B. U(conductive) of Various Parts of Your home
(1) Windows   _____   _____
(2) Exterior Doors   _____   _____
(3) Sliding glass doors   _____   _____
(4) Exterior walls only   _____   _____

(5) Ceilings   _____   _____
(6) Slab   _____   _____
(7) Wood floors   _____   _____
(8) Ring and bandboards   _____   _____
(9) Basement   _____   _____
(10 Crawl spaces   _____   _____
(11) Areas partly below grade and kneewalls
    (a) masonry   _____   _____
    (b) kneewalls   _____   _____

U(conductive) of Home   _____   _____

Note: This U(conductive) is not the total U_t of your home. We must next discover the amount of air infiltration in your home.

The method we give you in Section C, page 184 will give you an excellent feeling as to the amount of air turns you are experienceing in your home. From this math approach, you can then progress onto economical trade-offs which are discussed in Section D.

WORK SHEET TWO

Section C. Convective Heat Loss.

Table C-1.

(1) DD for your area _____

(2) No. of electricity units used in January _____

(3) No. of units of heating fuel used in January _____
(4) U*(conductive)* for your home _____

(5) Electricity consumption (in BTU) _____ BTU

(6) Other fuel consumption (in BTU) _____ BTU

(7) Heat gain from people (in BTU) _____ BTU

(8) Solar gain (in BTU) _____ BTU

(9) Total BTU available in the home _____ BTU

(10) U*(convective)* _____

(11) U*(convective) for one air turn per hour* _____

(12) Number of air turns per hour _____

190

WORK SHEET THREE

Section D. Trades, Heat Loss, Etc.

Table D-1.

(1) U(*conductive*) of your home _____

(2) U(*convective*) of your home _____

(3) U_t of your home _____

(4) Average low temperature in your area _____

(5) Average thermostat setting _____

(6) Average temperature difference _____

(7) Net output of furnace _____

(8) Original estimate of U of your home
   by furnace installer _____

Table D-2.

(1) Fuel consumed for one heating season _____

(2) DD year for your area _____

(3) U_t of your home _____

(4) Estimated fuel consumption for one
   heating season _____

(5) Percentage of net fuel consumption _____

Table D-3.

(1) Corrected fuel cost factor _____

(2) U_t of your home _____

(3) $U_t \times$ Your fuel cost factor _____

(4) U_t of your home after thermal correction _____

(5) U_t after correction $\times$ fuel cost factor _____

(6) Savings _____

APPENDICES

APPENDIX A. Calculating U of Air Infiltration as a Function of Wind Velocity

The following equation can be used to calculate air infiltration.

$$I = 60 \times Q \times C_p \times p \times \Delta T$$

I = U of air infiltration in cubic feet per hour per square foot of free open area, subject to wind velocity in mph

60 = factor for converting c.f.m. (cubic feet per minute) to c.f.h. (cubic feet per hour)

Q = c.f.m. subject to pressure resistance of wind striking opening at perpendicular (0.52). This resistance decreases when the direction of the wind striking the opening is at an angle less than perpendicular (0.25 to 0.35)

C_p = specific heat of air (0.240)

p = density of air (0.75 lb per cubic foot)

ΔT = fuel cost factor for a heating season or $(T_1 - T_2)$ temperature difference for one hour in BTU per hour

EXAMPLE:

At one mile per hour wind velocity (5280 feet per hour) on one square foot of free open space, the air infiltration for one hour per velocity of one mile per hour would be:

$$I = 60 \times \frac{5280}{60} \times 0.52 \times 0.240 \times 0.075$$

$$= 49.42$$

The cost of heating the air infiltration for one heating season for one square foot free opening would be expressed as:

$$\text{Cost per heating season} = 49.42 \times \text{fuel cost factor}$$

If the average velocity of wind in your area is 9.3 mph, then multiply one square foot by both 9.3 and the fuel cost factor to get the cost of air infiltration in one heating season.

APPENDIX B. Quick Analysis of Payback of a Solar Collector System

Solar insolation is dependent upon location (latitude), angle of collector to the sun, reflectance of solar rays from the face of the collector, emissivity of material used for the face of the collector, absorptivity of heat collector of the solar unit, heat loss of the solar collector to the sky, heat loss of the transfer lines to storage, and heat loss of the solar storage unit.

This demands a thorough knowledge of heat transfer and mechanical engineering. At best we will only give you a guideline for economical trade-offs. We highly recommend you hire a consulting engineer before you invest in any type of a solar collection system. At the very least, demand a certified testing of solar collection in YOUR AREA from the seller or manufacturer of the solar heating system. Rely not upon percentages but rather on actual collection rates interpreted in BTUs on a weekly or monthly rate.

Efficiency of a solar system decreases during the winter months because of heat loss to the sky, the low angle of the sun in the sky, and the heavy seasonal cloud cover. Solar heat collection is measured in BTUs.

Step-by-Step Calculations

1. The heating season consists of September through May. Calculate heat loss of your home in BTUs on a month to month basis or, better yet, follow our Thermal House concept of BTU heat loss as outlined in the Work Section. Instead of using your fuel cost factor, use the following on your U_t of the house:

Heat loss of your home (BTUs per month) = DD month $\times$ 24 $\times$ U_t of house

2. Invest in a copy of the NOAA annual report for degree days for your area (See Chapter 4). Do not use the percentage of sunshine in your area per month.

3. Discover the approximate latitude of your area and check the amount of daily BTU heat per square foot received from the sun.

4. Multiply the daily solar insolation (in BTUs) by the days in the month, and discount the same by the ESTIMATED efficiency of the solar collector as given in Table B-1.

Table B-1. Estimated Efficiency of Solar Collectors During the Heating Season.

September	40%
October	30%
November	30%
December	20%
January	20%
February	20%
March	30%
April	30%
May	40%

Also, check the percentage of sunshine as recorded by NOAA for any given month in your area and see if these values agree with the values in Table B-1. Remember, the efficiency of a collector could increase if the temperature of a collector is reduced by design.

5. Total the answer for Step 1 and divide the answer to Step 1 by the answer to Step 4. The resulting figure will give you the approximate size of collector you will need for your home.

6. Discover the square foot cost of the solar collector INSTALLED. This cost should include transfer systems, storage, and controls.

7. Divide the answer of Step 6 by annual fuel costs for your home as determined in the Work Section. This calculation will give your payback years without factoring in interest, breakage, and repairs.

APPENDIX C. Solar Insolation (in BTU)*

26 Degrees N. Latitude

Solstice	S	SE	SW	E	N	W	NE	NW	HOR.
June 22	50	524	524	873	312	872	619	619	2568
Mar./Sept.	990	870	870	733	0	733	280	289	2032
Dec. 22	1594	889	889	461	0	461	36	36	1168

30 Degrees N. Latitude

	S	SE	SW	E	N	W	NE	NW	HOR.
June 22	154	472	472	890	260	890	691	691	1294
Mar./Sept.	1116	905	905	721	0	721	260	260	1930
Dec. 22	1570	844	844	410	0	410	23	23	1008

34 Degrees N. Latitude

	S	SE	SW	E	N	W	NE	NW	HOR.
June 22	284	669	669	920	222	920	673	673	2598
Mar./Sept.	1228	935	935	708	0	708	231	231	1820
Dec. 22	1533	802	802	368	0	368	17	17	1696

38 Degrees N. Latitude

	S	SE	SW	E	N	W	NE	NW	HOR.
June 22	426	745	745	956	115	956	658	658	2592
Mar./Sept.	1330	839	839	691	0	691	209	209	1702
Dec. 22	1464	748	748	325	0	325	12	12	692

42 Degrees N. Latitude

	S	SE	SW	E	N	W	NE	NW	HOR.
June 22	568	820	820	987	111	980	653	653	2574
Mar./Sept.	1416	977	977	672	0	672	191	191	1572
Dec. 22	1362	677	677	277	0	277	8	8	538

46 Degrees N. Latitude

	S	SE	SW	E	N	W	NE	NW	HOR.
June 22	722	891	891	1012	226	1012	641	641	2544
Mar./Sept.	1484	985	985	653	0	653	174	174	1434
Dec. 22	1216	584	584	219	0	219	3	3	396

These figures represent BTUs per square foot of area per day, subject to direction of sunlight striking the collector. One can face a flat collector in only one direction but you will receive some benefit from other directions.

APPENDIX D. Calculating the Triangular Roof Correction Factor

1. Calculate the area of the attic floor by multiplying the length of the house by its width.

2. Calculate the U_t of the attic by multiplying the length and width by the U/ft^2.

3. Find the pitch of the roof (4/12, 5/12, 6/12, etc.). The pitch of the roof is designated by the numerator of the fraction which means the rise in inches for every 12 inches from the edge of roof to the center of the roof.

---

*Source of Calculations:
Ramsey, C. G., and Sleeper, H. R., *Architectural Graphic Standards*. New York: John Wiley & Sons, Inc., 1970.

4. Measure the height of the space over the outside wall to the bottom of the roof sheathing at the base of the floor of the attic.

The area along the edge of the attic contains less insulation than the center of the attic. Because of less insulation, this constitutes a thermal leak at least twice as great as in the center of the attic.

5. The base of the triangle can be found mathematically by subtracting the height of the wall edge from the height of the insulation and then by multiplying this difference by the inverse proportion of the pitch of the roof.

EXAMPLE:

Suppose that the pitch of the roof is 4/12, the insulation height is 6 inches, and the height at the edge of the attic wall to roof sheathing is 3.5 inches. Find the base of this triangle.

$$\text{Triangle base} \quad = \quad (6" - 3.5") \times \frac{12}{4}$$
$$= \quad 7.5 \text{ inches}$$

To convert the base of the triangle from inches to feet, divide by 12.

$$\text{Triangle base (in feet)} \quad = \quad 7.5 \text{ inches} \div 12$$
$$= \quad 0.625 \text{ feet}$$

6. Multiply the sum of the length of roof edge where the roof edge is close to the outside wall by the answer to Step 5. In a home with hip roofs or mansard roofs, there would be four sides to consider whereas with a gable roof there would be only two.

EXAMPLE:

Gable roof 60' long.

$$(60' \times 60') \times 0.625' \quad = \quad 75 \text{ square feet}$$

7. Deduct the answer of Step 6 from the total area of the roof.

EXAMPLE:

$$(24 \times 60) - 75 \quad = \quad 1365 \text{ square feet}$$

8 . To find the U_t of the roof with the trianglular correction, multiply the answer of Step 6 by U/ft^2 and also by 2. Then the answer of U/ft^2 to the net answer of Step 7.

EXAMPLE:

$$2(75 \times 0.06) + (1365 \times 0.06) \quad = \quad 90.9 \quad U_t \text{ of attic}$$

9 . Divide the answer from Step 2 into the answer from Step 8 to get the triangular correction factor.

EXAMPLE:

$$\frac{90.0}{(L \times w)(0.06)} \quad = \quad \frac{90.9}{86.4} \quad = \quad 1.05$$

Note the answer from Step 8 is the true U_t of the heat loss through the ceiling or the floor of the attic. This procedure gives us a more accurate look at heat loss through the ceiling area as we add insulation into the attic area. Be sure to follow through with sealing of air leaks into the attic area from the house below before adding any insulation.

Also, on a day when the snow is fresh on the roof, look for thermal leaks as shown by spotty melting of snow on the roof.

APPENDIX E. Calculating the Conductance Rate (U)
for One Air Turn per Hour in a Home

The equation for calculating the conductance rate for one air turn per hour in a home is given below:

$$\text{U per air turn per hour} = \frac{ft^3}{60} \times 1.1$$

EXAMPLE:
Suppose we have a 1200 ft^2 area with 8-ft ceilings. What is the conductance rate for one air turn per hour?

$$\text{U per air turn per hour} = \frac{1200 \times 8}{60} \times 1.1$$

$$= 175$$

To calculate the heat loss in BTUs for one air turn per hour, use this equation:

$$\text{Heat loss in BTUs per hour} = \text{U per air turn per hour} \times \text{temperature difference}$$

EXAMPLE:
Let's say the inside temperature is 70°F and the outside temperature is 20°F. What will be the heat loss in BTUs per air turn per hour?

$$\text{Heat loss in BTUs per hour} = (70 - 20) \times 175$$
$$= 8750 \text{ BTU per hour}$$

To convert the heat loss in BTUs per hour to BTUs per month or heating season, use one of the following equations:

(a) Heat loss in BTUs per month =

$$\text{U per air turn per hour} \times (\text{DD month} \times 24)$$

(b) Heat loss in BTUs per heating season =

$$\text{U per air turn per hour} \times (\text{DD year} \times 24)$$

EXAMPLE:
Let's say we have a DD year of 5400. What will be the heat loss in BTUs per heating season?

$$\text{Heat loss in BTUs per heating season} = 175 \times (5400 \times 24)$$
$$= 22\ 680\ 000 \text{ BTU per heating season}$$

APPENDIX F. Maximum Venting Area Required for Venting Crawl Spaces

To calculate the maximum venting area required for venting crawl spaces, use the following equation:

$$\text{Maximum venting area required for venting crawl spaces} = \frac{2L}{100} + \frac{A}{300}$$

L = total length of the outside crawl space walls in lineal feet
A = area of crawl space in square feet

EXAMPLE:

Calculate the maximum venting area required for venting a crawl space which has three outside walls. Two of these outside walls are 26 feet long and the other outside wall is 12 feet long.

$$\text{Maximum venting area required} = \frac{2(64)}{100} + \frac{(26)(12)}{300}$$

$$= 2.32 \text{ ft}^2 \text{ of vents required}$$

If we placed four vents in this crawl area, then each vent should be one-fourth of this area, or 0.58 ft² each.

Since most vents are sold in square inches, multiply the final ft² by 144 in order to find out the number of square inches required.

EXAMPLE:

Suppose the area of a required vent is known to be 0.58 ft². What is this area in square inches?

$$0.58 \text{ ft}^2 \times 144 = 83.52 \text{ in}^2$$

199

APPENDIX G. Calculating Attic Ventilation Requirements

Free Open Venting Required

Free open space of gable vents or roof top vents required to eliminate the migration of moisture into the attic area can easily be calculated. On homes with hip roofs, the side vents should be evenly distributed over the edges of the roof exposed to the attic.

For gable roofs, multiply the floor area of the attic crawl space by 0.0033.

EXAMPLE:

Suppose the floor area of an attic crawl space is 1000 ft^2. How much vent area will be required?

$$\text{Vent area required} = 1000 \text{ ft}^2 \times 0.0033$$
$$= 3.33 \text{ ft}^2$$

Since a minimum of two gable vents is required, each gable vent should be one-half of 3.33 ft^2, or 1.66 ft^2.

Venting with Fans

Per 1000 c.f.m. rating of fan:

1. For wood louvers with ½" hardware cloth having 40% minimum free area, required venting area = 2.27 ft^2

2. For metal louvers with ½" hardware cloth having 50% minimum free area, required venting area = 1.82 ft^2

3. For plain opening covered with ½" hardware cloth having 80% minimum free area, required venting area = 1.14 ft^2

4. For automatic or manual shutters having 90% minimum free area, required venting area = 1.01 ft^2

APPENDIX H. Fresh Air Required for Sizes and Types of Fireplaces

The following equations can be used to calculate the air required for various sizes and types of fireplaces. Your answer will tell you the c.f.m. required to sustain the fire in the fireplace. In these equations, let

H = height from the top of hearth to bottom of facing
B = depth of fireplace burning area (times) $2/3H - 4''$
W = Width of fireplace opening and/or side opening
L = Length of fireplace opening

1. Open front and/or side

$$\text{Fresh air required} = (L + W) \times H \times 60$$

2. Open front and back

$$\text{Fresh air required} = 2L \times H \times 60$$

3. Open on three sides

$$\text{Fresh air required} = (2L + W) \times H \times 60$$

4. Open on four sides

$$\text{Fresh air required} = 3.14 \times (B + 8'') \times H \times 60$$

From the c.f.m. calculated above, you can calculate the heat loss (in BTUs) due to infiltration of air to sustain the fire in the firebox according to the following equation:

$$\text{Heat loss per minute} = \text{c.f.m.} \times 1.1 \times T.D.$$

(Recall that T.D. is the temperature difference between the room and outdoors.)

EXAMPLE:

Suppose the c.f.m. is 360 in the fireplace, room temperature is 70°F, and the temperature outdoors is 20°F. What will be the heat loss in BTUs per minute?

$$\text{Heat loss per minute} = 360 \times 1.1 \times (70 - 20)$$
$$= 19\,800 \text{ BTU per minute}$$

This would be subject to the heat radiated from the fire in the firebox into the room.

---

*Ramsey, C. G., and Sleeper, H. R., *Architectural Graphic Standards*. New York: John Wiley & Sons, Inc., 1970.

APPENDIX I. Temperature Conversion and Important Standard Temperatures

TEMPERATURE CONVERSION

Fahrenheit to Celsius (Centigrade):
$$°C = (°F - 32°)0.555$$

Celsius to Fahrenheit:
$$°F = (°C \times 1.8) + 32°$$

Important Standard Temperatures

Constant	Celsius Temp.	Fahrenheit Temp.
Absolute zero	$-271.11°$	$-459.58°$
Water freezes	$0.00°$	$+32°$
Water boils	$+100°$	$+212°$

APPENDIX J. Density of Wood

Density of Wood in Pounds per Cubic Foot*
(12% moisture content)

Birch, Red Oak	44
Cedar	22
Cypress	32
Douglas Fir	34
Fir, White	27
Hemlock	28-29
Maple (Hard)	42
Oak (White)	47
Pine (Northern)	25
Pine (Long Leaf)	29
Pine (Ponderosa, Spruce)	28
Pine (Short Leaf)	36
Poplar (Yellow)	28
Walnut (Black)	38

---

*Ramsey, C. G., and Sleeper, H. R., *Architectural Graphic Standards.* New York: John Wiley & Sons, Inc., 1970.

APPENDIX K. Degree Days for Major Cities in the United States

This list of cities across the United States gives degree days representing various high and low temperatures over one heating season. We have purposely not listed monthly reports over the full year. With the exception of Alaska and few of more northern states, heat loss in the milder months of April, Many, and September would be insignificant.

Note how January in each state is the coldest month of the year. The reason for this is that during the month of December the ground had been cooling because of low solar insolation. However, in February the air and ground begin to warm up slightly.

The Degree-Day method has been used for many years. The origination of the degree-day method was for the natural gas and fuel oil suppliers at the time many home owners had coal stokers for furnaces. With the degree day method, the fuel oil suppliers could estimate storage supplies required and had an economic basis for comparing coal with natural gas and fuel oil. With just very few exceptions, coal furnaces are not used in this country. So, the natural gas companies and fuel oil companies did a good job of selling their products.

Normal Mean Degree Days Heating

State/City	Annual	Oct.	Nov.	Dec.	Jan.	Feb.	Mar.	State/City	Annual	Oct.	Nov.	Dec.	Jan.	Feb.	Mar.
ALABAMA								**GEORGIA**							
Birmingham	2551	93	363	555	592	462	363	Atlanta	2983	127	414	626	639	529	437
Mobile	1560	22	213	357	415	300	211	Savannah	1819	47	246	437	437	353	254
ALASKA								**IDAHO**							
Fairbanks	14 279	1203	1833	2254	2359	1901	1739	Boise	5809	415	792	1017	1113	854	722
								Idaho Falls	8760	648	1107	1432	1600	1291	1107
ARIZONA								**ILLINOIS**							
Flagstaff	7152	558	867	1073	1169	991	911	Chicago	6155	326	753	1113	1209	1044	890
Phoenix	1765	22	234	415	474	328	217	Springfield	5429	291	696	1023	1135	935	769
Yuma	1217	0	148	319	363	228	130								
ARKANSAS								**INDIANA**							
Little Rock	3219	127	465	716	756	577	434	Fort Wayne	6205	378	783	1135	1178	1028	890
								Indianapolis	5699	316	723	1051	1113	949	809
CALIFORNIA															
Burbank	1646	43	177	301	366	277	239	**IOWA**							
Eureka	4643	329	414	499	546	470	505	Des Moines	6808	363	837	1231	1398	1165	967
Mt. Shasta	5722	406	696	902	983	784	738	Sioux City	6951	369	867	1240	1435	1198	989
San Diego	1439	37	123	251	313	249	202								
San Francisco	3015	143	306	462	508	395	363	**KANSAS**							
								Dodge City	4986	251	666	939	1051	840	719
COLORADO								Topeka	5182	270	672	980	1122	893	722
Denver	6283	428	819	1035	1132	938	887								
								KENTUCKY							
CONNECTICUT								Covington	5265	291	669	983	1035	893	756
Hartford	6172	372	711	1119	1209	1061	899	Louisville	4660	248	609	890	930	818	682
New Haven	5897	347	648	1011	1097	991	871								
								LOUISIANA							
DELAWARE								Baton Rouge	1560	31	216	369	409	294	208
Wilmington	4930	270	588	927	980	874	735	New Orelans	1385	19	192	322	363	258	192
FLORIDA								**MAINE**							
Miami Beach	141	0	0	40	56	36	9	Caribou	9767	682	1044	1535	1690	1470	1308
Pensacola	1463	19	195	353	400	277	183	Portland	7511	508	807	1215	1339	1182	1042
Tampa	683	0	60	171	202	148	102								

State/City	Annual	Oct.	Nov.	Dec.	Jan.	Feb.	Mar.
MARYLAND							
Baltimore	4654	264	585	905	936	820	679
MASSACHUSETTS							
Boston	5634	316	603	983	1088	972	846
Pittsfield	7578	524	831	1231	1339	1196	1063
Worcester	6969	450	774	1172	1271	1123	998
MICHIGAN							
Detroit	6232	360	738	1088	1181	1058	936
Escanaba	8481	539	924	1293	1445	1296	1203
Flint	7377	465	843	1212	1330	1198	1066
Grand Rapids	6894	434	804	1147	1259	1134	1011
Marquette	8393	527	936	1268	1411	1268	1187
MINNESOTA							
Duluth	10 000	632	1131	1581	1745	1518	1355
Minneapolis	8382	505	1014	1454	1631	1380	1166
Saint Cloud	8879	549	1065	1500	1702	1445	1221
MISSISSIPPI							
Jackson	2239	65	315	502	546	414	310
MISSOURI							
St. Joseph	5484	285	708	1039	1172	949	769
St. Louis	4900	251	627	936	1026	848	704
MONTANA							
Billings	7049	487	897	1135	1296	1100	970
Havre	8700	595	1065	1367	1584	1364	1181
Miles City	7723	502	972	1296	1504	1252	1057
NEBRASKA							
Lincoln	5864	301	726	1066	1237	1016	834
Norfolk	6979	397	873	1234	1414	1179	983
Omaha	6612	357	828	1175	1355	1126	939
NEVADA							
Elko	7433	561	924	1197	1314	1036	911
Las Vegas	2709	78	387	617	688	487	335
Reno	6332	490	801	1026	1073	823	729
NEW HAMPSHIRE							
Concord	7383	505	822	1240	1358	1184	1032
Mt. Washington Obs.	13 817	1057	1341	1742	1820	1663	1652
NEW JERSEY							
Atlantic City	4812	251	549	880	936	848	741
Newark	4859	248	573	921	983	876	729
Trenton	4980	264	576	924	989	885	753
NEW MEXICO							
Albuquerque	4348	229	642	868	930	703	595
Raton	6228	431	825	1048	1116	904	834
Silver City	3705	183	525	729	791	605	518

State/City	Annual	Oct.	Nov.	Dec.	Jan.	Feb.	Ma
NEW YORK							
Albany	6875	440	777	1194	1311	1156	99
Buffalo	7062	440	777	1156	1256	1145	103
Rochester	6748	415	747	1125	1234	1123	101
Syracuse	6756	415	744	1153	1271	1140	100
NORTH CAROLINA							
Ashville	4042	245	555	775	784	683	59
Charlotte	3191	124	438	691	691	582	48
Raleigh	3393	164	450	716	725	616	48
NORTH DAKOTA							
Bismark	8851	577	1083	1463	1708	1442	120
Fargo	9226	574	1107	1569	1789	1520	126
OHIO							
Cincinnati	4806	248	612	921	970	837	70
Cleveland	6351	384	738	1088	1159	1047	91
Columbus	5660	347	714	1039	1088	949	80
OKLAHOMA							
Oklahoma City	3725	164	498	766	868	664	52
Tulsa	3860	158	522	787	893	683	53
OREGON							
Meacham	7874	580	918	1091	1209	1005	98
Portland	4635	335	597	735	825	644	58
Sexton Summitt	6254	443	666	874	958	809	818
PENNSYLVANIA							
Erie	6451	391	714	1063	1169	1081	97
Philadelphia	5101	291	621	964	1014	890	744
Pittsburgh	5987	375	726	1063	1119	1002	874
RHODE ISLAND							
Providence	5954	372	660	1023	1110	988	868
SOUTH CAROLINA							
Charleston	2033	59	282	471	487	389	291
SOUTH DAKOTA							
Huron	8223	508	1014	1432	1628	1355	1125
Rapid City	7345	481	897	1172	1333	1145	1051
Sioux Falls	7839	462	972	1361	1544	1285	1082
TENNESSEE							
Chattanooga	3254	143	468	698	722	577	453
Memphis	3232	130	447	698	729	585	456
TEXAS							
Abilene	2624	99	366	586	642	470	347
Dallas	2363	62	321	524	601	440	319
Waco	2030	43	270	456	536	389	270

State/City	Annual	Oct.	Nov.	Dec.	Jan.	Feb.	Mar.	State/City	Annual	Oct.	Nov.	Dec.	Jan.	Feb.	Mar.
UTAH								**WEST VIRGINIA**							
Salt Lake City	6052	419	849	1082	1172	910	763	Charleston	4476	254	591	865	880	770	648
Wendover	5778	372	822	1091	1178	902	729	Huntington	4446	257	585	856	880	764	636
								Parkersburg	4754	264	606	905	942	826	691
VERMONT															
Burlington	8269	539	891	1349	1513	1333	1187	**WISCONSIN**							
								Green Bay	8029	484	924	1333	1494	1313	1141
VIRGINIA								La Crosse	7589	437	924	1339	1504	1277	1070
Lynchburg	4166	223	540	822	849	731	605	Milwaukee	7635	471	876	1252	1376	1193	1054
Norfolk	3421	138	408	698	738	655	533								
								WYOMING							
WASHINGTON								Cheyenne	7278	543	924	1101	1228	1056	1011
Seattle	4838	384	624	763	831	655	608	Lander	7870	555	1020	1299	1417	1145	1017
Spokane	6655	493	879	1082	1231	980	834	Sheridan	7683	539	948	1200	1355	1154	1054
Stampede Pass	9283	701	1008	1178	1287	1075	1085								
WASHINGTON D.C.															
Dulles Airport	5010	352	574	917	1098	935	576								

APPENDIX L. Conversion of R to U

The R value of a combination of materials is called R_{Total} (R_t) per square foot of area. To convert R_t to U_t, use the equation:

$$U = 1/R$$

EXAMPLE:
Find the R_t and U_t of a wall with R-11 insulation in the wall cavity.

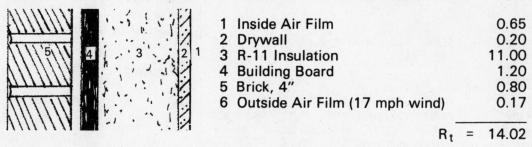

1	Inside Air Film	0.65
2	Drywall	0.20
3	R-11 Insulation	11.00
4	Building Board	1.20
5	Brick, 4"	0.80
6	Outside Air Film (17 mph wind)	0.17

$$R_t = 14.02$$

To convert R_t to U_t,

$$U_t = 1/R_t$$
$$= 1/14.02 = 0.071$$

Do this for floors, ceilings, or any other section of your home. Be sure to use the correct R factor for heat flow direction.

CONVERSION TABLE OF R FACTOR TO U FOR ONE SQUARE FOOT AREA

When R is	U is	When R is	U is
.10	10.00	17.00	.058
.20	5.00	18.00	.055
.30	3.33	19.00	.052
.40	2.50	20.00	.050
.50	2.00	21.00	0.47
.60	1.66	22.00	.045
.70	1.42	23.00	.043
.80	1.25	24.00	.041
.90	1.11	25.00	.040
1.00	1.00	26.00	.038
2.00	.500	27.00	.037
3.00	.333	28.00	.035
4.00	.250	29.00	.034
5.00	.200	30.00	.033
6.00	.166	31.00	.032
7.00	.142	32.00	.031
8.00	.125	33.00	.030
9.00	.111	34.00	.029
10.00	.100	35.00	.028
11.00	.090	36.00	.027
12.00	.083	37.00	.027
13.00	.076	38.00	.026
14.00	.071	39.00	.027
15.00	.066	40.00	.025
16.00	.062		

APPENDIX M. Heat Transmission of Glass (Vertical & Horizontal)*

Note: the difference between the summer and winter ratings arise
because of the direction of the flow of heat.

Vertical Panes, Exterior	Season	U	R
Single Glass	winter	1.13	0.84
	summer	1.06	0.94
Insulated Glass			
3/16" air space	winter	0.69	1.44
	summer	0.64	1.56
1/4" air space	winter	0.65	1.55
	summer	0.61	1.65
1/2" air space	winter	0.58	1.72
	summer	0.56	1.79
Insulated Glass (3 lights)			
1/4" air space	winter	0.47	2.13
	summer	0.45	2.22
1/2" air space	winter	0.36	2.78
	summer	0.35	2.86
Glass Blocks			
6" × 6" × 4"	winter	0.60	1.67
	summer	0.57	1.76
8" × 8" × 4"	winter	0.56	1.79
	summer	0.54	1.85
12" × 12" × 4"	winter	0.52	1.92
	summer	0.50	2.00
12" × 12" × 2"	winter	0.60	1.67
	summer	0.57	1.76
Single Plastic Sheet			
	winter	1.09	0.92
	summer	1.00	1.00

Horizontal Glass Exterior.	Season	U	R
Single Glass	winter	1.22	0.82
	summer	0.83	1.20
Insulated Glass (2 lights)			
3/16" air space	winter	0.75	1.34
	summer	0.49	2.04
1/4" air space	winter	0.70	1.43
	summer	0.46	2.17
1/2" air space	winter	0.66	1.52
	summer	0.44	2.27
Glass Block			
11" × 11" × 3"	winter	0.53	1.89
	summer	0.35	2.86
12" × 12" × 4"	winter	0.51	1.96
	summer	0.34	2.94
Plastic Bubble			
Single walled	winter	1.15	0.87
	summer	0.80	1.25
Double walled	winter	0.70	1.43
	summer	0.46	2.17

*Ramsey, C. G., and Sleeper, H. R., *Architectural Graphic Standards.* New York: John Wiley & Sons, Inc., 1970.

APPENDIX N. Resistance Values for Building Materials*

Description			Thermal Resistance (R)		
Position of Air Space	Heat Flow	Air Space Thickness, in.	Bright Aluminum Foil	Aluminum Painted Paper	Non-Reflective
No. 1 Still Air Surfaces					
Horizontal	Up		1.32	1.10	0.61
45°Slope	Up		1.37	1.14	0.62
Vertical	Horiz.		1.70	1,35	0.68
45° Slope	Down		2.22	1.67	0.76
Horizontal	Down		4.55	2.70	0.92
No. 2 Air Spaces					
Horizontal	Up (Winter)	¾ to 4	2.06	1.62	0.85
Horizontal	Up (Summer)	¾ to 4	2.75	1.87	0.80
45° Slope	Up (Winter)	¾ to 4	2.22	1.71	0.88
Vertical	Horiz. (Winter)	¾ to 4	2.62	1.94	0.94
Vertical	Horiz. (Summer)	¾ to 4	3.44	2.16	0.91
45° Slope	Down (Summer)	¾ to 4	4.36	2.50	0.90
Horizontal	Down (Winter)	¾	3.55	2.39	1.02
Horizontal	Down (Summer)	¾	3.25	2.08	0.84
Horizontal	Down (Winter)	1½	5.74	3.21	1.14
Horizontal	Down (Summer)	1½	5.24	2.76	0.93
Horizontal	Down (Winter)	4	8.94	4.02	1.23
Horizontal	Down (Summer)	4	8.08	3.38	0.99
No. 3 Moving Air Surfaces (Any Position or Direction					
15 mph Wind (Winter)					0.17
7½ mph Wind (Summer)					0.25

Description		Thermal	Resistance (R	
		Density lb/cu.ft.	Per Inch of Thickness	For Thicknes Listed
No. 4 Building Board, Boards, Panels, Sheathing, etc.				
Asbestos-cement board		120	0.25	
Asbestos-cement board—⅛-in.		120		0.03
Gypsum or plaster board—⅜-in.		50		0.31
Gypsum or plaster board—½-in.		50		0.45
Plywood		34	1.25	
Plywood—¼-in.		34		0.31
Plywood—⅜-in.		34		0.47
Plywood—½-in.		34		0.63
Plywood—⅝-in.		34		0.78
Plywood or wood panels—¾-in.				0.94
Wood fiber board, laminated or homogenous		26	2.38	
		31	2.00	
		33	1.82	
Wood fiber, hardboard type		65	0.72	
Wood fiber, hardboard type—¼-in.		65		0.18
Wood, fir or pine sheathing—25/32-in.				0.98
Wood, fir or pine—1⅝-in.				2.03

* (Used with permission of The American Society of Heating, Refrigerating and Air-Conditioning Engineers)

208

Description	Density lb/cu.ft.	Thermal Resistance (R)	
		Per Inch of Thickness	For Thickness Listed
No. 5 Building Paper			
Vapor-permeable felt			0.06
Vapor-seal, two layers 15 lb felt			0.12
Vapor-seal, plastic film			Negl
No. 6 Flooring Materials			
Carpet and fibrous pad			2.08
Carpet and rubber pad			1.23
Cork tile—⅛-in.			0.28
Floor tile or linoleum—average value—⅛-in.			0.05
Terrazzo—1-in.			0.08
Wood subfloor—25/32-in.			0.98
Wood, hardwood finish—¾-in.			0.68
No. 7 Insulating materials, Blanket and Batt			
Cotton fiber	0.8—2.0	3.85	
Mineral wool, fibrous form, processed from rock, slag, or glass	1.5—4.0	3.70	
Wood fiber	3.2—3.6	4.00	
No. 8 Insulating Materials, Board			
Glass fiber	9.5—11.0	4.00	
Wood or cane fiber Acoustical tile—½-in.			1.19
Wood or cane fiber Acoustical tile—¾-in.			1.78
Wood or cane fiber Interior finish, (plank, tile, lath)	15.0	2.86	
Wood or cane fiber Interior finish, (plank, tile, lath)—½-in.	15.0		1.43
Roof deck slab, approximately—1½-in.			4.17
Roof deck slab, approximately—2-in.			5.56
Roof deck slab, approximately—3-in.			8.33
Sheathing, impregnated or coated	20.0	2.63	
Sheathing, impregnated or coated—½-in.	20.0		1.32
Sheathing, impregnated or coated—25/32-in	20.0		2.06
No. 9 Insulating Materials, Board and Slabs			
Cellular glass	9.0	2.50	
Expanded Urethane		5.88	
Expanded rubber	4.5	4.55	
Expanded Polystyrene (bead foam)	1.6	3.45	
Wood shredded, cemented in preformed slabs	22.0	1.82	
Mineral wool with resin binder	15.0	3.45	
Mineral wool with asphalt binder	15.0	3.22	
Styrofoam®		5.50	
No. 10 Insulating Materials, Loose Fill			
Macerated paper or pulp products (cellulose)	2.5—3.5	3.57	
Mineral wool, glass, slag, or rock	2.0—5.0	3.33	
Sawdust or shavings	8.0—15.0	2.22	
Silica Aerogel	7.6	5.88	
Vermiculite, expanded	7.0—8.2	2.08	
Wood fiber, redwood, hemlock, or fir	2.0—3.5	3.33	
Wood fiber, redwood bark	3.0	3.22	
Wood fiber, redwood bark	4.0	3.57	
Wood fiber, redwood bark	4.5	3.84	

Resistance Values for Common Building and Insulating Materials

Description	Density lb/cu.ft.	Thermal Resistance (R) Per Inch of Thickness	For Thickness Listed
No. 11 Roof Insulation, Preformed, for Use Above Deck			
Approximately—½-in.			1.39
Approximately—1-in.			2.78
Approximately—1½-in.			4.17
Approximately—2-in.			5.26
Approximately—2½-in.			6.67
Approximately—3-in.			8.33
No. 12 Masonry Materials, Concretes			
Cement mortar	116	0.20	
Gypsum-fiber concrete, 87½% gypsum, 12½% wood chips	51	0.60	
Lightweight aggregates including:			
expanded shale	120	0.19	
clay or slate	100	0.28	
expanded slags	80	0.40	
cinders	60	0.59	
perlite	40	0.86	
vermiculite	30	1.11	
cellular concretes	20	1.43	
Sand and gravel or stone aggregate, oven dried	140	0.11	
Sand and gravel or stone aggregate, not dried	140	0.08	
Stucco	116	0.20	
No. 13 Plastering Materials			
Cement plaster, sand aggregate	116	0.20	
Cement plaster, sand aggregate—½-in.			0.10
Cement plaster, sand aggregate—¾-in.			0.15
Gypsum plaster, lightweight aggregate—½-in.	45		0.32
Gypsum plaster, lightweight aggregate—⅝-in.	45		0.39
Gypsum plaster, lightweight aggregate on metal lath—¾-in.			
Gypsum plaster, perlite aggregate	45	0.67	
Gypsum plaster, sand aggregate	105	0.18	
Gypsum plaster, sand aggregate—½-in.	105		0.09
Gypsum plaster, sand aggregate—⅝-in.	105		0.11
Gypsum plaster, sand aggregate on metal lath—¾-in.			0.10
Gypsum plaster, sand aggregate on wood lath			0.40
Gypsum plaster, vermiculite aggregate	45	0.59	
No. 14 Masonry Units			
Brick, common	120	0.20	
Brick, face	130	0.11	
Hollow clay tile, one cell deep—3-in.			0.80
Hollow clay tile, one cell deep—4-in.			1.11
Hollow clay tile, two cells deep—6-in.			1.52
Hollow clay tile, two cells deep—8-in.			1.85
Hollow clay tile, two cells deep—10-in.			2.22
Hollow clay tile, three cells deep—12-in.			2.50
Stone, lime or sand		0.08	
Gypsum partition tile, 3-in. × 30-in.—solid			1.26
Gypsum partition tile, 3-in. × 12-in. × 30-in.—4-cell			1.35
Gypsum partition tile, 4-in × 12-in. × 30-in.—3-cell			1.67

210

Description	Density lb/cu.ft.	Thermal Resistance (R) Per Inch of Thickness	For Thickness Listed
No. 15 Concrete Blocks			
Sand and gravel aggregate, three oval core—4-in.			0.71
Sand and gravel aggregate, three oval core—8-in			1.11
Sand and gravel aggregate, three oval core—12-in.			1.28
Cinder aggregate, three oval core—3-in.			0.86
Cinder aggregate, three oval core 4-in.			1.11
Cinder aggregate, three oval core—8-in.			1.72
Cinder aggregate, three oval core—12-in.			1.89
Sand and gravel aggregate, two core—8-in. 36 lb.			1.04
Sand and gravel aggregate, two core—8-in. 36 lb.—with filled cores			1.93
Lightweight aggregate, expanded shale, clay, slate or slag; pumice—3-in.			1.27
Lightweight aggregate (etc.)—4-in.			1.50
Lightweight aggregate (etc.)—8-in.			2.00
Lightweight aggregate (etc.)—12-in.			2.27
Lightweight aggregate, expanded shale, clay, slate or slag, pumice—2-core, 8-in. 24 lb.			2.18
with filled cores			5.03
3-core, 6-in. 19-lb.			1.65
with filled cores			2.99
3-core, 12-in. 38-lb.			2.48
with filled cores			5.82
No. 16 Roofing			
Asbestos-cement shingles	120		0.21
Asphalt roll roofing	70		0.15
Asphalt shingles	70		0.44
Built-up roofing—⅜-in.	70		0.33
Slate—½-in.			0.05
Sheet Metal		Negl	
Wood shingles			0.94
No. 17 Siding Materials (On Flat Surface)			
Wood shingles, 16-in, 7½-in. exposure			0.87
Wood shingles, double, 16-in., 12-in. exposure			1.19
Wood shingles, plus insulation 5/16-in. backer board			1.40
Asbestos-cement siding, ¼-in., lapped or shingles			0.21
Asphalt roll siding			0.15
Asphalt insulating siding (½-in. board)			1.46
Wood siding, drop, 1-in. × 8-in.			0.79
Wood siding, bevel, ½-in. × 8-in., lapped			0.81
Wood siding, bevel, ¾-in. × 10-in., lapped			1.05
Wood siding, plywood, ⅜-in., lapped			0.59
Structural glass			0.10
Woods			
Maple, oak, and similar hardwoods	45	0.91	
Fir, pine, and similar soft woods	32	1.25	
Fir, pine, and similar soft woods—25/32-in.	32		0.98
Fir, pine, and similar soft woods—1⅝-in.	32		2.03
Fir, pine, and similar soft woods—2⅝-in.	32		3.28
Fir, pine, and similar soft woods—3⅝-in.	32		4.55

APPENDIX O. Heat Loss of Ducts in the Heat Transfer System

Refer to Chapter 13 to get the correct degree-day factors for calculating costs, however, to estimate the total heat transfer rate of the house (U_t), subtract the temperature of the basement (estimated at 62°F) from the temperature in the duct for a particular system. This will give heat loss per hour per lineal foot of duct.

These are the most popular duct sizes. The U values are per lineal foot. Don't forget to factor in the correct DD year when figuring costs. If you want to calculate the heat loss per hour, subtract the basement temperature from the temperature in the heat duct and multiply the difference by the U/lineal foot. You will find the losses high and, in fact, the heat ducts and the hot water lines are actually supplying substantial heat to the basement.

(Temp of Duct – Temp of Basement) × U/lin. ft = BTU/hr/lin. ft.

Duct	Zero Insulation	R-4	R-7
4" round	1.26	0.21	0.132
5" round	1.58	0.269	0.166
6" round	1.91	0.32	0.20
8" round	2.59	0.43	0.267
4" × 12"	3.17	0.53	0.332
6" × 12"	3.65	0.62	0.466
8" × 12"	4.02	0.684	0.421
8" × 14"	4.46	0.92	0.468
8" × 16"	4.87	1.01	0.511
8" × 22"	6.09	1.03	0.639

APPENDIX P. Heat Loss of Hot Water Lines

There are two basic sizes of water lines used in the home—½" and ¾". Not only are the hot water lines emitting heat but the cold water lines are absorbing heat (acting as a heat sink). Here are listed the U values per lineal foot of copper water lines without insulation.

To calculate the heat loss per hour, subtract the temperature of the hot water from the temperature of the basement.

EXAMPLE:

(Average basement temperature is 62°F, average water from hot water tank is 150°F, the difference is:

$$150 - 62 = 88$$

U/lineal foot of ½" hot water line with no insulation is 0.158. By multiplying the temperature difference by the U/foot,

$$(88 \times 0.158) = 13.90 \text{ BTUs per hour per lineal foot}$$

Let's say you have 100 feet of pipe and the hot water is running one hour,

$$1 \text{ hr} \times 100 \text{ ft} \times 13.9 \text{ BTU/hr/lin. ft} = 1390 \text{ BTU}$$

Interestingly enough, right next to the hot water tank about five feet away on the water line (cold and hot) this goes on all day and all night at a rate of 974 393 BTU/yr! R-4 insulation would cut this to 80 171 BTU/yr.

Heat Transmission Rate (U) of Copper Hot Water Lines per Lineal Foot

Size of line	Zero Insulation	R-4	R-7
½"	0.158	0.026	0.016
¾"	0.196	0.032	0.020

BIBLIOGRAPHY

Ambrose, E. R., *Heat Pumps and Electric Heating*. New York: John Wiley & Sons, Inc., 1966.

Brinkworth, B. J., *Solar Energy for Man*. London: The Compton Press, 1972.

Condon, E. U., and Odishaw, H., *Handbook of Physics, 2nd Ed*. New York: McGraw-Hill Book Co., Inc., 1967.

Daniels, F., *Direct Use of the Sun's Energy*. New York: Ballentine Books, 1964.

Duffie, J. A., and Beckman, W. A., *Solar Energy Thermal Processes*. New York: John Wiley & Sons, 1974.

Handbook of Fundamentals. New York: American Society of Heating, Refrigeration and Air Conditioning Engineers (ASHRAE), 1972.

Holman, J. P., *Heat Transfer, erd Ed*. New York: McGraw-Hill Book Co., Inc., 1972.

Manual J. National Environmental Systems Contractors Association, Chicago, 1967.

Ramsey, C. G., and Sleeper, H. R., *Architectural Graphic Standards, 5th Ed*. New York: John Wiley & Sons, Inc., 1970.

Shortley, G., and Williams, D., *Elements of Physics, 2nd Ed*. New York: McGraw-Hill Book Co., Inc., 1967.

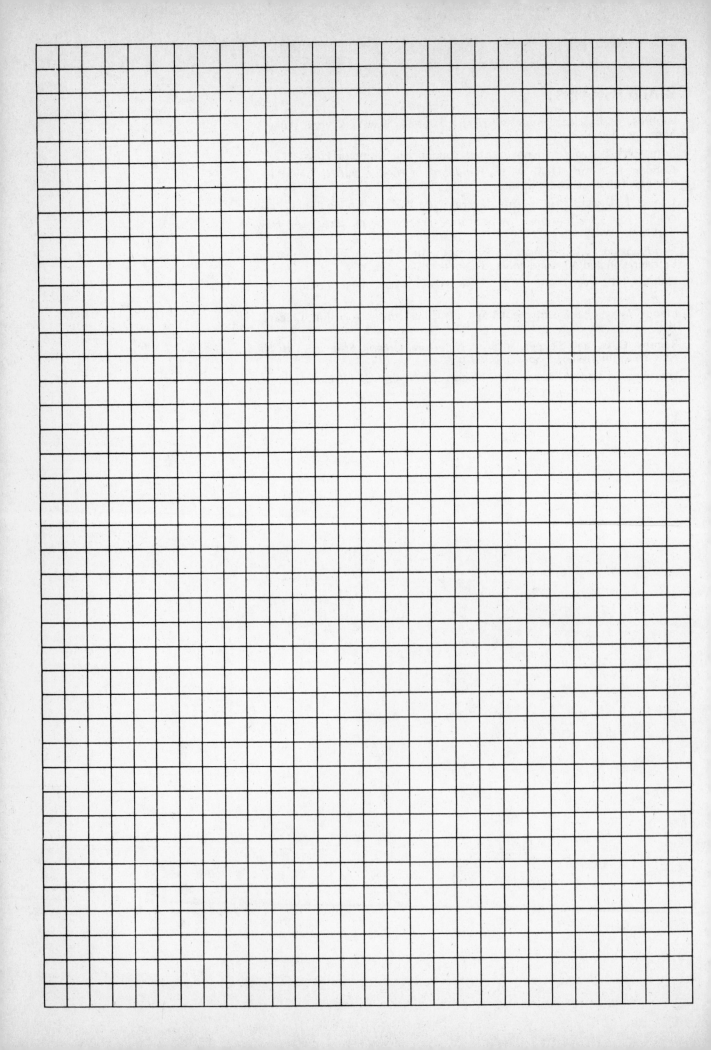

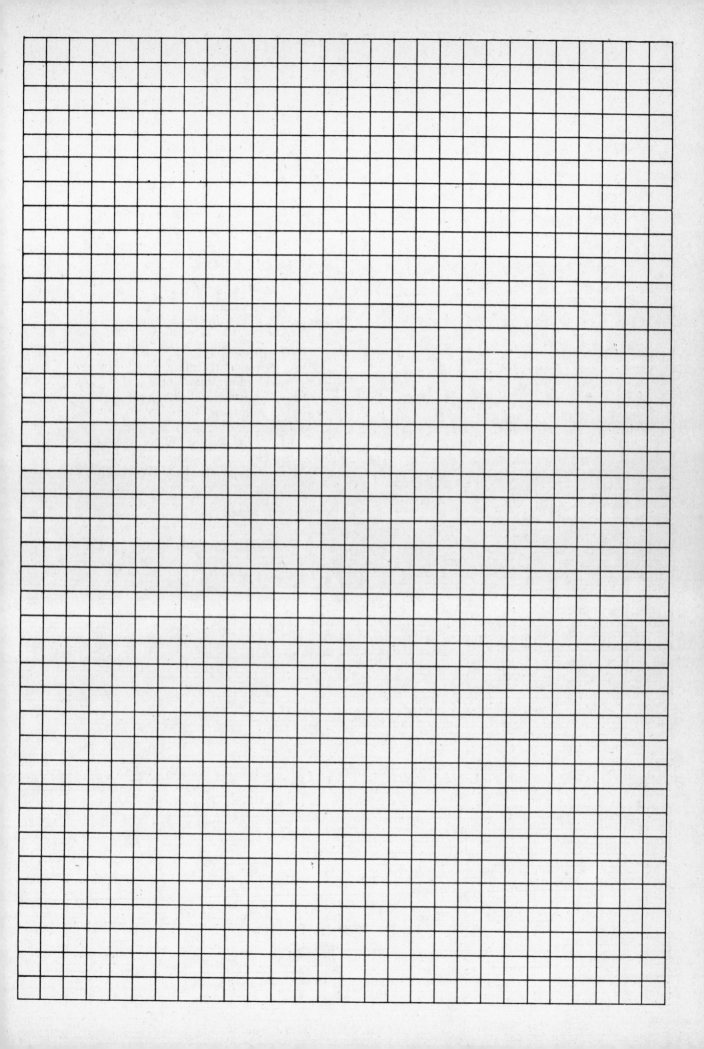

DEDICATION

To my wife,
Patricia Louise
for her patience and understanding.

To my three children,
Diana, Bobby and Timmy
who, like other children, may face a real
danger of fuel and energy shortage for
themselves and their children.

To Dr. Richard D. Bailey, Ph.D.
of the Ohio State University, whose patience
and kindness led me through the Thermal Woods.

Illustrations by John Murphy

Photographs by John Murphy

Typography by Beaver Press, Inc., M. Huber